THE WILDMAN, THE EARTH AND THE STARS

An Astrology of Masculine Archetypes

February 00
Beaverton

To KATHY,
Release your Wildwoman!

THE WILDMAN, THE EARTH AND THE STARS

An Astrology of Masculine Archetypes

DANIEL E. LOREY

Delphi Press, Inc., Oak Park, Illinois

Published 1994 by Delphi Press, Inc., Oak Park, Illinois and Quadrant Publications, Franklin Square, New York.

ISBN 1-878980-13-0

Library of Congress Catalogue Number 93-73575

99 98 97 96 95 94 6 5 4 3 2 1

Contents

To Antonette, Erin and Michael, my three biggest admirers.
Your support has made all the difference in the world.
I love you all.

And to all my mentors for planting the seeds.

Acknowledgements

Much of the archetypal descriptions and terminology used in this book comes from the work of Robert Moore and Douglas Gillette and their book King, Warrior, Magician, Lover. Grateful acknowledgement is made to Harper San Francisco for permission to quote and paraphrase selected passages and to reproduce figures from their work. Poems by Robert Bly are reproduced by permission of Doubleday.

Special thanks to Karen Jackson of Delphi Press, Liz Davidson and Chris Harnesk for all of their help in producing this book. Many thanks to Lillian Lewis for her brilliant cover illustration. Thanks to Douglas Gillette for contributing the Foreword and for his generous time and support and to Robert Moore for his enthusiastic acceptance and support of my ideas. A special thanks to Lois Rodden for all her assistance in verifying birth data sources. To Robert and Ruth Bly for their warm support, encouragement and cooperation. To my father for all his help in manuscript production and computer expertise and to my family for all their support. To Toni, Erin and Mike for believing in me. Special thanks to Pam and Janet for really understanding me. To Lori Stonehill-Matthews for believing in my work before anyone else knew. John Van Zandt for his miscellaneous help along the way. To all the Izzo clan, too numerous to mention, for helping this old boy understand the meaning of acceptance. Special thanks to Carol Hart, God rest your soul, for introducing me to the woman I love. I know somewhere you are smiling! Thanks to Rick Hart and the rest of the men in my support network for being both friends and mentors. I would like to acknowledge and thank the following list of people for contributing to my overall values and philosophy of life. In different ways, you have all contributed unknowingly to this book as well: Carl Jung, Donald Bradley, Cyril Fagan, John Bradshaw, Alice Miller, Lucia Capacchione, John Lee, Michel and Francoise Gauquelin, Krishnamurti, Joseph Campbell, Schwaller de

Lubicz, John Anthony West, James Hillman, Michael Meade, Robert K.G. Temple, Zecharia Sitchin, Richard C. Hoagland, Frank Zappa, Peter Gabriel, Enya and Sting.

Foreword

A fundamental assumption of astrology, as I understand it, is that human beings—we in our essence, as well as in the events of our lives—are microcosms of the universe. We mirror and reflect the gigantic structures and forces which shape and drive the vast whole. We are concentrations of those titanic elements, both in our bodies and in our souls.

Amazingly, though they discredit astrology along with other occult spiritual practices, more orthodox spiritualities have agreed with this basic intuition. Mystics, prophets and theologians of virtually all of the world's traditional religions have long put forth such ideas as "God is a circle whose center is everywhere and whose circumference is nowhere" and "each human being is a spark from the Divine Fire, of the same substance and essence as God."

Equally amazing, at least to me, modern philosophy, cosmology and even subatomic physics are arriving at the same conclusion. Alfred North Whitehead, the greatest twentieth-century philosopher, has proposed a theory which would explain "causation at a distance." The new physics and cosmologies are increasingly speaking of the world of time and space as a holographic universe—that is, the whole is contained fully in each of its parts. The Big Bang, and the unimaginable world that preceded it, are still with us, as us; and what was then infinitesimally small is now merely writ large. The primal unity has evolved into inconceivable multiplicity without, however, having lost its unity.

Carl Jung, along with Sigmund Freud one of the founders of all modern psychological theory and practice, grasped this same essential concept and consciously built bridges between modern science and the ancient spiritualities wherever he could. In particular, his notion of the collective unconscious and, at its center, the Self, resonates with modern physics and cosmology, Whiteheadian philosophy and the so-called occult spiritualities.

In the collective unconscious, according to Jung, we are all inextricably tied to one another and the whole vast universe. It could even be said that, in keeping with the more orthodox mystical traditions within the world's religions, at a deep level we are all one. Cardinal Nicholas of Cusa said this. So did the Sufis, Gnostics and many others. The Hindus say, "Thou *art* That!"

At very least there *must* be an intimate correspondence between the way our minds work and the "external" world. If there were not, we could not function within the larger universe.

In my work with Robert Moore concerning the dynamics and structure of the male psyche, we have come upon the idea that this psyche is fundamentally quadrated, that is, divided into four complimentary energies or archetypes—King, Warrior, Magician, and Lover. These are the four basic gradients, or lines of perception, feeling, reflection and action around which our lives—both in terms of our being and in terms of our doing—are organized.

It just so happens that these four organizing principles in the male psyche (and in the female psyche too) correspond both to the structures of the brain—in primal form, the structures of the limbic system—and to the virtually universal myths of the cosmos. In the limbic system we all have affiliative, aversive, switching and leadership neuronal sub-systems which correspond respectively to the Lover, Warrior, Magician and King/Queen psychological potentials. In the myths of the cosmos we notice, too, the strong tendency to experience the world as quadrated. As a refinement, largely of Jungian insights, our discovery confirms Jung's reaffirmation of the ancient dictum "As above so below" or, as he modified it, "As within so without."

Since Moore's and my work has been applied mainly to the workings of the male psyche, it has come to be associated primarily with the men's movement, or, as some prefer to call this shift in the collective male psyche, "men's work." It is certainly true that, up to this point, much of men's work has been inspired and informed primarily by a Jungian view of the world; by art and poetry which can easily be interpreted by such a view and, specifically, by the king, warrior, magician, lover model of the male soul.

In this book, Daniel Lorey has brilliantly brought together all of these interrelated themes—the mystical scientific notions of a holographic universe and the correspondence between microcosm and macrocosm, Jungian interpretive tools, Moore's and my refinement of those tools, specifically as applied to the male soul and elements of the men's movement. He has achieved this synthesis in the interests of a fresh rationale and new applications for the ancient wisdom of astrology.

Daniel Lorey has moved the powerful interpretive tool of astrology from a pre-modern context, through the fires of modern science, into the dawning post-modern era. In the post-modern era, we are coming to know that the ancient myths and spiritual intuitions are true—not in the literal, historical sense in which many people still "believe," (e.g., the Genesis myth), but rather in the sense that they are true to the actual workings of the human soul and its interactions with the cosmos.

Douglas Gillette, M.A., M-Div.
Chicago, Illinois
October 1993

Preface

> "In terms of service to the human race, the typical psychologist and the typical astrologer are only half as effective as they could be, if that much. Let us pray they soon combine their wits."
>
> —Garth Allen[1]

The reasons and motivations for my writing this book are many. Close friends and colleagues have been urging me for years to write a book based on my ideas and methods. Although encompassing many areas of thought, this book primarily reflects my love for both astrology and psychology. Part of my passion is to forge a usable partnership between these two fields of thought.

Both astrology and psychology seek the same end: to better understand the human soul and its unique process of individuation and maturation. These processes occur within the boundaries of the larger cosmos which contain and sustain the human essence.

Carl Jung ventured into unifying these ideas. Only a select few knew of his deep interest in the field of astrology. He was never one to profess such interests openly for fear of tarnishing his reputation within the psychological community. I wonder how many more eminent psychologists are also "closet" astrologers!

Astrology is plagued by an inability to offer a concise, clear and cohesive method of telling a person anything meaningful about who they really are. It is either oversimplified into daily newspaper horoscopes, or hidden behind seemingly obscurative mathematics. It has therefore remained a minimally understood and respected field by most of the population.

I myself must confess that my early relationship to the study of astrology was one of love/hate. I knew there were valuable insights to be gleaned from this art and science, but I was unable to sort through all the confusing methods of interpreting the birth chart. There were many times during my early studies where I walked away from astrology in sheer frustration. The methods designed to help me understand my craft were failing miserably through their constant contradiction. I was lucky enough to happen upon two exceptionally brilliant mentors whose work helped me to sort through the mountains of ideas swimming through my head. I am referring to the research of Cyril Fagan and Donald Bradley (alias Garth Allen). Their work is invaluable, yet obscure, and is now mostly out of print.

The unavailability of their material is a major impetus behind this book. I feel that I owe it to them to keep the best of their ideas alive and available. They both were well educated in the fields of Freudian and Jungian psychology and made major strides towards combining these with astrology.

Cyril Fagan was personally fascinated, in the Freudian sense, with his client's sexual proclivities. He wrote extensively about which specific astrological patterns, he believed, could be shown to accompany certain sexual preferences such as homosexuality and deviations such as sadomasochism. He was the first astrologer, to my knowledge, to entertain the thought of such parallels with sexual Freudian psychology.

Garth Allen, in his booklet *Taking the Kid Gloves Off Astrology*, made a more diverse study of parallels between the astrological planets and their direct influence on the various stages of psychological development in childhood. He showed how Jupiter influenced the stage of "oral fixation" and Saturn determined the stage of "anal fixation" etc. This was the first broad and disciplined psychological study done of the planets.

Both of these teachers paved the way for my particular slant on astrology, which prefers a foundation built solidly upon psychological principles. It was, however, the wonderfully brilliant and concise work of Robert Moore and Douglas Gillette that rounded out my understanding of astrology. They introduced me to their theories on Jung's work involving archetypes and the quadrated psyche.

The archetypes, as I understand them, can best be described in this way. The archetypes are to the human soul what the organs are to the human body. Each is a sub-system with its own specific strengths and abilities. Just as the tissue of the liver is specialized to perform certain tasks, so the makeup of each archetype is also specialized.

The liver is subservient to the needs of the physical organism, which outweigh its own priorities. The same can be said of an archetype. The agenda of an archetype must remain subservient to the needs of the Self and the human soul's larger agenda for self-actualization. It is critical that this scenario of subservience be present. This is the only way that we can maintain a state of wholeness and balance, both physical and psychological.

In recent years there has been a resurgence of interest in Jungian psychology and its discussions of the archetypes, especially in the field of masculine psychology and in the men's movement. Men such as the poet Robert Bly, and Robert Moore of the Chicago Theological Seminary have written extensively in this area. The work of Moore in particular, shines with pure genius. He is a Jungian psychologist who, in his work on the four central archetypes, has succeeded (albeit unknowingly) in nailing down the meanings of the inner planets of astrology!

The inner planets are those closest to the Sun: Mercury, Venus, Earth, and Mars. They pertain to the more personal aspects of the human personality. In reading Moore and Gillette's work on masculine archetypes, I was stunned by the incredible revelation that the planets are the actual physical "depositories" of the archetypes of which they write. I was excited to think that the astrological chart could be used as a personalized map to show each person which particular archetypes were strong within them and, most importantly, *why*.

This offers the possibility of taking a lot of the guess work out of determining which of the archetypes are prominent within your personality and which are absent or de-emphasized. This can all be determined through the astrological techniques of angularity and aspect interpretation. Without the added benefit of this astrological data, one is left to guess as to which archetypes are strongest within themselves.

During the course of my exploring the meanings of these inner planets with you, I shall be referring extensively to Robert Moore and Douglas Gillette's book, *King, Warrior, Magician, Lover: Rediscovering the Archetypes of the Mature Masculine.* I recommend their work to any serious astrologer who truly wants to get a handle on the psychology behind these archetypes (inner planets).

This book will be found to echo in decidedly masculine terms and language because it was inspired from such a strongly masculine perspective on the archetypes. Any woman reading this book will better understand the men in her life as a result. She can also apply the information to her own life by simply substituting the equivalent Goddesses in place of any references to Gods. My next book will deal with a more rounded out "gender specific" astrology that will thoroughly address the element of sexuality within astrology.

Within this book, one will also find many references to the recent recovery movement. This new field of "the people's psychology" has been very effective in reaching the population at large. People like John Bradshaw have helped to introduce the public to the concept of the "inner child." This information is central to this book as well.

The material of this book has been in my head for a number of years now, just waiting to come out. I consider myself to be a kind of research reference librarian. I do not proclaim this material to be completely original. I have been influenced by the work of many brilliant mentors over the years. We are all influenced by the larger collective, of which we are only a part.

Keeping this in mind, we shall start by reviewing the planets. I will go much deeper into all of their meanings, adding newfound knowledge from many sources. In an orderly fashion, we shall start at the center with the personal planets. From there we will work our way to the outer moral and spiritual planets.

Along the way, I will introduce the concept of the Archetypal Tree and help you to construct your own understanding of its importance in organizing the planets. This "Tree," though bearing much resemblance to the Kabalic Tree of Life, is different and has its own special significance. It is not meant to invalidate that system at all. Instead, it is meant to impart its own teaching.

The whole purpose of placing the planets (archetypes) into a larger schematic diagram is to help the student better understand the diverse inter-relatedness of these seemingly unrelated energy patterns. The Warrior archetype (Mars), instead of being viewed as an abstract concept, can now be visually related to as the perfect polar opposite to the Lover archetype (Venus, see page 10).

Without this additional perspective, one runs the risk of missing the forest for the trees in the course of their seeking to better understand the nature of archetypes. The "Tree" helps, on an immediate visual level, to more fully convey the concepts of Yin and Yang as well as the multi-leveled nature of the human psyche. It offers the opportunity, I believe, to transport our understanding of archetypes to the threshold of holographic comprehension.

The Archetypal Tree is the result of 15 years of research and synthesis on my part. I am excited to finally be presenting these ideas to the astrological and psychological communities. The additional connections with human physiology should help to broaden our overall understanding of ourselves as divine organisms.

I shall also introduce a basic common sense numerology as it applies to the planets. The core of my theories in this avenue were inspired by the brilliant work of John Addey on the nature of harmonics. I have, in my own work, taken this a step further by connecting each aspect (harmonic) to a particular planet. I believe this is more in keeping with pure Pythagorean principles.

In my work, I find renewed meaning to the old idea of macrocosm/ microcosm that pervades current trends of thought in both psychology (family systems theory, etc.), and the sciences (astrophysics and holography, etc.). Astrology has always been based in the concept of "as above, so below." I feel the time is ripe for all these fields to be woven into a spectacular tapestry that enriches the lives of all who behold it.

It pleases me to author a book intent on just such a purpose.

Daniel E. Lorey, IV
Franklin Square, NY
October 1993

"The Archetypal Tree"
by Daniel Lorey IV ©1992

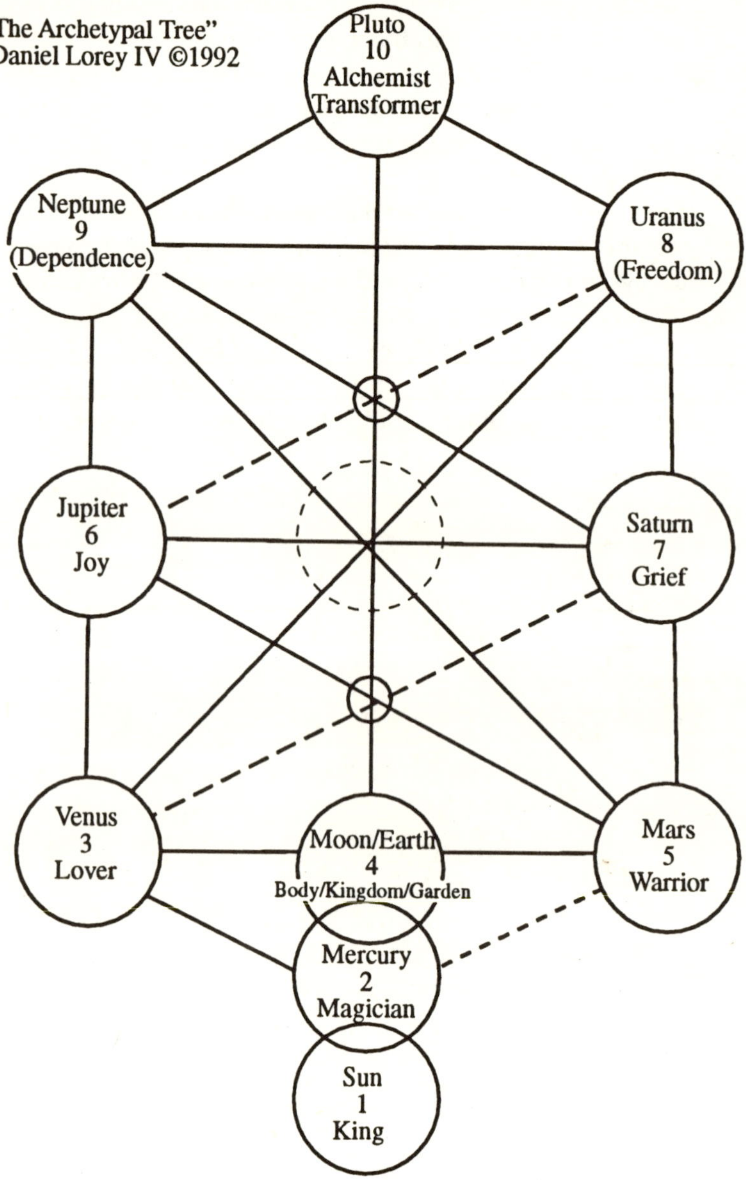

Introduction

The planets are to astrology what the archetypes are to psychology. An archetype is considered to be a basic unchangeable and essential component of the human psyche (soul). From the beginning of time, the planets have always been the spine and guts of astrology. In order to understand the system presented in this book, you must begin by understanding the powerful parallel between archetype and planet.

The inner, or personal, planets are the essence of what makes up the human psyche. They are the central core, the foundation out of which the healthy ego grows. The outer planets are the seasonings that flavor us with spiritual maturity and moral fiber on our journey through life. These two groups are separated by the asteroid belt, a clear physical indication that they are vastly different in their significance.

The inner planets are the Sun, Mercury, Venus, Mars. Traditional astrology is based in a geocentric perspective—seeing the Earth as the center of the universe. The circular chart is the sky above and below the Earth. Subsequently, the Earth does not appear as a planet in the chart and is usually not considered an influence. However, I include the Earth as an archetypal influence. The Earth and her days and seasons are important to our sense of grounding both spiritually and physically.

The inner planets represent the hardware of the human computer. They are absolutely central to the human psyche. This is essential for us to understand, as far too many astrologers focus on the powerful and more dramatic influences of the outer planets, writing the inner group off as boring and mundane. The outer planets represent the software for our computer, offering additional programs for the human experience. They pertain to values, principles and awareness that we add to our foundation.

The crucial thing to realize here is that you cannot boot-up your software when your hardware is not functioning correctly. If your central circuits are not properly integrated, then the whole system never gets up and running.

The archetypes and the inner planets are linked both in their symbology and in their very real and present energies. The Sun is the King; The Warrior, Mars; The Magician, Mercury; The Lover, Venus. And the Earth is of course the primal source for humanity, which is linked to the Wild Man.

These five central elements form the "hub" of the human soul and its experiences. This is depicted beautifully in the cover design of this book. The Earth/Wildman is at the center depicting the Egocentric design of human consciousness. Surrounding this center are the four primary archetypes that influence and shape our human destiny. This is the blueprint of what Carl Jung called the quadrated nature of human consciousness. He brilliantly documented man's universal fascination with four-fold patterns of expression that can be found in countless cultures throughout the whole of our human history.

The essence of astrology, no matter the method of interpretation, is quite simple: The astrologer casts an astrological birth chart in an attempt to capture and represent a moment in the dynamic "dance" of planets as they move around the Earth. It is much the same as attempting to take a photograph of something that is alive and in motion. The photograph, at best, simply hopes to convey the essence of what it captures. The astrological picture, as we will see, is three dimensional. The astrologer suffers an immediate restriction when he attempts to draw this 3-D reality onto a two dimensional piece of paper!

To understand the three dimensionality of a chart, the best method is a simple exercise in creative visualization. This basic technique can prevent you from being confused about these concepts as we proceed further.

Imagine yourself standing outside in a wide open field. You are facing directly South with your hands stretched out to your sides like a bird. Through orienting yourself in this way, you will be better able to completely understand the way that planets appear to visually move around the Earth during the course of the day. Turn your head and look directly to your left, down the length of your left arm and out over your finger tips to the eastern horizon. This is the place where the Sun first appears every morning at sunrise. This point is known to astrologers as the *ascendant*. All planets will rise here in the course of their daily travel around the Earth.

Since most people are familiar with the motion of the Sun, we will use this heavenly body to represent the motion of any planetary body as it travels around the Earth. They all follow this same pattern.

The first thing to remember is that all celestial bodies move in a clockwise direction around the Earth. Continuing with our visualization, the Sun would, upon rising in the east, start to rise higher and higher above the Earth as it also begins to arc over towards the south (directly in front of us). When the sun has climbed to its highest point in the sky, it will be due south and the time of day will be high noon. Astrologers call this location the *mid-heaven*, or *upper meridian*, or M.C. for short.

From this point onward, the Sun will gradually begin to sink or fall lower and lower in the sky until it starts to approach the western horizon. This is where it sets every evening. In our visualization, the Sun will now appear directly over the fingertips of our right hand. Astrologers call this point the *descendant*.

The remainder of the Sun's daily path occurs during the night hours and takes it underneath the Earth. The Sun will continue to sink until it reaches the lowest point of its travels. It would now be located in the general direction underneath our feet and directly behind us to the North. This coincides with midnight and is referred to by astrologers as the *lower meridian*, or I.C. for short (fig. 1).

Astrologers, in their attempt to assign significance to the exact location of each planet, have divided this daily circle into twelve smaller subunits called *houses*. Each house has come to represent a very specific definition. Planets, located within a particular house's confines, are thus associated with its respective definition.

Through this method, your average astrologer will proceed to classify and define your personality based on where the planets fall in your own personal birth chart. The chart is cast for the exact moment of your entry into this world and is thus believed to contain a total representation of the energies that imprinted themselves indelibly upon your psyche during the birth crisis.

I personally accept this theory of a synchronistic imprinting that occurs during the birth experience. The incarnation of a spirit into a fleshy vessel is *the* monumental occurrence in the evolution and course of each human life. The position and alignment of the planets (archetypes) at that crucial moment are thus directly influential and significant for that particular person's life.

As far as the methods used by the astrologer to interpret the exact meaning of the planetary arrangements, I find no credibility in the standard and popular method of using the 12 houses to define a human personality. I have, instead, developed my own system of interpreting

Figure 1

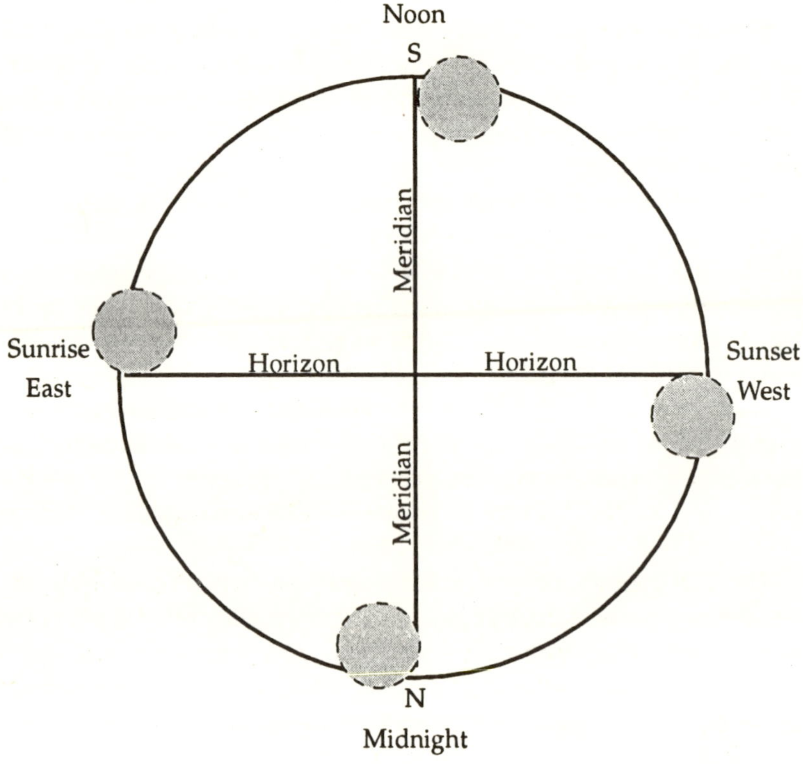

Planets placed here are *most* active

Gauquelin "Power Spots"

the planets through defining them according to their placement within the four basic quadrants.

It has long been agreed upon by astrologers that the *four angles* of the chart are the most potent locations in the mundane sphere. These are the four cardinal directions; North (I.C.), South (M.C.), East (ascendant), and West (descendant). They are the only points in the mundane sphere that I consider valid and potent, *because they truly exist*. I consider the argument for the other house cusps to be an impotent one.

The four quarters and cardinal directions are notions that appear in many world religions. The 12 houses of traditional astrology divert attention from this very important point: *The circle that comprises an astrological chart is an image of the Earth.*

This methodology deviates notably from standard astrological practice, but demands serious consideration. I propose a bold new method of chart interpretation that radically departs from older and more traditional systems. It is less esoteric in nature and therefore is more accessible and understandable. It is Earth-centered, and therefore it is important to begin with a deep and thorough explanation of the Earth's four angles.

The two large divisional axes, which create the four angles, are worth exploring in further detail. The first axis is called the Meridian or time marker. This is the line of demarcation between Midnight till Noon (when the Sun is rising) and Noon till Midnight (when it is falling). It splits the daily circle vertically down the middle and signifies the left brain/right brain split of our consciousness. The Eastern (rising) half of the meridian is left brain and the Western (setting) half of the meridian is right brain (fig. 2).

The entire meridian carries a solar *I Am* quality to it. Planets found on the upper meridian (M.C.) represent our outer, visible sense of I Am-ness. Planets located on the lower meridian (I.C.) denote our sense of inner, private I Am-ness. The M.C. is related to the principles of the King archetype, and its two representatives: Sun and Jupiter. The I.C. is related to the qualities of the Magician archetype, and his three allies: Mercury, Saturn, and Pluto.

The second axis is called the Horizon. It is created by the actual body of the Earth which serves to cut the heaven in two. Half lies below us, incapable of being perceived. This is representative of the unconscious mind or netherworld of mythology. The other half lies above the Earth, signifying our conscious mind, or that which is out in the open. The upper half of the chart correlates, physiologically, to the cerebrum and the lower half to the cerebellum (fig. 3).

Figure 2

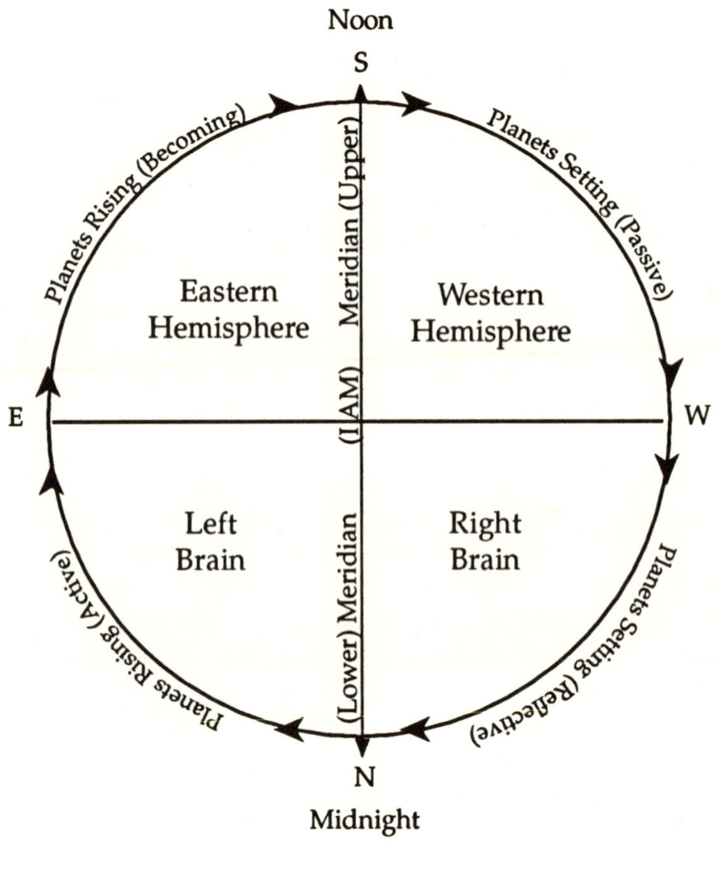
Noon
S
Planets Rising (Becoming)
Meridian (Upper)
Planets Setting (Passive)
Eastern Hemisphere
Western Hemisphere
E
(I AM)
W
Left Brain
Right Brain
Planets Rising (Active)
(Lower) Meridian
Planets Setting (Reflective)
N
Midnight

Figure 3

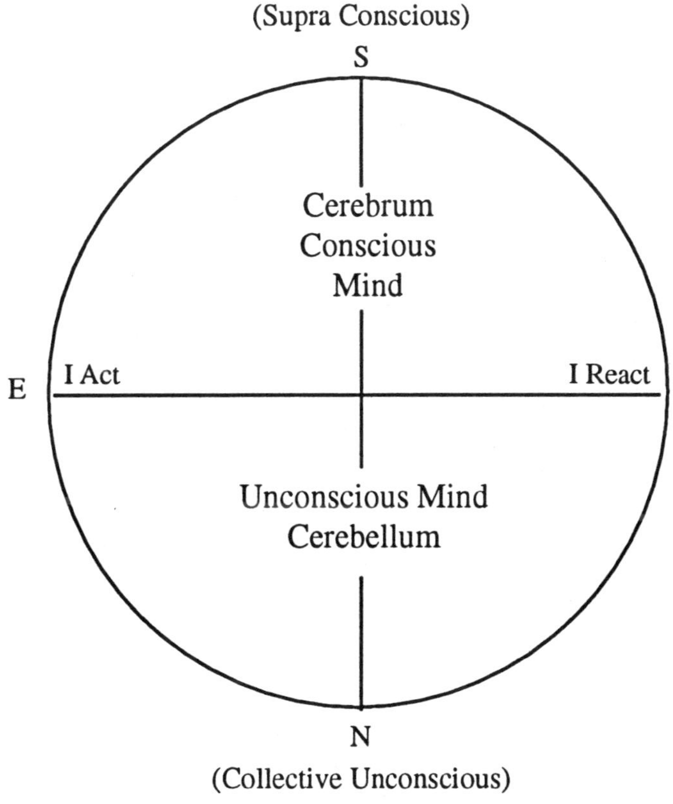
(Supra Conscious)
S
Cerebrum
Conscious
Mind
E
I Act
I React
Unconscious Mind
Cerebellum
N
(Collective Unconscious)

The entire axis of the horizon represents the lunar stimulus-response nature of the psyche. The Ascendant corresponds to our *I Act* impulse. It is ruled by the Warrior archetype and his two spokesmen, Mars and Uranus. The Descendant represents the *I React* response. It is ruled by the Lover archetype and its two envoys, Venus and Neptune.

This simple quadrated structure offers a wealth of information. Hidden within its simplicity can be found the psychological types developed by Carl Jung, introversion and extroversion, and the principles of the rational versus irrational. This allows for four basic combinations between all these preferences.

Each of the four quadrants in the chart correlates to one of the four human archetypes (fig. 4). The first quadrant (moving clockwise from the ascendant) is that of the Warrior and relates to the rational extrovert. Planets in this zone of one's birth chart are under the general influence of the Warrior. He is objectively oriented in a rational, calculating way. The Warrior is mentally detached from his environment.

Continuing clockwise, the second zone resonates with the King archetype. He is known as the irrational extrovert. The King is also outwardly concerned with his realm, but he is not detached like the Warrior. He is passionately involved with his kingdom and feels all the joy and grief of his people. He intuitively sacrifices himself for his people. The Warrior would see this as irrational!

The third quadrant relates to the Lover. This psychological type is known as the irrational introvert. The Lover's energy is personal and focused on his own inner, subjective world. He is unconcerned that others may view him as irrational and out of control. This archetype is intuitively surrendering to something much deeper, which is profoundly spiritual.

The last sector corresponds to the Magician archetype. Here we encounter the rational introvert. He is also concerned with his own subjective world, but in a logical and intellectual way. The Magician turns his discerning faculties inward upon himself, seeking to better understand his own soul through this process.

How one's planets are distributed throughout the circle will determine the general inclination of the personality. When the planets are highly concentrated within one or two quadrants of the chart, this will bias the way in which the individual perceives and responds to the world.

This method of viewing the chart will, I believe, offer much more personal and meaningful insights into an individual's psyche. (The astrological term for the individual being analyzed in a chart is the

Figure 4

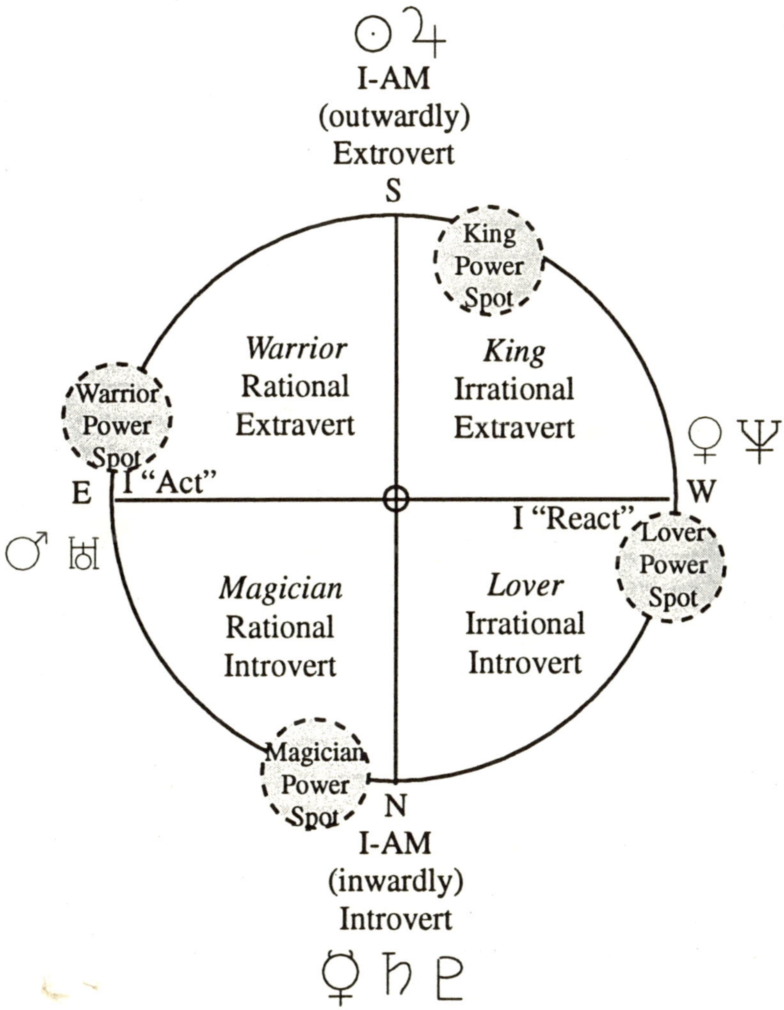

☉ ♃
I-AM
(outwardly)
Extrovert
S
King Power Spot
Warrior
Rational
Extravert
King
Irrational
Extravert
♀ ♆
Warrior Power Spot
E
I "Act"
W
I "React"
Lover Power Spot
♂ ♅
Magician
Rational
Introvert
Lover
Irrational
Introvert
Magician Power Spot
N
I-AM
(inwardly)
Introvert
☿ ♄ ♇

native.) I see this as being preferable to the unrelated trivialities of the twelve houses, (money, children, inheritance, clubs, etc.). These things are only secondary to the native himself. I feel that these areas of focus serve only to take us further away from, rather than closer to, an understanding of the person.

The 12 house method is identical to my "quadrant" system in only one respect. They both assign constant meanings or characteristics to specific regions of the circle. These assignments do not change in either system. Their differences arise from the fact that my quadrant system holds true to the four-fold nature of the human soul and the clockwise direction of planets as they circle the Earth.

The 12 house method follows the irrational premise that the Earth's circle should be broken up into 12 sections that are given meanings relating to the 12 signs of the zodiac. These 12 houses are then laid out in a counter clockwise direction, which completely goes against the natural "clockwise" motion of the planets in their daily travel around the Earth!

There are other credible and respectable studies that have independently arrived at some of the same conclusions as myself, most notably the work of Michel and Francoise Gauquelin on placement of planets. Most astrologers, using the 12 house system, have had a difficult time reconciling the differences between their methods and the irrefutable statistical research of the Gauquelins. The Gauquelins have done exhaustive statistical research on the significance of angularity, drawing conclusions that are brilliant but much too vast to explore within the context of this book. A simplified description of the essence of their research, however, must be noted here. They have shown that planets just above the ascendant or just past the midheaven were situated in "power spots." This was also true of planets just past the descendant and I.C., but to a lesser degree.

These power spots act as windows that allow the energies of planets found in those locations to gain access to the outside world by manifesting as traits within the individual. Those planets take center stage in the way others perceive us. They are the energies most likely to shine out from within our psyches and be seen by others.

These four windows give further credence to the quadrated nature of the psyche. When planetary archetypes are found located within these "power zones," they lock powerfully into the individual's ego structure. If Mercury is in the rising hot spot, for example, the person will be overly identified with the Magician archetype in their own personal definition of who they are. It might even be said that they are adversely "possessed" by Hermes and incapable of distancing their ego from the Magus archetype. If there are no other planetary archetypes present within any of the four power zones, Hermes may dominate or possess all aspects of the person's life.

Let us take just one of these four power zones and show how it can deeply empower any archetype (for better or worse) that is found within its domain. We shall work with the Warrior power zone, located just above the ascendant. If the Sun (King archetype) is located here, the person will manifest many traits of the King in an active, assertive and willful fashion. They may be compassionate and bless others, if their King is healthy, or tyrannically oppress and curse others, if their King is wounded. The one certainty throughout is that the King archetype will manifest itself in some form or other.

If we find Venus (the Lover) located within the rising power zone, this person will manifest the Lover in many ways. They are "touchy-feely" kind of people who enjoy, and need, to make physical contact with everyone they meet. This can range from a simple comforting hand upon your shoulder to all out seduction if they find you attractive. A lot will depend on the health or woundedness of the archetype.

When Mars resides within the Warrior power zone, the result should be easy to intuit. These natives are often classified as "go getters". Their drive towards personal achievement can be so intense that they are often viewed as obnoxious, brutal and blunt in their dealings with others. Unless this trait is tempered by other factors within their chart, they will be pegged as aggressors or as having "brass balls."

Paying keen attention to these angular planets is one of the key ways in which my approach varies greatly from standard astrological methods. These Gauquelin power zones are not considered angular and dynamic in traditional astrology. They occupy roughly the same positions as the "cadent" houses which are not considered to be dynamic in their expression. I feel this is one of the major weaknesses of the 12 house system. This obscuring of the true power locations of the chart throws a wet blanket over the flames of understanding and seriously hampers the astrologer in his task.

I have just given you a small taste of how I work with angularity when interpreting a chart. This method will be expanded upon, in more depth, at the end of each of the planetary chapters. This will give you a complete understanding of the nature of each of the planets when they are found on each of the four angles.

Another concept, important to understanding the relationship of the planets to each other, is that of aspects. Aspects are angular relations between planets as seen in the natal chart. Common aspects are squares (90° of arc), trines (120° of arc), and oppositions (180°). Aspects are simply the relationship that planets have to each other based purely on their position. Two planets will blend with a certain "flavor" depending on this angular relationship.

If the Sun and Moon are positioned 180° apart (this opposition is known as the full moon phase) they will resonate differently than if they were separated by 90° (this square is also the first quarter phase). All these planetary aspects are viewed from the vantage point of the Earth. Aspects are purely numerical harmonics in terms of their overall expression.

A *Grand* Configuration occurs when planets are seen in *patterns* of aspects, for example, a Grand Trine indicates that three planets in the chart are each 120° apart from the other and if lines were drawn to connect them, they would form an equilateral triangle.

The Conjunction is the most common aspect. It is, therefore, the most frequently found aspect in any astrological chart. Then comes the Opposition, Grand Trine, Grand Square, Grand Quintile, Grand Sextile, etc. Each time we increase the ante by one, (by adding another planet to the picture) the probability of having the whole pattern perfectly represented becomes more and more of a rarity. Each "Grand Configuration" becomes a less common occurrence, with each planet (foci) that we add.

The power of these configurations, when fully present, increases with each planet we add. That is, a complete Grand Square, in the chart, is more powerful than a complete Grand Trine, etc. The reason for this is through the simple addition of another planet (archetypal generator) to the pattern. This provides the structure with an increase in total energy output. A Grand Sextile, for example, would represent an awesome power structure within the psyche of that person.

All these structures, composed of multiple archetypes/planets, are indicative of advanced "integrated circuits" within the soul of that native. I believe they are notches in our belt of evolution. As a result of lessons learned or not learned through past life experiences we carry integrated power structures within our makeup. Their purpose is to work in a group effort to help urge us on towards self-actualization. They are an inner reality map of collective strengths which we have achieved and earned through past efforts.

These aspects, whether acting alone or in group effort, serve to help us define our own personal issues. For example, two people may each have the Sun in the rising power zone. One may be a compassionate person who blesses and empowers others, while the other may be a subversive tyrant who undermines others and overpowers them.

The difference in how each man's King archetype manifests can be found in the aspects to their respective Suns. The first man might have Sun conjunct Venus and the second might have Sun square Pluto. Each planetary aspect offers various potentialities that seek to manifest in our lives. Some aspects lend themselves to harmonious expression while other are more of a struggle to manage. In the course of the text, we shall find that much can be gleaned from their patterns.

This book unfolds in a very deliberate fashion. Chapters 1 through 10 will introduce the planets to those who are unfamiliar with them. I have incorporated much new information, gathered by the recent Voyager missions, which will actually serve to round out your overall understanding of the outer planets.

In the later chapters, I also offer a sizable helping of new information in the areas of metaphysics and medical astrology. These are areas that are sorely in need of updating.

We shall discover in the course of this book the absolute genius in the way the solar system has been ordered and laid out. This same wisdom is inherent within the design of humans as well. The universe is one big hologram. Our solar system is simply a huge holographic representation of the human psyche, as seen on a much larger scale. Within its design is the wisdom of the human soul externalized.

We shall start at the center with the Sun and work our way outward in the exact order that the planets are found. Each successive chapter will build upon the knowledge contained within the previous ones. It is therefore important not to skip around as you read. There is a glossary of terms found at the end of the book that will help you with any unfamiliar words.

CHAPTER ONE

The Sun, The King

☉ The Sun has always been associated with the archetype of The King. It is an energy of one-ness and order. In ancient Egypt he was Ra, the Sun-King, who traveled across the arc of the heavens in his celestial boat, in order to view all of creation and bless his Kingdom. All the lesser gods (planets) served him. The Egyptian myth is only one of many that reflects this theme as it manifests in the nature of the solar system.

The Sun is the brightest and most powerful object in our world. It is the center of the solar system and the anchor to which all of creation is tied. The Sun is composed primarily of hydrogen, which is the basic building block of the whole created universe.

From this simplicity, it generates a fusion reaction that emits light and heat. It is a huge radiator and giver of life. The Sun-King represents sacrifice. He expends himself so that his Kingdom may be blessed by his light and flourish.

Because the Sun has to do with the concept of one-ness and fusion, its energy is also represented by the conjunction aspect. All conjunctions, in a chart, carry a solar flavor within them. They represent the fusing together of two (or more) celestial bodies into a subjective one-ness. Boundaries collapse and the archetypes of the conjunct planets melt together into a radiating power source, much like the sun.

We encounter the essence of this archetype when we enter the world as a newborn infant. We all come into this world as a "Divine Child," that pure spark of brilliance very akin to the Sun. This is the infantile, undeveloped energy of the King made flesh.

We see this phenomenon reflected in the myths of the Divine Child. The stories of Jesus, Moses and Horus all have this theme running through them. There is an innocent child, destined for greatness, entering into a hostile world that wants to destroy him.

The old order is threatened by him. Herod rises up to slay the infants. Set (the "dark one") searches for Horus in order to kill him. In all these cases, the child is protected by the female (the mother). Mary whisks Jesus away in time, Isis suckles Horus amidst the papyrus plants of the Nile, and Pharaoh's daughter hides Moses.

All these myths point out two things. The Divine Child is truly a genuine all powerful King and yet, at the same time, he is totally helpless and in need of protection. He contains the seed of a King and must be tended to and nurtured until he can stand on his own. The Divine Child must also be taught and disciplined. He will eventually aspire to Kingship through the rites of initiation. Jesus, Moses, Plato, Pythagoras, were all initiated before they became leaders.

The Pyramid

At this point I need to introduce the concept of the pyramidal structure and how it relates to our understanding of the four central archetypes. I became aware of this analogy through the work of Robert Moore and Douglas Gillette, especially, *King, Warrior, Magician, Lover: Rediscovering the Archetypes of the Mature Masculine.*[1] Their development of this concept is brilliant and lucid and merits some overview at this point.

According to Moore and Gillette, we can better understand the human psyche if we view its structure as being akin to that of a pyramid. Each of the four sides represents one of the mature archetypes, in the male psyche, they are: King, Warrior, Magician, and Lover. Each also has a planetary correlation: The Sun represents the King; Mercury, the Magician; Venus, the Lover; and Mars, the Warrior. Each side (archetype) has a bi-polar shadow form at its base (fig. 1a). As this immature energy of the shadow is educated and initiated, it refines itself and rises to its mature form at the apex of the side.[2]

We humans are actually "living pyramids" which, just like plants, must have a root system to nourish our growth. The pyramid we are aware of consciously is actually part of a double pyramid or octahedron. The other invisible half is projecting straight downward into the Earth (fig. 1b).

This is the unconscious, shadow half of our psyche. From its rich depth we nourish and feed our conscious manifest self. It is as essential to our growth and health as the root system is to a tree. Part of personal initiation and healing is learning how to go down into our dark side and re-connect to the split-off, shadow fragments of our personalities. As we

Figure 1a

Taken from *King-Warrior-Magician-Lover*

Pages 18-19

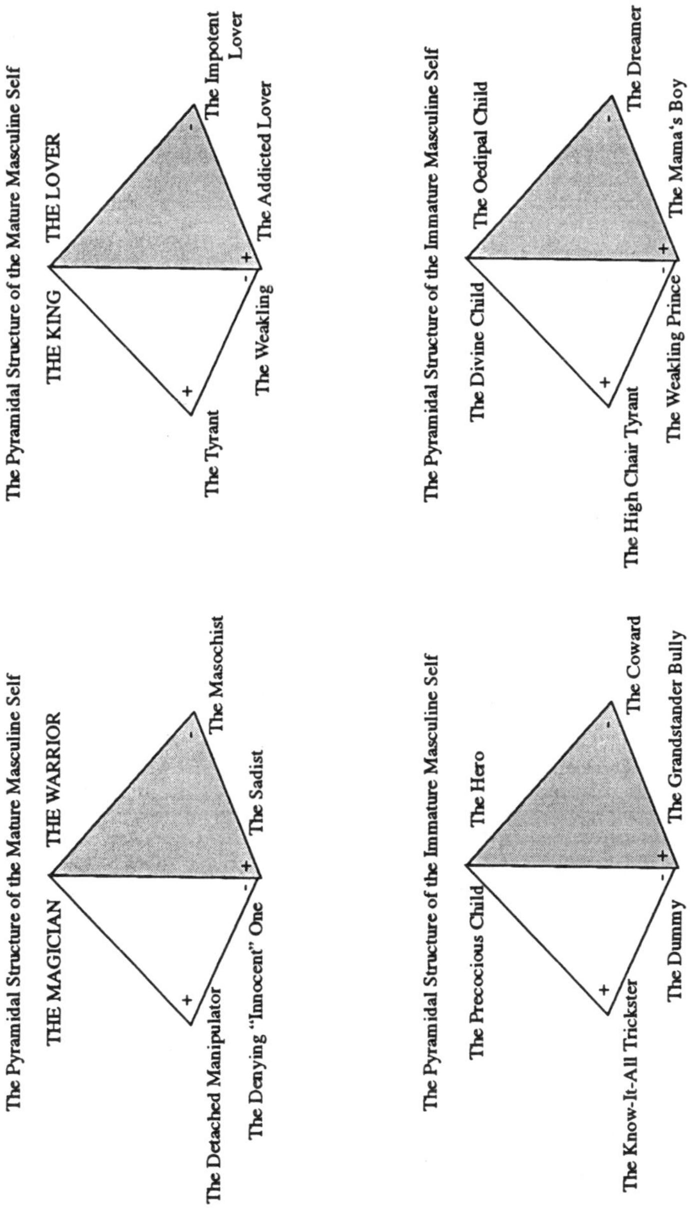

Figure 1b

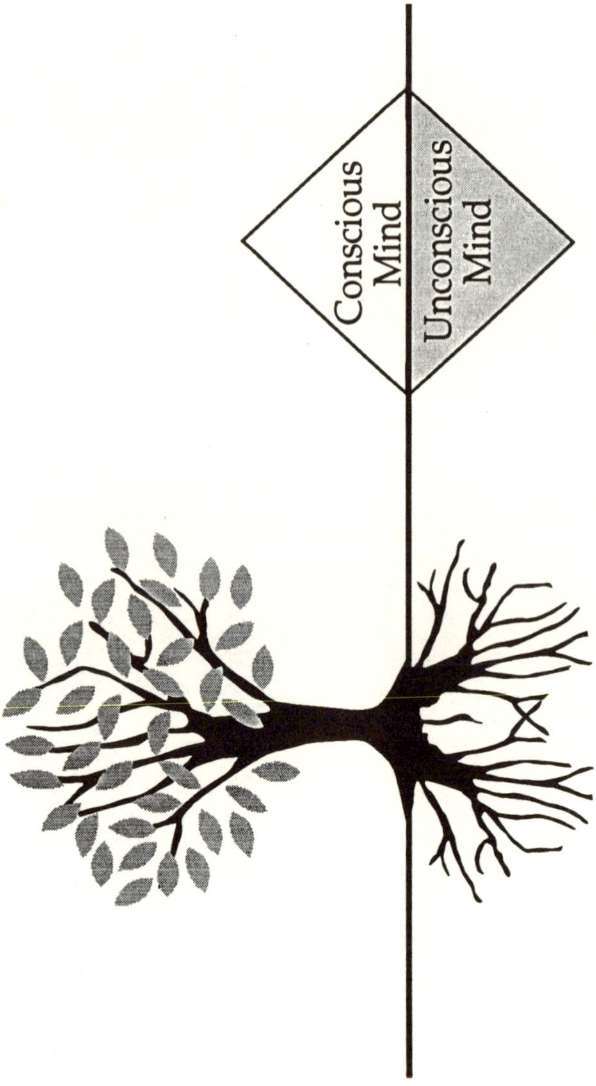

discover in the process of studying our archetypal astrology, most of us are only a fraction of who we were meant to be.

Psychic Wounds = Immaturity (Adult Children)

The developing archetypes of children should mature into a healthy foundational pyramid, upon which the adult pyramid of archetypes can be built. All ancient civilizations built their pyramids upon earlier pre-existing ones, rather than destroying the efforts of the earlier builders. The adult psyche reflects this very same idea. Underneath its pyramid of the four adult archetypes lies the smaller pyramid of the four childhood archetypes (fig. 1c).

We encounter, in childhood, a major problem if these infantile archetypes are not acknowledged, loved and matured. If instead we are raised by abusive and neglectful parents who lack the wisdom to recognize our divine archetypes, these child selves become wounded and fragmented. Their development is drastically thwarted as major chunks of them split-off and go into hiding in the unconscious. The body grows and matures leaving large sections of the soul behind. Wounded children remain largely immature on an inner psychic level. This results in the, now well known, adult child syndrome. The work of Alice Miller[3] and John Bradshaw[4] is paramount in coming to understand the full impact of these psychic wounds. They both allude to it as soul murder.

The bi-polar shadow forms of each archetype, are a direct result of this psychic wounding or shaming that occurs to us early in child development. Some of us have been more affected by this phenomenon than others. I believe we all have unresolved issues and wounds centering around these four archetypes. This is especially true in this age of spiritual ignorance, where initiation has all but disappeared.

Robert Moore has a realistic way of looking at this predicament. He feels that it's not a matter of *if* we are manifesting any of the shadow forms. It's really just a question of *how* we are manifesting them! Having shadows (wounds) is part of being human.[5]

If we turn to the concept of the Archetypal Tree, we can see that the inner planet archetypes form the foundation of the tree. This foundation is the launching pad from which we ascend into the ideals embodied by the outer planets. If we are to fully self-actualize, we must tend to these wounds hidden within the unconscious half of this base-structure.

Many of us have much pain associated with the shame of never having had our Divine Child (Sun-King) recognized adequately by our

Figure 1c

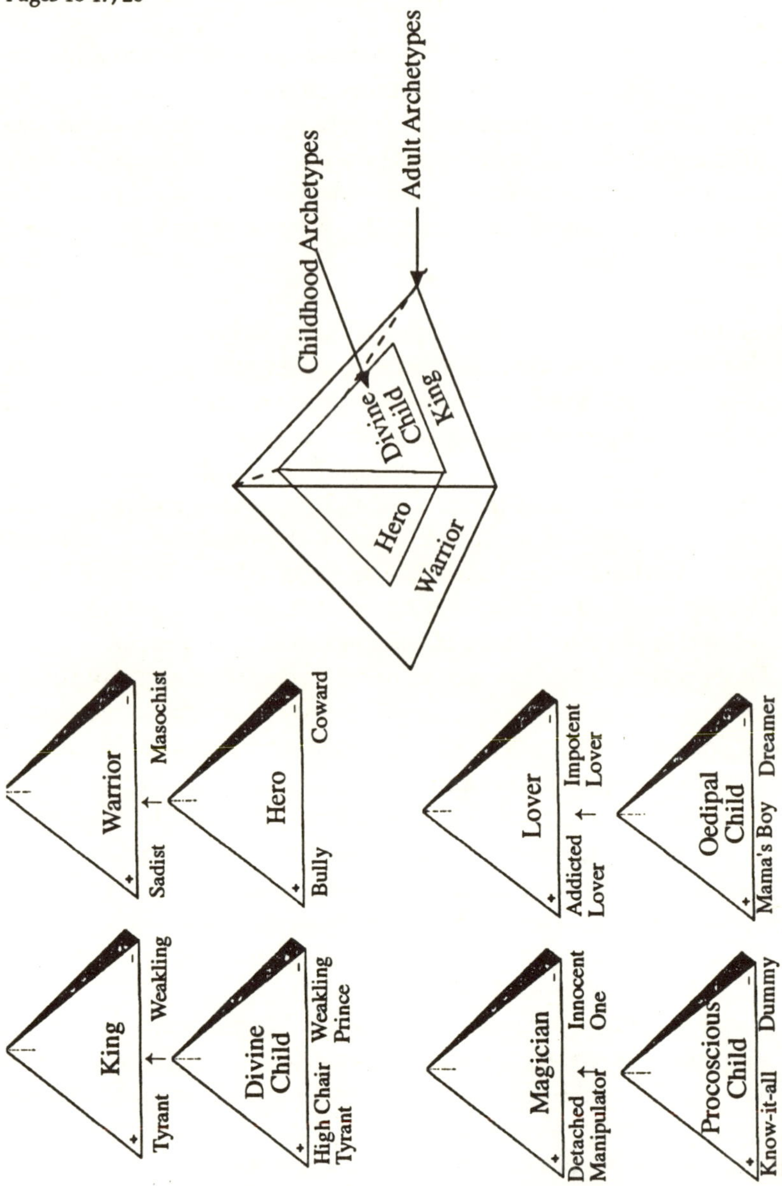
Childhood Archetypes
Adult Archetypes
Divine Child
King
Hero
Warrior
King
Tyrant
Weakling
Divine Child
High Chair Tyrant
Weakling Prince
Warrior
Sadist
Masochist
Hero
Bully
Coward
Magician
Detached Manipulator
Innocent One
Procoscious Child
Know-it-all Trickster
Dummy
Lover
Addicted Lover
Impotent Lover
Oedipal Child
Mama's Boy
Dreamer

parents. If the parent fails to see, value and love the Divine Child nature within their children, it splits off into the shadow of the unconscious and manifests either as the positive pole (high chair tyrant), or the negative pole (weakling prince).

The child's psyche moves to protect itself from the pain of this shame and rejection by separating from it (splitting it off). He either ascends high up into the high chair, or hides deep within the closet of the unconscious. He becomes "more than" or "less than," overinflated or underinflated. He never achieves proper maturation through healthy mirroring, blessing and teaching. Thus we have the beginnings of what Moore and Gillette call "infantile grandiosity." This is a false or distorted greatness, because the child's "true greatness" has never been acknowledged, fostered and disciplined.

Most of us are very out of touch with healthy, mature, adult Sun-King energy. Many adults carry the immature shadow parts of childhood directly into their adult life virtually unchanged. The energy of the High Chair Tyrant shows up in adulthood as the overinflated corporate executive who exploits and abuses others. He berates and squashes all of the beauty within his employees. Like Herod, he seeks to kill all signs of freshness, creativity and life. He is sensitive to criticism, because he is vigilantly trying to hide his own wound from the world. Inwardly he is really weak and impotent.[6]

The key to developing a healthy sense of the adult King, is to go back to the point of the original wound. Robert Bly calls this "the descent downward into the ashes of our grief."[7] We must establish a relationship with the wounded Divine Child within us. This can be done by befriending him in a number of ways: active imagination, invoking him and inner dialoguing, etc.

We must acknowledge him and invite him to leave the shadows of his shame. He can then come out into the light where there can be a relationship. It means "helping him down from the high chair" as Robert Moore so aptly puts it. Only then can we begin to parent this Divine Child to eventually become a healthy adult King in this world.

As we heal our Sun-King wounds, we will start to experience King energy in its fullness. Our personality will become more organized, structured and calm. We will start to feel more comfortably centered within our own bodies (kingdoms). This is what has been called Maat (right order) by the Egyptians. King energy signifies fertility and blessing. He always affirms and acknowledges good deeds and actions. He is a channel for the King in the other world.

All us Earthly kings must never associate ourselves with *the* King. To do so is sheer suicide. We are only meant to be stewards of King energy say Moore and Gillette.[8] All of us are living in limited containers (bodies) that act as containment vessels or stepdown transformers, if you will. We were never designed to handle a "full load." If that were the case, we would have been born on the Sun. Everyone knows what happens to those who fly too close!

Our proper place is here on Earth as stewards of a satellite in the King's domain. Part of adult initiation is to learn to accept one's proper place in relation to the King. We cannot be the King, unless we want to fry our circuits. We can, however, act as noble servants and teachers of his wisdom and creativity. We also can pass on his legacy, but we may never claim ownership of it.

The King also has to do with genetics and the passing on of the legacy through reproduction and lineage. This is where the whole concept of the royal bloodline comes from. He represents the genetically encoded wisdom locked in the chromosomes at the center of every cell. It is truly exquisite how nature holographically represents itself on so many different levels. From the atom, to the cell, to the solar system: Sun-King energy always represents itself at the center.

It is my belief that we are foolishly toying with the very essence of Kingly (divine) energy by dabbling in nuclear physics and genetic engineering. This, to me, is evidence of infantile grandiosity in the form of the high chair tyrant and the Magician shadow: the "know it all" (see Chapter 2). These scientists actually believe that they can improve on the true greatness and perfection found in nature. I liken these men to children playing with dynamite! How many more mutant viruses and Chernobyls do we need before we, as a race, can learn our proper place?

Humanity is rapidly de-evolving, because we have lost the conscious connection to our King archetype. Ours is a time where Kings are laughed at as being unnecessary and disregarded in our ignorance. We have chosen to ignore the value of Sun-King energy for so long now, that we have lost much of the valuable teachings passed down through the oral traditions of many tribal cultures.

This was the whole purpose behind the Sun worship of Ra, Aten, Mithra and Apollo, etc. All the ancient cultures taught and stressed to their children to always maintain a conscious connection to their source of divinity and life. In turn, they learned true humility and spirituality through knowing their proper place and their limitations as human beings.

I encourage you to develop your own personal ritual process, one that allows you to connect to the Sun energy in your inner make-up. Invoke the King, through the use of symbols and pictures, to help access a "feel" for his energy. Establish contact with the wounded Divine Child. The more you can heal and befriend him, the more you will be able to move truly forward. You will be helping him to mature into a strong, healthy, balanced force in your life that knows its place in the scheme of creation.

The Sun and the Four Angles

To see how Sun energy operates in the life of an individual, you can examine its position in the natal chart. The King archetype is particularly strong if the Sun is found in any of the four power zones. It must be mentioned that there is a enormous difference between a planet being located in a particular quadrant as opposed to being found within that *quadrant's* power zone. One quick example will serve to clarify.

In the introduction, I gave an example of the types of traits that will manifest when the Sun is found within the power zone of the Warrior quadrant. One might expect these same traits to be present if the Sun was located *anywhere* within the Warrior quadrant. This is not always the case, however, and I must explain why.

The power zones represent the "hot spots" within each quadrant where that quadrant's influence is likely to affect the planet found there. If the Sun was found in the "background" of the Warrior quadrant (midway between the ascendant and midheaven), then the influence of this quadrant upon the Sun would not be discernible at all. It would be drowned out by other more dominant influences.

The only exception would be if the Sun was connected, via a major aspect, (square, opposition, etc.) to some other planet that *was* located within one of the four power zones. The Sun could then find expression, indirectly, through this other angular archetype. The Warrior traits, attributable to the Sun's placement within that quadrant, might then be somewhat apparent to others because of this indirect avenue of expression.

Because of these complexities, I will confine myself exclusively to discussion of the planetary archetypes only when they are located within the four power zones. The "peak point" of power, within each of these power zones, is located 12-15 degrees past each angle when moving in a clockwise direction. This phenomenon must be seen as a bell curve in terms of the zone's ability to help planets manifest their nature. The manifesting ability of the zones will fall off, in either direction, as we move away from this peak point. This will help you to gauge the relative strength of any planet in terms of angularity.

The Sun in the King Power Zone

When located just past the midheaven, the Sun is truly empowered. This is the time of day when the Earth has reached its peak temperature as a result of the Sun's physical influence. It would logically follow that all other influences, attributable to the Sun, would also be at their peak. The King is perched regally on his throne in the fullest sense of that phrase!

A person with this arrangement has wonderful potential for leadership. The King archetype (the Sun) is located within his own quadrant's power zone! As a result, this native will have a strong need to have their King seen and admired by others. They seek to lead, bless and empower others. They also desire, and usually achieve, massive success in their careers. The Sun's vision of prosperity seeks to take others along for the ride.

These people have tremendous stamina, personal magnetism and charisma. Others naturally look to them as authority figures and they feel quite comfortable in that role. This feeds their rather large Egos. In its negative expression, this can often lead to shadow forms of the King such as grandiosity and tyrannical tendencies.

If the King is wounded within this person, they can often turn out to be a self-serving King. This can manifest as the "back stabbing" young executive who is climbing the corporate ladder towards success. He views everyone else as a potential threat to his power and seeks to squash them in whatever underhanded method he can think of.

The Sun in the Lover Power Zone

When the Sun is found at the descendant, or just below, he is resting comfortably within the Lover's domain. The Sun represents the central purpose of our lives. In this particular setup, that purpose is strongly colored by the priorities of the Lover power zone.

These natives get their primary sense of purpose through "relationship" and intimacy with those closest to them. They are most comfortable in marriage or a committed relationship. This setup fuels their central purpose. These people feel empowered in the role of provider to their spouse and children. These provisions can be either emotional, monetary or both. The healthy King seeks to give to his loved ones. He lives for his family.

When the King is wounded, a different scenario emerges. These natives will often become enmeshed within their loved one's lives, using them for their own narcissistic gratification. The family, as he sees it, lives for him. They can tyrannically oppress their spouse and/or children's feelings by terrorizing them with their own. They seek to dominate and control every aspect of their family's life.

The Sun in the Magician Power Zone

This is the most introverted of the four zones and stands diametrically opposed to the place where the Sun is most empowered in an outward sense (the midheaven). The extroverted nature of the King is thus turned inward upon oneself. The results of this can vary widely from one person to the next.

Because this zone is buried far down within the unconscious region of the chart, it may be said that this person's true purpose will probably be obscured from other's sight and possibly even their own. They can often feel uncomfortably vague about where their sense of personal power lies. Without introspection, it may remain hidden indefinitely.

These natives need to take much time for self-reflection in order to uncover their King within. Meditation and spiritual practices are crucial for them. Their sense of power and purpose is directly connected to the dark inner world of the Magician. Without searching for it there, they will remain essentially powerless at their core despite any outward attempts to convince others to the contrary.

If they hook up with their inner King, they can make excellent priests and counselors because of their rich familiarity with the inner world. The richness of their King will bless others in this way. If they are wounded, they may remain purposeless enigmas to themselves and others, missing the mark of their true calling.

The Sun in the Warrior Power Zone

Persons with this setup will shine like the sunrise. They carry the promise of a new day dawning. These natives are often crusaders for whatever their cause may be. They actively seek to go out and take the message of their King's purpose to as many people as they can reach. The Warrior influence of this zone adds a feeling of personal quest to whatever their King's purpose might be.

This arrangement adds immense physical stamina and an unconquerable spirit. They feel that they can achieve anything and often do! These people usually keep an incredibly busy schedule and live a very active physical lifestyle. If their King is healthy, they seek to energize those around them with this inexhaustible sense of enthusiasm. We enjoy being around these natives because they bless us with their abounding energy and animation.

If the King is wounded to any degree, this can lead to a personality that bulldozes others with its inherent will. They refuse to be considerate of others rights and boundaries and will often manipulate others to their own ends. These people can be very self interested to the point of considering themselves completely separate and above everyone else. They can be extremely impatient and intolerant of others.

These scenarios will be modified by other factors in the chart. For example: if there are other angular archetypes, they will also have a leading role in the personality as well. Such an arrangement will serve to moderate these definitions to some degree. The Sun can also be involved in one or more major aspects to other planets. This, in turn, will also modify the expression of the King archetype in some manner.

These definitions, therefore, are meant to aid you with interpreting charts where *only one* planet/archetype is in an angular power zone. They are simplified in that respect and will require some modification, on your part, when other factors are present. The ability to juggle multiple angular planets in your delineations will improve as you read more charts and develop your astrological intuition. These guideline definitions are provided to give you a starting point.

In addition to having an angular placement of the Sun within these four power zones and/or a powerfully aspected Sun, there are two other phenomenon that can create an indirect attunement with the King archetype within one's personality. The interesting fact is that in either of these cases the Sun does not even have to be involved per se.

The first of these would be if there was a large number of planets residing within the King's quadrant. The Sun need not be among them. If there were, let us say, seven planets packed into the King quadrant of the chart, then this native would manifest an indirect attunement to the

King archetype because of this arrangement. They would manifest a predisposition towards pursuit of power, sovereignty and recognition of such. The subtleties of this orientation would be determined by the planets occupying the King quadrant.

The final scenario involves the King's aspect. Earlier we mentioned that the Sun-King was attuned to the energy of the conjunction aspect. In this regard, we can say that persons whose charts contain a predominant conjunction of two or more planets will manifest King-like personality traits that will radiate from this alternate source. A gifted blessing issues forth from any conjunction that modulates itself with a type of dignity befitting the King archetype itself.

When interpreting a conjunction aspect in the chart, strive to view the respective planets as fused into a collective amalgam. Remember that the native will lack any objective ability to separate the two influences in his mind. It is much like the old dilemma of the Reeses Peanut Butter Cup commercial: Did you get peanut butter on my chocolate or did I get chocolate in your peanut butter?

Let us say, for example, that you come across a chart with a Jupiter/Neptune conjunction. This native will be naturally expansive and optimistic (Jupiter) towards matters of spirituality and mysticism (Neptune). Their sense of religion and faith (Jupiter) will be deeply woven into the ecstatically sublime mysteries of pure spirituality (Neptune). These people will be anything but status quo in the usual Jupiterian context. Neptune will preclude any chance of that.

Whichever combinations of planets you encounter in conjunction with each other, come to see them as pooling their resources together. This will put you well on the way to mastering the interpretation of conjunctions. All conjunctions offer the potentiality for a wonderful gift to spring forth and bless the world. Whether this potentiality is ever fully realized and manifested is up to the native. We all have many potentialities, yet some of us may never actualize them.

These alternate sources are important to look for when reading a client's chart. Just because their Sun appears relatively weak, due to its background position and/or a complete lack of aspects to other planets, does not mean that this person is devoid of King energy. Look for the alternative indicators before making this assessment. The way in which their King manifests may be in one of these more subtle forms.

CHAPTER TWO

Mercury, The Magician

Mercury is the second world we encounter as we move away from the primary world, the central, unified focus of the Sun-King. It therefore, most obviously, represents the concept of two-ness or *awareness of separation*. Mercury has come to represent all duality and separation.

Here we have the powerful bi-polar energy of the opposition aspect represented very clearly. Picture an imaginary solar system with just the Sun and Mercury. We have two objects in perpetual opposition, as Mercury dances around the Sun. He is always in the company of the King.

Each is aware of his separateness as they face each other. This dualistic nature of Mercury can be seen even in its physics. His orbit is the most extreme and elliptical of all the planets except Pluto. The temperature (415° C) of his world is the hottest of all the planets, except Venus. Mercury is also, however, one of the coldest places (170° C) in the entire solar system! The black and white principle of extremes, is even reflected in its range of temperatures!

It is worth mentioning that recent astronomical data now points strongly towards the possible existence of a polar ice cap on Mercury! The more we examine this eccentric little world, the more fascinating discoveries we are finding along the way.

The core concept of Mercury is *awareness of space or separation*. This awareness leads directly to linear thought, logic, objectivity and all the dynamics of intelligence. There is a striving towards balance (inter-relationship) inherent within the nature of the opposition. The opposition is the most powerful aspect after the conjunction. All conjunctions are subjective and all oppositions are objective by nature (as is Mercury).

Mercury, in the developing infant's psyche, represents the phase of the "Precocious Child," as described by Moore and Gillette.[1] As this archetype unfolds, within the child, we see the beginnings of curiosity about the separateness or objectiveness of life. His mind is quickened and he is eager to learn about things. Mercury is also the quickest of the planets, making a complete orbit around the sun in 88 days. In his curiosity, he wants to know the why and how of everything. Because of Mercury's affinity with two-ness, the Mercurial child wishes to share his discoveries and knowledge with others. His excitement, innocence and wonder about life are infectious to those around him. He has a sense of adventure and delights in exploring the unexplored.

Under the influence of this archetype we become pioneers of life's mysteries, which seem never ending to us. We want to know what makes everything tick—including ourselves. The energy of Mercury is dualistic. He can be introverted and ponderous as well as extroverted and eager to share his world with others. We find that due to Mercury's close powerful relationship to the Sun-King, Mercury's archetype of the Precocious Child is closely mingled with that of the Sun's Divine Child. During the first two years of life, these energies are developing and coexisting, along with the archetype of Venus. All three arrive (awaken), before the age of two.

I believe that as each planet completes its first cycle (orbit), and returns again to its natal position, it then becomes officially part of our human experience. This marks the initiation of that archetype into our growing psychic complexity. We have been baptized into its reality, so to speak.

It is then ours to keep. Becoming personal, it is now woven into our experience. Just as a tree grows rings that reflect its age, so do we on an inner psychic level. The archetypes unfold and our consciousness expands outward (fig 2a).

According to Moore and Gillette, when the Mercurial child does not have his sense of curiosity and intelligence acknowledged and seen by his parents, it also splits-off into its unconscious, bi-polar, shadow parts. He winds up becoming a "Know-It-All Trickster" (more than), or a "Dummy" (less than). All archetypes, when wounded or fractured in this way, become destructive energy towards others and ultimately oneself.[2]

The Know-It-All Trickster starts to maliciously deceive others and hide the truth and knowledge he once so eagerly shared with them. He becomes a manipulator in the world of thought, using it to protect his wound and to hurt others. He projects an aura of mental superiority and delights in exposing other's weaknesses with verbal assaults and laughter.

If the child has been wounded in both the Divine Child and Precocious Child archetypes, he is then even more driven by his shadows as

Figure 2a

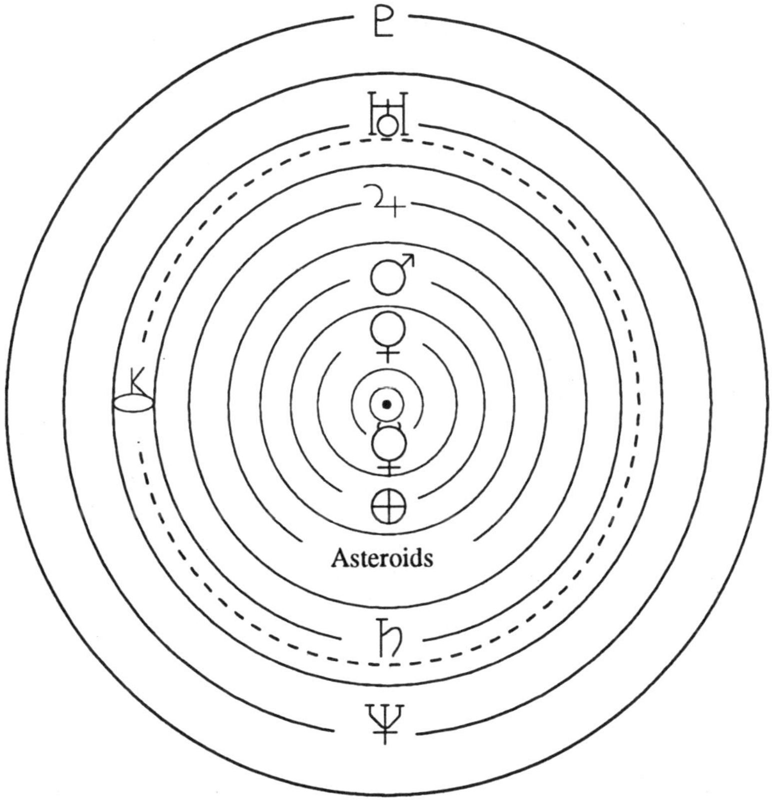

they work in tandem much of the time. It is essential to establish a relationship with the Trickster. We need to establish an open line of communication with whichever part of the shadow we feel we are manifesting.

If it is the Dummy with which we are identified, then we hide behind a (sometimes) feigned sense of ineptitude. This is a very passively aggressive way of manipulating others while seeming innocent. Here we have the child who plays stupid so that his mother will help him with his homework. He grows up to be the man who purposely shrinks the laundry so that his exasperated wife will do it from then on.

These energies develop because of the wound. To heal the wound, we have to talk to and acknowledge our shadows. In order to have the healthy, mature (adult) archetype of Mercury unfold, the child archetype must be helped down from his grandiosity. This now allows him to grow and become educated or initiated into the adult archetype.

The fully mature adult archetype of Mercury is that of the Magician or Magi. The court magician, according to Moore and Gillette, was the King's psychotherapist. He helped the Sun-King keep a clear head about things, giving him perspective. He sees through denial and delusions, helping us make the intelligent choice.[3] Mr. Spock is a perfect example of a Mercurial type. He even has the magical ability to merge with others' minds.

Mercury is positioned on the middle pillar of the Archetypal Tree, just above the Sun. The middle pillar, as a whole, represents a conduit for the passing on of different things. With the Sun, it is the passing on of divinity through the genetic code of wisdom. Mercury passes on pure knowledge in the form of symbol, language, mathematics, mythology and astrology. Remember that the Biblical three wise men were in fact Magi, or astrologers!

Continuing up the middle pillar, we have the Earth, which represents the garden or kingdom where life itself is passed on and becomes manifest. Further on up the pillar is Pluto, who represents a higher octave of Mercury. He is the fully ascended magician, or alchemist, who has the power to pass on anything. So the central pillar represents the path of impartial clarity where the opposites are balanced, and spiritual wisdom flows freely. It is the aorta of spiritual life-force flowing out of the Sun-King himself.

The Magician archetype is very powerful because of its proximity to the Sun. In many cultures the Magician wields more power and respect than the King! A shaman is often revered more than the chief of the tribe.

In ancient Egypt, during the 18th dynasty, the magician-priests of Amen-Ra's temple were more powerful than the Pharaoh.

Eventually this led to the reform of Akhenaten who re-established Sun worship as the sole religion throughout the land. There are many pictures of him where he is seen worshiping the Sun with his wife Nefertiti. He was a true Earthly King who had a healthy relationship with the King in the other world. The point here is that all archetypes serve the King, even the Magician.

The Magician is the conduit of the King. All Royal wisdom is filtered through him. He is the aqueduct that transports the Kingly waters of knowledge down to Earth. For this very reason, he is situated between the King and the Kingdom (Earth) on the middle pillar of the Tree.

In the human body, Mercury rules the central nervous system which is the actual vessel through which the King's conscious light flows. The dualistic nature of Mercury is blatantly obvious in the actual physiology and mechanics of the central nervous system. The brain itself is split into left and right hemispheres. Our neurons transport their electrical impulses through a complex biochemical exchange of ions between two electrolytes: sodium and potassium. The Magician networks, routes and channels the King's unfathomable wisdom in much the same way our central nervous system controls and directs our consciousness. He is the one closest to the secret keys of wisdom. The Egyptian Magician-priest Imhotep is a good historical example.

It is worth noting that in most ancient cultures all Magicians and Shamans were priests. It was essential to their survival for them to have a sense of spirituality and humility. In this way they could handle the immense responsibility of the power with which they were entrusted. The Magician is, in essence, the King's right hand man, the central scrutinizer of his realm.

It is for this reason that Mercury also rules the pineal gland, which is the central regulator of the mid-brain. This gland is the only known tissue in the body that contains photosensitive cells similar to the retina of the eye, a strange capability for a gland buried in the middle of the skull. Perhaps it is capable of receiving more than just the visible light spectrum. Mercury rules the mechanics of this gland and Pluto rules the awareness or consciousness which it imparts.

The Magician archetype is an essential component of all technologies and crafts that are dualistic in nature. The modern day chess master maneuvers within the black and white world of pure tactics. The entire computer industry relies on its fundamental binary code of ones and zeros.

The Magician gets to observe the realm and all incoming data. He is the one who gets to balance the energies of all the archetypes within our psyche. Mercury is the chief editor whose job it is to report directly to the King with his final copy, after he has all the data compiled at his fingertips. He also is the one who get to return with the King's decision. He is, in actuality, an interpreter for the King, a spokesperson, or his private press secretary.

The shadow of the Magician is the progression from the Trickster to the Detached Manipulator. There are the many temptations that the Magician will encounter as he seeks to refine himself and move closer to the King. The more power he gains, the more temptation he will feel to misuse it in manipulative ways. The path of the black magician is always open to him. This is the test that Luke Skywalker passed by forsaking the dark side of the force.

The fully mature Magician assists the King in maintaining Right Order. He helps keep the peace. If our Magician is weak (wounded), we find chaos creeping into our lives from all quarters. The wounded Magician can find himself feeling much like the boy in "Peter and the Dike." He tries to maintain order, but lacks a sufficient number of fingers!

Mercury rules all Hermetic traditions. Like a "hermetically sealed" jar, he needs a secretive, contained space for his ritual process. All selective, or private clubs and organizations fall under his urge. He delights in secret codes, passwords, pledges, keys, cryptic gestures, etc. Names and nick-names are solely Mercurial by nature. They allow him to identify and control those whom he lets enter his sacred space.

We find this connection of Hermes with contained spaces to be illustrated quite obviously in Greek mythology. The god Hermes was actually born in a cave! Chiron, another magician, also made his home in a cave. This was the Greek's way of showing the need for containment of hermetic knowledge.

Even in our modern world, we find the same need for containment of Mercurial energy. In western culture, we see this old world magician lurking under the guise of the psychologist and the scientist. Both of these professionals are capable of releasing powerful and potentially devastating energies.

It is for this very reason that the psychologist operates in his own sacred space, one on one with his client. He has the knowledge and training to help release and invoke powerful cathartic emotional experiences within his patients. He has the ability to help facilitate healing with his craft, but is equally capable of wreaking havoc through irresponsibly allowing counter-transference to occur. The need for boundaries and ethics is paramount.

The same holds true for today's scientists. They too must work within contained sacred space, so that the powerful forces released can be controlled and harnessed properly. Here we see the need for a "containment vessel" around today's nuclear power plants!

In both these modern day scenarios, we see the absolute need for complete and thorough training in the crafts of the twentieth century Magician. Without strict enforcement of such guidelines, we end up with mutant viruses and sexually abused analysands.

Initiation is essential for the true Magician. He needs to be guided and disciplined at every step of his growth. All the middle pillar archetypes (Mercury, Earth, Moon, Pluto) have a direct line to God (the Sun). The Magician must, therefore, be ushered into his knowledge gradually, so as not to cause damage through ignorance. This is the principle behind all the Hermetic traditions of the past. Christ, Buddha, Socrates and Plato all had disciples. Herein lies the value of the oral transmission of knowledge. There is a personal connection with the master teacher. Knowledge must always have a personal touch to it. We are then more likely to use it in humane ways.

Mercury and the Four Angles

Mercury in the King Power Zone

When the planet Mercury (Magician archetype) is located within the power zone of the King, the person is likely to choose a career, or calling in which they can bestow the gift of their Magician's talents upon the world. They often will end up in the communications field in some capacity. These natives are openly gregarious and have the gift of gab. They enjoy every aspect of exchanging information or goods. Many will become psychotherapists.

Excellent career choices include: All the media arts (television, radio and journalism), teaching, stocks and bonds, merchandising, sales and advertising. They also love all aspects of travel and computer technology. Mathematics and statistical research come naturally to them. The Mercurial type craves data in any form and is gifted in its interpretation. Many are multilingual.

As gifted as the healthy Magician can be for society, the unhealthy version delivers to us all of the shady con artists and charlatans that populate these respective fields of endeavor. These natives are the professional sociopaths that blight our society with their selfish manipulation of knowledge and information for the purpose of their own ends. The shadow Magician lies behind the recent explosion of insider trading on Wall Street, direct marketing fraud and 900 number scams. He specializes in the realm of easy money. Buyer beware!

Mercury in the Lover Power Zone

A person with Mercury located in the Lover's power spot will seek to use their communication skills to secure their Lover needs at all costs. They often become peacemakers through their strong desire to maintain intimacy amongst family members. If anyone is quarreling, they will seek to patch things up through acting as a third party and negotiating between them. They have a knack for sugar coating their words and making everyone happy in the end.

These natives will seek a partner in relationship with whom they can communicate. This is of paramount importance to them. They crave mental stimulation through their mate and will therefore only be attracted to persons with marked intelligence and wit. They are extremely intelligent themselves, yet only those who know them intimately will be aware of this. They will not flaunt it like those who have Mercury residing in the King zone.

When the wounds and shadows of this current type manifest themselves, we have the con artist Trickster playing his manipulative games within the realm of relationship. These people can pull the wool completely over the eyes of even those closest to them. They will manipulate, cajole and distract in any manner that works effectively with their partner. Their motives will emanate mostly out of jealousy or fear of abandonment.

Mercury in the Magician Power Zone

This planet is most at home in this location. Hermes retreats to his cave and ponders the secrets of life. This introspective setup can encourage the native to pursue spiritual matters or any form of uninterrupted mental fascination. The Magician seeks power through knowledge. He believes that if he reads enough books he will figure it all out! These people are experts at secretly observing life and understanding its inner workings.

Many gifted psychotherapists and researchers have Mercury placed here. This arrangement will also show up in anyone who prefers to silently marvel at life such as the monk or priest. It may also play a hand in the personality of the occultist who enjoys the manipulative seduction of ritual magic.

Because of this fascination with the obscured and unconscious, these natives will have a natural curiosity about the dream world and its interpretation. They may grow to excel in this area. Because this power zone is so introverted, any planets located there may be difficult to sense. If wounded, they can easily act out unconsciously without anyone else even knowing.

These wounded natives, with Mercury angular and unconscious, can be the most devious of Tricksters. They are terrified to communicate their deepest observations and prefer secrecy and silence. They often do their manipulating through this form of non-involvement or detachment. They may clearly see someone heading for disaster, yet will say nothing to warn them. Their inner sense of power comes from knowing they could have changed the outcome.

Mercury in the Warrior Power Zone

Here, in complete contrast to the previous type, Mercury explodes on the scene in this rising hot spot. These natives manifest Mercury in every breath they take. They actively seek out knowledge for the sake of simply wanting to know the truth, the whole truth and nothing but the truth!

They gravitate towards reading, education and language with an absolute fire. These natives are dexterous with their hands, perky, outgoing and communicate with enthusiasm. Their quest is to turn the whole world on to knowledge and learning. They love being in touch with everyone and everything. Most have a great sense of humor, and are often mischievous practical jokers. They can burn with nervous energy at times. The energy of the Warrior power zone can overdrive their minds like a runaway train.

These people also make excellent salespersons and public speakers. They have an amazing ability to make an extremely dominant impression on all who cross their path. Here we find the poet who can powerfully sway a large gathering with his eloquent mastery of the written and spoken word (Robert Bly's chart as discussed in Chapter 14 provides an excellent illustration of this). His passion and love of language, as a means to wisdom, cannot escape even the most numb at heart.

In its shadow form, this type of person is verbally dominant and seldom lets you get in a word edgewise. Here we see the politician who talks right over the journalist's question as he bullies his way through the press conference. He is a master of twisting words around to suit his purpose. His sly ability to distract others from their train of thought, coupled with his belligerent will, are no match for most. He simply runs circles around them.

In addition to these four angular placements of Mercury, we can also find evidence of a prominent Magician archetype through a large number of planets occupying the Magician quadrant. If a chart contains five or more planets within this quadrant, then the native may be seen to possess a strong sense of the Magus archetype within their personality regardless of whether the planet Mercury is very prominent or not.

Another way in which a well developed Magician archetype can manifest is through a marked presence of opposition aspects in the chart. This dualistic aspect resonates with the very "objective awareness" inherent within the Magician archetype. Two or more oppositions in the chart, especially if angular, will earmark the native as having a well developed sense of the Magician archetype. This remains true even if Mercury is not part of either opposition. When it comes to interpreting the opposition aspect, it helps to keep certain concepts in mind. Remember that the opposition represents the maximum split or separation that can occur between two planets. This distancing or detachment offers maximum opportunity for objective clarity. The potentiality, in this case, is for full awareness and wisdom.

Yet one must balance the two forces involved or they will constantly keep you off-center in some fashion. Because the opposition is a binary split of two planets, it will also contain the possibility of creating a schizoid split or fracture between the two archetypes composing the opposition. If one balances the two forces involved, wisdom and awareness are the rewards. If he fails to fully integrate the two, schizoid shadow fragments will likely plague this native.

No other aspect will generate psychological projection more powerfully that the opposition. The challenge is to own and integrate both halves without projecting onto others. This means that we must stop blaming others and pointing the finger. "Judge not, lest ye be judged."

Let us say that a man has an opposition of Mars and Venus in his chart. He is likely to acknowledge and embrace the qualities of the Warrior within himself (Mars). But without equal recognition of his Lover (Venus), he is very likely to project this archetype's energy onto the women in his life and expect them to embody it for him. Yet through this opposition, he also has the potentiality to fully realize both the masculine (Mars) and feminine (Venus) as existing powerfully within himself. The chore at hand is to heal the illusion of this apparent split.

CHAPTER THREE

Venus, The Lover

Venus is the third planet (archetype) that we encounter as our awareness continues to expand outward. It represents three-ness and the balance or harmony we experience through this trinity. Here we have the *aesthetic* world of form and felt thought that the child begins to experience as he expands beyond the archetype of Mercury. For the first time, the child begins to feel the joy and pleasure inherent within his world. His *sensual* receptors start to unfold as this third archetype comes into being.

Imagine a solar system with three bodies: Sun, Mercury and Venus. We now have the opportunity for a perfect triangle, or Grand Trine to exist! The Grand Trine is the perfect expression of what Venus adds to the equation. The equilateral triangle is the strongest structural component that can be achieved in nature. That is why Buckminster Fuller used this basic form to create the geodesic dome. It has a harmonious stability inherent within its simple triune structure that represents a motion towards *reconciliation* and *relationship*. This sense of security brings about the harmony, love and pleasure within the archetype of Venus.

So it is the Trine, and especially the Grand Trine, that resonates with the very energies of this archetype. People with Grand Trines in their chart are operating from a Venusian perspective, regardless of whether this planet Venus is involved or not. The planets composing a person's Great Trine are joined together by a Venusian force.

A Grand Trine is usually reflective of forces (planets) that we have learned to harmonize in a smooth, gentle and loving way. It is our hidden gift, or talent that we have already polished and perfected. This is our private joy, our true bliss and the very oyster of our accomplishments, a resource to aid in our evolution. Here we have a well of strength, full of lessons learned from previous life experiences.

Venus has the most circular orbit of all the planets. In this simple fact we have further proof of its harmonious nature. Ease and grace are reflected by the very way in which this celestial body carries itself through its orbit. It is from this sense of comfort and security that the child begins to venture out and soak up the pleasures filtering through his awakening senses. His world becomes sensual.

With the unfolding of each new archetype, the child becomes more and more dependent on healthy mirroring. The arrival of Venus, coinciding with the return of the planet to its natal position, sparks the awareness of love through a love object. This is the narcissistic period where good mirroring is absolutely essential. In fact, there is no better symbol for Venus then that of a mirror! The child must see all his parts reflected back through the parent's eyes. The unreflected parts split off into the unconscious. It is during the Venusian phase, that our sensual nature runs the risk of being wounded through non-acknowledgement.

Moore and Gillette call the healthy archetype "the Lover" and its immature archetype, the "Oedipal Child" (in more generic terms, it could be called the "Narcissistic Child").[1] Garth Allen elaborated this point very well in his book, writing extensively about the narcissistic needs that can be directly linked to the planet Venus.[2]

I see this as a period where both boys and girls need to cathect, or fuse with a love object. It usually tends to be the parent of the opposite sex. This is a time where the child desperately needs to bond with an object of a nurturing and loving nature. There begins to develop an insatiable desire for love and attention. The child needs to be acknowledged as lovable. He wants to be held and made to feel good about his need for stroking. Venus is our need to love and be loved, to touch and be touched. We all yearn to be an object of veneration to others. It is our craving to indulge in our sensual nature and rejoice at the experience of being in our bodies. This is a most difficult archetype to accept. There is so much denial, disapproval and repressive shaming of the body's erotic impulses conveyed to most children by their parents. Being wounded is virtually inevitable in our modern world.

I'm sure that there is a wounded Lover in most everyone today. The results are obvious with all the sexual dysfunction and addiction in society. The most common sexual dysfunction today is disorder of desire, or a serious lack of sensual response to the energy of Eros. This is because so much of the Lover archetype has split off into the unconscious, having been shamed or abused into hiding.

The amount of sexual abuse in our society is only now starting to reveal itself. Through support and acknowledgement, crippled Lovers are finally coming out of the shadows and revealing their wounds to the light of day. If there is such a thing as an endangered species amongst the archetypes, it would have to be the Lover.

In the process of opening ourselves up to love, we make ourselves the most vulnerable. It is this vulnerability that has been so viciously crushed and destroyed throughout history. We hate vulnerability in this society. That is why the abuse of women and children is so widespread. The Lover is the archetype that is easiest to wound and most difficult to heal.

Moore and Gillette have labeled the two immature bi-polar shadow forms of the Lover the "Mama's Boy" and the "Dreamer."[3] The child which has not had its sensual nature properly acknowledged by the parent will become "bound" to them in a desperate attempt to become the apple of their eye. They try to be "more than" by overcompensating for their fears of being unlovable. The child will attempt to win the parent's love through all sorts of measures. They will stop at nothing.

The "Mama's Boy" will eventually grow into adulthood where he will carry this complex wound into the full blown adult manifestation of the shadow, which Moore and Gillette call the "Addicted Lover."[4] Sex and love addiction is a serious problem that, like sexual abuse, is only now starting to become more fully apparent. These adults have huge holes in their psyches that have been carried since childhood.

The other alternative left open to the child is to become "less than" by retreating into their private thoughts. They numb out their bodies in order to escape the shaming wounds to their souls. Instead they become a romantic "Dreamer" who retreats from human relationships entirely. He finds safety in his private thoughts where he can create the perfect paradise. It is here that he and his "dream lover" can live happily ever after.

This private world can lend itself to many forms of obsession and addiction. In order to create the illusion of a lover, the Dreamer will often resort to using pornography, fetishes, masturbation and even cross-dressing. He is actually terrified of the real thing, so he settles for substitutes.

Unhealed, the Dreamer eventually becomes the adult shadow form of the "Impotent Lover." Moore and Gillette explain that because children fail to achieve possession of the love object, they then retreat in defeat. Within the isolating shadows of their imagination they hide from further pain. They usually live "quiet lives of desperation," dominated by fear, loneliness and celibacy.[5]

I think by this point we can clearly see the types of damage that can and do happen to the archetypes. It also becomes clear why most astrologers have a relatively poor working knowledge of the "personal planets." It is because virtually all of us have large chunks of the King, Magician, Lover and Warrior archetypes missing from our conscious awareness. They are tucked away in the unconscious, concealing our wounds and uninitiated ignorance.

The Lover is absolutely essential to our health and well being. This Venus archetype has rulership over the "venous" blood that is rich in carbon dioxide. The atmosphere of the planet Venus is composed primarily of carbon dioxide! Again we see correlation on the physical level.

According to Edgar Cayce, Venus also rules the thymus gland a major physiological regulator and part of the immune system.[6] I believe this to be true, because Love = Harmony = Health = Immunity. It is also the endocrine gland closest to the heart, which has always been associated with love. The fact that the Thymus gland shrinks so much in adulthood might be proof of the wounds that our Lover sustains in childhood. It is also an interesting parallel to notice the alarming increase in immune deficiency disorders now plaguing our culture.

This is all part of the heavy price we are paying as a culture for our collective inhumanity towards each other. The sins of the fathers shall be visited onto the sons. Sin is a Western term for what the Buddhists call ignorance. The only way out of this mess is through knowledge, the inner knowledge found through the process of education and initiation.

We must all become students, or disciples, of our own inner nature once again. To heal the Lover, we must seek out true nurturing from others and seek to nurture them as well. Many of us may have to learn this process virtually from scratch!

We can start by befriending the wounded Lover within ourselves and helping him down from the high chair of his wounded infantile grandiosity. We need to parent him and develop a bridge of trust once again. This can best be done through community support. The Lover responds best to community, because it learns most effectively through the mirroring faces of others.

There is an emerging wave of support groups of all kinds springing up across the country. We have men's gatherings, women's groups, veteran's support, incest survivors, adult children, etc. There is also private group therapy and church groups. Anybody with an interest or issue can find support groups for help. I believe groups are essential for healing the wounded Lover.

Healing the Lover allows him to unfold in his fullness and we may begin to experience our passion for maybe the very first time. Herein lies our sense of enjoyment and play. Many of us have lost our spontaneity and the ability to just frolic! The healthy Lover allows us to experience the joys and pleasures of our body, without shame. When we connect with our bodies, we connect with all of creation. We gain empathy from this awareness that leads to an experience of spiritual oneness. The Lover approaches very close to the creative passionate fires of the unconscious. We've all heard the term, "He was a hot lover." It is worth noting that Venus is the hottest planet in the entire solar system (470°C)!

The Hindus knew of the connection between the Lover, sex and spirituality. This was the whole purpose behind the development and practice of tantra. The true Lover wants to become one with the mystery of life and creation by riding the waves of ecstasy experienced within his very being. He yearns to collapse all boundaries and merge with the entire cosmos. His appetite is insatiable, his thirst unquenchable.

Garth Allen has many valuable insights of Venus in his book and we shall note some of the more critical ones here.[7] The world of Venus has always been associated with sweetness. Lovers use a whole collection of pronouns and nicknames to describe their Love object: sweetie-pie, sugar, honey-bun, cookie, lollipop, etc. These words also expose the most popular form of love substitute: food! Venus rules the pancreatic enzymes that break down complex carbohydrates into simple sugars.

When our Lover is starved, and we have no partner available, many of us will use food to fill the void. Overeaters who habitually reach for sweets are probably catering to their wounded Lover. It is this deep need within us, which craves things sweet, cozy, warm and safe, that will drive us to find substitutes for the real thing.

Another common substitute is having a pet. There is a second collection of nicknames for love objects centered exclusively around cute, young animals: kitten, chick, duckie, lassie, lamb. If the Lover has no love object to call by these names, he will often substitute a pet. Allen points out that the word puppy actually means "child substitute." There are other Latin variations that show the connection: puppet (animated doll), pupus (child), etc.[8]

The Lover represents the nurturing relationship between Mother and Child regardless of our gender. We all have this basic need to love and be loved. Robert Bly and Robert Moore both point out that a lack of masculine sweetness, or nurturing masculinity, is the underlying reason why most men are incapable of giving much tenderness. It is essential for young boys to receive "mothering" from their fathers. Moore says: "If you're a young man and you're not being admired by an older man, you're being hurt."[9]

As men, it is essential for us to associate with and learn from older nurturing males. I praise the pioneering work of men like Robert Bly, Michael Meade, Robert Moore, Douglas Gillette and John Lee in this regard. Part of being a healthy man is to give and receive love and nurturing from other men. We must eliminate the homophobia that so powerfully stifles men from expressing their vulnerability.

There are other symbolic ways in which we can allow the Lover to express his nature in our daily lives. Garth Allen points out two of these: baking and gardening.[10] Both entail the process of creating something from scratch and helping it to grow through our care and nurturing. I have recently become aware of my emerging Lover through developing a bonsai garden. I feel very attached to each tree. They have all taken on different personalities, much like children!

Any kind of creative nurturing venture allows the Lover to emerge and grow within us. Volunteer work, nursing and all healing work such as massage, therapeutic touch, and convalescent care. It was the creative and healing powers of Venus that allowed Isis to heal Osiris and Christ to raise Lazarus from the dead.

According to Cyril Fagan, the Bennu (Phoenix) was the Egyptian name for Venus! The Phoenix bird symbolizes resurrection from his own ashes. Venus would rise fresh and new out of the Sun's corona, to become the morning star once again, after a brief period of gestation in the underworld. Love springs eternal!

The power of love is capable of softening even the toughest of psychological defenses, much the way water can dissolve large granite rocks in a stream. The soft triumphs over the hard. How many tough people have you seen melt while gazing at a newborn's face! People go "ga ga" when their Lover engages and surfaces. Many lovers actually talk baby talk with each other!

The Chinese philosophy of Taoism is very much in touch with the nature of the Lover. Taoists praise the nature of water as being closest to "The Way." Those qualities which they mention are softness, passivity and receptivity. The Lover is much like a sponge that soaks up the holy waters of life-force energy.

It is worth noting a very subtle, and easily overlooked, connection between the Lover archetype and this very common compound known as water. In the beginning of the chapter, we stressed the connection between the Lover, the triangle and the number three. Water is a triangle shaped molecule composed of three atoms (one oxygen atom and two atoms of hydrogen).

In Greek mythology, Aphrodite (Venus) was born out of the ocean. According to the legend, she was carried ashore by the gentle west wind. She was also accompanied by the three Graces in her arrival. The Graces were the three goddesses who collectively acted as the friends and protectors of all things graceful and beautiful. Here we see yet another mythological verification of the connection between the Lover, the number three and the western direction or angle.

Venus has much to do with the "seat of the soul," which is the chest, heart and lungs. God breathed the breath of life into the nostrils of man. The Hebrew word for soul is NePheSH, which means: "breath" or "one who breathes." The Egyptians had two words for soul: Nifu or breath, and Ankh which meant "life" and "breath," or "the breath of life."

A newborn's first sign of life is his first breath or in-spiration, where his spirit comes into his body. Upon dying; we ex-pire, breathing our last breath or expiration. Our spirit exits the body. The very process of breathing is called respiration. We re-spirit ourselves with every breath!

The Lover instinctively knows this connection of Spirit- Life-Energy and the breath. A Lover, when he is experiencing pleasure, will breathe more deeply. This is all part of making Love, as he heaves huge quantities of invigorating spirit-energy into his body. He will often experience his chest heating up as the power of Eros-Life-Spirit flows into his lungs.

This can happen even if he is passively receiving pleasure. It has nothing to do with physical exertion. One of the most erotic experiences, I can recall, was receiving a lung full of air from one of my lovers while she and I were embraced in a kiss. Our inner Lovers danced as the breath passed back and forth between our lungs.

The Lover needs an uninhibited, safe environment to allow his amorous nature to come out. Moore and Gillette point out that the Latin words "amor" and "roma" are diametric in both meaning and spelling. This is a phenomenon that is very common in ancient cultures. Amor means "passionate experience" and roma means "duty, responsibility, law and order."

We must learn how to balance these extremes with wisdom, and common sense. The amorous nature of the Lover, left unchecked, will turn totally promiscuous. The Lover, like all archetypes, must serve the King and heed to his wisdom and prudence. Too much of anything is ultimately imbalanced and destructive.

We place Venus at the bottom of the left pillar in the Archetypal Tree. It shares the first horizontal axis with its polar opposite, Mars. These two always counterbalance each other in nature. The whole concept of the Archetypal Tree stresses balance and harmony, of which the Lover is just a part.

Venus and the Four Angles

Venus in the King Power Zone

Persons with this arrangement will often gravitate towards a profession where there Lover archetype can have a major input. This might include such choices as nursing, veterinary medicine, high fashion and modeling, as well as counseling. This would especially include a preference for group therapy as this allows the Lover to offer plenty of input. These therapists have a real knack for generating a true feeling of group community and safety.

The essential ingredient is that these natives absolutely need to involve their Lover archetype in their career in order to be truly happy with their lives. They must sense a general feeling of giving and receiving love or admiration in their public life. Without this, they will feel emotionally dead inside and quickly become depressed. These people must offer the blessing of their Lover's gift to the world in some capacity. This is the purpose for which they live.

A wounded or shadow expression of the Lover in this power zone is the person who narcissistically expects the world to admire and love them simply because they feel that they deserve it. They can be extremely vain. This is quite evident in today's top fashion models and entertainment figures. They identify with themselves strictly in terms of their physical beauty. The shadow of Venus lazily feels that she can simply float through life on her good looks.

There are many rock and pop stars today who maintain their popularity not through any musical talent, but strictly because of their image. The hair, clothes, makeup and glitter are their ticket to fame and fortune. When all these accouterments are stripped away, what usually remains is mediocre musical ability at best. This is the facade behind which the wounded Lover will hide.

Venus in the Lover Power Zone

The Goddess of love is most comfortable in this location. These people love to be in love! They live for the complete fulfillment of all their sensual needs. These natives simply ooze with sensuality. They yearn to be around others and yearn for others to be with them. If left alone, they feel empty inside and unstimulated. They will usually always have a significant other in their life even if this person is viewed as only temporary.

Here the love needs are fulfilled exclusively through relationship, whereas in the previous type they were fulfilled through career or profession. These are the important distinctions to be made from angle to angle. This present type will often feel completely content with simply being the apple of their lover's eye. Unless other motivational factors are present in the chart, these people will be driven by the simple desire to keep the flames of their relationship burning forever. Their overwhelming desirability to their partner can often insure this.

In its shadow form, this arrangement can be the perfect setup for love addiction in its many forms. The wounded Lover within these natives will often bow to any of the demands of their partner. They will dress up in any manner of pornographic paraphernalia and prostitute themselves in countless ways simply because they fear abandonment.

These wounded natives will often find themselves performing sexual acts that might normally revolt them. They grow to become professional seducers because they know that this will insure the future of their relationship. Codependency will flourish as they conform and acquiesce to any and all demands of their partner. They will ultimately sell their soul to gratify their sensual needs. This often includes drifting into the world of drugs and alcohol.

Venus in the Magician Power Zone

Venus goes underground in this setup. These natives will feel very shy and awkward about their sensual needs. Love, to them is a very sacred and private matter. So private, in fact, that they may have real difficulty in approaching another person whom they find desirable. The Lover archetype instead will turn its passion towards the inner world of personal introspection. These people will often fall in love with the inner whispers of their own psyche.

This type will often content themselves with reading or writing exquisite poetry (in private of course!) for hours on end. They are natural day dreamers and have a rich inner fantasy life. Many would prefer to stay home alone on a Friday night and rent a romantic video. The depth to which they understand and sense their inner Lover is immense and, as a result, they are terrified to share it with anyone for fear of rejection or abandonment. These fears are bigger than life to them and will dictate the whole of their emotional choices.

If the Lover is wounded in this particular arrangement, the native may choose long periods of celibacy in between their failed attempts at relationship. They do not understand the workings of intimacy too well. Inside their heads they have it all worked out, but when they get involved with a real, live, flesh and blood person, the whole thing seems to run amuck! As a result they are inwardly anxious about touching or being touched. They feel a strong upwelling of sensuality which triggers a fear of losing control.

This dilemma stems from the oil and water nature of the Lover and Magician energies. The Lover is irrational and analog in nature. The Magician is logical and digital in nature. These natives will therefore strive to logically understand love. This is a fruitless pursuit, as we all know, because love cannot be pinned down and understood in this manner. Learning this lesson will begin the healing process for these people. They must dive deep within themselves to become fully conscious of their Lover archetype.

Venus in the Warrior Power Zone

This arrangement forces the usually passive Lover archetype into an assertive role. These natives have a forthright way of relating to people. Others will find them very warm and cozy to be around. They are capable of seducing others simply with there physical presence. These people will think nothing of extending themselves to others physically by embracing them warmly upon first meeting them.

As a result of this sensual directness, these natives are seldom without friends and are most always involved in a sexual relationship. They see what they want and they simply go after it. Their quest is to pursue their own sensual comfort and pleasure nature. They see nothing wrong in being direct and up front about their desires. These natives can be very aggressively uninhibited.

In its shadow form, these natives can often become the great seducers of society. They will often build a Don Juan reputation as their list of conquests grows. This is true of women as well. Either sex can easily become actively promiscuous in their pursuit of personal pleasure. The tendency is to use the opposite sex for sensual and sexual gratification.

These wounded natives often run the risk of leaving many devastated hearts in their wake. Their Lover simply runs roughshod over many an unsuspecting victim. In their endless aggressive pursuit of pleasure, they will rarely stop to look back at the results of their actions. The guilt is simply too great for them to handle.

A person with five or more planets located within the Lover quadrant will also manifest a strong attunement to this archetype regardless of whether Venus is angular or not. This subtle secondary indicator must not be overlooked. If this phenomenon combines with an angular Venus, then the emphasis on the Lover archetype is even stronger as a result.

The final indicator that must be noted is the presence of two or more trine aspects within the chart. This will also herald an attunement to the Lover archetype. One special arrangement is if the chart contains a grand trine. If so, this will act as a tremendous generator of Lover energy. We may safely deduce that this native has a specialized attunement to the harmonic of the Lover archetype. The specifics of this can be determined by the planets which form the grand trine.

When interpreting trines in the chart, come to see them as offering potentiality for a harmonious relationship between the two planets involved. There is an opportunity for an effortless flow of cooperation to exist between the two archetypes that compose the trine. They usually can work well together within the psyche without causing any major rifts.

The one drawback of this aspect is that is can flow so smoothly that we are completely unaware of its potential or presence within us! When drifting upon its currents, we can often be lulled to sleep. This false sense of security can often leave us spoiled and lazy. Trines are often where we can be found to be resting on our laurels psychologically. The challenge is to avoid sloth and contentment.

Let us say that we encounter a chart with a trine between Mercury and Mars. This native will have a wealth of Warrior energy (Mars) that will be effortlessly channeled into Mercurial pursuits. They will be energetic and tireless speakers and readers. Normally Mars, when combined with Mercury, would cause the person to express themselves to others in a blunt and obnoxious manner frequently laced with profanity. However, the smoothing Venusian influence of the Trine will usually prevent any such manifestation in this case. The aspect always dictates the terms of the relationship between the two planets.

CHAPTER FOUR

The Earth, The Moon and The Wildman

The next stop on our outward spiral journey of initiation is the place we call home. Here we find the Garden of Eden where life flourishes abundantly. It is only on Earth that spirit touches down and becomes realized into matter. This is the full manifestation of the dance of life.

The breath of the King blows across the face of the Earth and stirs the dust of matter to form shapes. Spirit takes on flesh and incarnates. From the rich organic soup of our oceans life was born. Water is a perfect electrolyte. We humans and the Earth are composed predominantly of this essential element. The Earth is a living electromagnetic wet-cell battery and so are we.

We find the Earth situated above Mercury on the central pillar of the Archetypal Tree, with Venus and Mars to either side. This is the fourth sphere in our outward travel from the Sun. The Earth and Moon have to do with four-ness and the quarters of a circle. This produces the Square (90°) aspect and more importantly, the Grand Square.

Here on Earth we find the dynamic, constantly moving energy of life. The square is the most dynamic and challenging aspect, as is life itself. The Grand Square is the complete realization of the number four with each corner being occupied by a planet.

Life on Earth is deeply rooted in a fourfold reality. Our very DNA structure is composed of four primary proteins. (More on this in Chapter 11). We divide our year into four seasons. The lunar phase is also divided into quarters. The human heart has four chambers. We even build our houses with four walls, and arrange them in larger quadrated groups we call blocks. Carl Jung was one of the first to notice the universal human obsession with four-fold consciousness. He found the use of Mandalas, fourfold drawings of the universe, to be widespread within countless cultures from the Tibetans to the Navaho Indians.

The very symbol for the Earth reveals the number four. It is the four quarters of the King's domain, the four elements and the four central archetypes. (We have yet to expound on the Mars- Warrior archetype, the subject of the next chapter.)

The Earth is the center, with the four archetypes gathered around. The symbol for the Earth could also represent the cross-hairs on a scope. They are the intersection of the two Great Axes, the Meridian (time), and the Horizon (space). Human astrology is Geocentric (Earth-centered) in nature, because the Earth is the seat of our limited human Ego or consciousness.

We are limited by the two cross-hairs of time and space. This is the cross of matter, upon which we are crucified. All our trials and tribulations take place here. People with the Grand Square (or Grand Cross) in their charts know this feeling well. I can speak from experience, because my own chart contains a Grand Cross. Random square aspects in the birth chart are indicative of struggle and challenge. The Grand square is perfect, in the Pythagorean sense, by representing the full essence of four-ness: Dynamic energy and challenging struggles. It is simply trial by fire.

The cerebellum is our subconscious, instinctual brain that controls our autonomic nervous system functions such as heartbeat, digestion, elimination, etc. This all comes under the rulership of the Moon/Earth. It is important to always see the Earth and Moon as an inseparable unit. They are married in purpose.

Even though the Earth contains the oceans from which life arose, the Moon generates the rhythms of the tides that move all organisms to reproduce and mate. Without the Moon, the oceans would have remained stagnant and lifeless. Contained within its 28 day "circle dance" is that powerful primordial instinct that drives all creatures to procreate. It is also intimately linked to the 28 day menstrual cycle of female fertility.

It has been proven repeatedly that in cultures where women do not live exposed to artificial light, they ovulate with the full moon phase and menstruate with the dark moon. Women living or working in close proximity will also menstruate at about the same time. Imagine, then, the awe of our tribal ancestors at that time when the moon was dark and all the women bled. It is for this reason that the Moon came to be linked with women's mysteries.

The Earth and Moon have also, in modern times, been regarded as feminine. Most mythologies surrounding them are feminine based. The

Egyptians, interestingly enough, saw the Earth as masculine (Geb) and the Moon as predominantly feminine (Isis-Hathor). This is in keeping with the oriental principle behind macrobiotics. The central object was Yang (masculine), and the object surrounding or encircling it was Yin (feminine). The Earth is therefore Yin in its relationship to the Sun, but Yang in its relationship to the Moon!

The Egyptians at times associated the Moon with the masculine gods Thoth and Osiris. Osiris was the husband/brother of Isis. There is a wonderful lunar myth about Osiris in which his "dark" brother Set was out hunting by the light of the Moon. He comes upon the body of Osiris and cuts it into fourteen pieces. He then disperses the different parts throughout Egypt so that Isis cannot find them.

There is much more to this story as it continues. In this section, however, we see the body of Osiris (the Moon) being sliced into fourteen pieces, signifying the 14 days of the waning Moon. Darkness (Set) slowly consumes the Moon's light. Osiris eventually is resurrected by Isis. He represents the power of resurrection and perpetual renewal within nature.

The Osirian myth embodies the awesome powers within nature. He is seen as fertile and potent, usually depicted with a fully erect phallus. His body was often green and/or black, depicting fertile soil and vegetable-plant life. He represents the fertile, wild and untameable instincts to reproduce and perpetuate nature.

Other archetypes of the Earth-Moon, of sacrifice, death and resurrection, abound. In *Iron John*, Robert Bly introduces the archetype of the Wildman.[1] The characteristics of the Wildman are virtually identical to those of Osiris. The Wildman is also a descendent of the Green Man of the forest, and Cernunnos, the Horned God of ancient European Pagan traditions.

It may seem strange that the feminine Moon would have any connection to the masculine archetype of Wildman. But the archetype of the Moon is ultimately androgynous, being both Isis and Osiris. It is the source of spontaneity and regeneration. In the story "Iron John," the key to the Wildman's cage is hidden underneath the mother's pillow! We must dive down into the depths of the mother's realm, the female within ourselves to retrieve and liberate our Wildman archetype.

The Moon-Earth are situated like a fulcrum, balancing the axis that joins Mars and Venus on our Tree. Neither Venus or Mars, in and of itself, represents procreation or sex. Venus represents sensuality and yearning. Mars constitutes the willpower necessary to consummate the act and to possess the object of beauty. The meeting of these two energies can only take place on Earth under the watchful blessing of the Moon!

This is the sacred marriage ceremony that occurs here within the Earthly Temple. Only within flesh can the holy spirit make its home. All our instincts and body memories are stored within the dark archives of our autonomic nervous system, ruled by the Moon. Countless millennia of collective evolutionary experiences are contained within the wisdom of our cerebellum and medulla oblongata.

The wisdom of these memories can be accessed by re-connecting to our bodies and nature itself. The Wildman emerges from deep within the forest, to howl, dance and make love under the full Moon. He frees our soul so that we may breathe deeply and truly know what it means to be alive and re-born!

In this capacity, the Wildman archetype can also be seen to correlate with the mythology of the god Dionysus. He was the Greek god of wild, mystical, passionate expression and even madness. He was a god of vegetation, specifically the grape vine. Dionysus embodied the same concepts of death, dismemberment, rebirth and renewal as both Osiris and Jesus did. In fact, many of the miracles and parables associated with Jesus involved the making of wine and the planting of vineyards!

People who invoked Dionysus often consumed large amounts of wine so as to alter their consciousness and allow him to express his nature through them. This was often consummated in wild orgies of untamed passion and dance. In the Middle Ages, the Moon came to be associated with madness and frenzy. This is the origin of the words lunacy and lunatic.

The quadrated symbolism found in Christian theology can be seen in both the central symbol of the crucifix and the four gospels. In Egypt, Osiris was surrounded and protected by his four children. One of his primary symbols was the Djed pillar. This was the equivalent of the Christian cross. It was the tree in which Osiris was buried and later resurrected. At the top of this pillar were carved four tiers or levels.

All of these various cultures' mythologies were striving to express the same archetypal pattern or concept. Jung updated all this and named it the eternal child archetype. It represents that vibrant, youthful innocence and pliability that adapts and flows with the direction of eternal renewal. This occurred through periodic and cyclical death. It was viewed as "seasonal" in nature and is deeply connected with the rhythms of the Earth and its Moon.

Within the female psyche, there is an equivalent Wild Woman archetype.[2] The Greeks named this goddess/archetype Artemis. She was a wild moon goddess who was the protectress of nature and the forests. She fiercely guarded over the animals of nature with her bow and arrow. Diane Fossey, the scientist depicted in *Gorillas in the Mist*, is an excellent example of an Artemis type. Their instinctual nature prefers communion with animals and nature to that of other humans.

This perennial Wildman archetype, at its best, teaches us respect for our bodies and for nature—the Earth. When our Lunar-Wildman nature is wounded through shaming, abuse or neglect, we numb our bodies. We lose respect for the Earth and for ourselves. This has led to the plague of degeneration that currently engulfs mankind and threatens the health of the planet. I'm not sure which we are destroying faster, the Earth or ourselves. Our legacy is one of deforestation, pollution, global warming, cancer, heart disease, and AIDS. The time is now for the Osiris-Wildman, Artemis-Wild Woman archetype to make a comeback. We are ready to reclaim our health, our physicality and our connectedness to the cycles and seasons of the Earth.

The Native Americans know the Wildman on a first name basis. Most Pagan cultures are well educated in his importance. We need to develop a healthy respect for archetypes, mythology, ritual, initiation and the rites of passage. We are the stewards of the garden. It's time to face our sacred responsibility.

There is one final symbol of power connected with the Earth and the Wildman. This is the Pyramid. The word means "fire within." This fire is the very spark of life burning within our flesh and bones.

The Pyramid is the purest symbol for the realm of the Earthly Kingdom. It also represents the inner realm of our soul's kingdom. Moore and Gillette's work has helped us to visualize this inner pyramid of archetypes. With the exploring of Mars in the next chapter, we will have covered all four sides of the structure. The Earth-Moon archetype represents the fifth side of the Pyramid, the base, or foundation upon which it rests! I truly believe that the Great Pyramid, in Egypt, was an initiation temple back in ancient times. It is perfectly aligned with the four cardinal points. Osiris was often shown with the gods of the four directions at his command. He was Lord of the four quarters. The Great Pyramid was a temple for the initiation into the Osirian Mysteries. This profound experience was the Egyptian equivalent of the Eleusinian mysteries surrounding the abduction of Persephone by the god Pluto. The lesson is essentially the same in both myths. The participant came away with a personal revelation into the deeper meaning of both life and death. From the wisdom and security imparted by this experience, the disciple could now live his life with a powerful inner courage and purpose. He is finally ready to make full use of the next archetype, the next inner planet on the outward spiral of initiation.

The Moon and the Four Angles

Moon in the King Power Zone

When a person has the Moon located just past the midheaven of the chart, they will seek (and receive) their own personal sense of regeneration and renewal through their career. They are identified highly with their public self and are very conscious of how others react to them. The adaptability of the Moon, as reflected in its phases, allows them to wear many faces in public.

The Moon embodies both the eternal child and the adapted child. These natives are aware of a deep inner sense of feeling naked and secretly vulnerable in public settings. They will often scurry quickly to hide this from others. Yet it is this very trait, of dynamic vulnerability, that others are drawn to in them. They have the potential to excel as professional actors or performers, where they can easily portray the complete field of human emotions. When they are publicly accepted and embraced for their talent in this regard, then their career will flourish and so will they. If they are rejected and fall out of the public's graces, then they feel like the martyred Christ in being condemned to a fatal crucifixion. In fact their careers can often go through many cyclic deaths and rebirths based on public acceptance.

This archetype does not contain a related shadow as do the other four. It simply fluctuates eternally between regeneration and degeneration. Any shadow manifestations will be due to the Moon's association with other planet archetypes via various aspects. The Moon will simply accentuate or de-accentuate these flickering shadows that emanate from elsewhere in the chart.

Moon in the Lover Power Zone

The native, whose chart contains this arrangement, will receive their personal sense of death and rebirth through relationships. Much of their self worth and esteem will rise and fall on the level of success contained within their relationship to spouse or significant other. This can also extend to close family members who can easily rock their boat as well.

They view it as essential, to their emotional growth and well being, that they be involved in a healthy thriving relationship. These natives will look powerfully to this source in order to receive most of their validation about themselves. Their partner can often, unknowingly, make or break them through a simple passing comment. All of their vulnerability lies nestled within the domain of their relationship.

It is through this emotional roller coaster that these natives eventually rise from the ashes like the phoenix. Just like the previous type will eventually come to sense their true public worth in between the rising and falling of public opinion, so this present type will also gain a growing sense of their innate "loveability" that remains unaffected by their external relationships.

Moon in the Magician Power Zone

Persons with this placement of the Moon will receive their personal sense of regeneration from inner critical reflection and meditation. They feel emotionally vulnerable and often rocked by the intensity of their own feelings and images. They often embark on their own inner journey of personal crucifixion and resurrection. (See the chart of Carl Jung in the final chapter for a poignant example).

These natives almost always have a powerful first hand awareness of the inner principle of spiritual regeneration. They very often will gravitate towards the direction of Christianity, possibly joining the priesthood as a result. Many others, like Jung, will gravitate towards psychotherapy in some form. They believe deeply in the human's ability to heal and regenerate his own soul.

Persons with this arrangement will also feel a tremendous closeness to nature and animal life. They will imbibe a strong sense of regeneration from being out in the woods. Many will have numerous pets and plants in their home to help recreate this feeling.

Moon in the Warrior Power Zone

When the Moon is rising in this power zone, the native will receive an inner sense of regeneration from physical and/or emotional activity. In fact, they can drive themselves in a seemingly endless fashion day in and day out. Many often become full-blown workaholics, never knowing when to quit.

This person may feel involuntarily thrust into battle. Emotionally they are terrified at how vulnerable they feel. Often times, as a result, they will prefer to operate out of their "adapted" mode. They are quite capable of putting on the happy face and fooling others. The best defense is a good offense in their minds. Their aggressive adapted mode serves to protect them.

These persons can excel at acting because of their aggressive and dynamic ability to switch masks as needed. They can make excellent drama coaches and love to actively involve themselves in various forms of role play. Many of the newer forms of therapy, such as psycho drama, will appeal to them as both a participant but more preferably as a director of such.

This type of person cannot help but manifest all of their idiosyncrasies for others to see. They are assertively personable and very flexible in group settings. These natives have a good ability to quickly an efficiently size other people up through their strong attunement to their immediate environment. They have the potential to subtlety dominate others through their strong emotional charisma.

As there is no quadrant assigned to the Lunar/Wildman archetype, we must look to its aspect for evidence of its presence in a chart. Whenever there are two or more square aspects in a birthchart, we can be sure that the Wildman archetype is present within the personality even if the Moon is not in the thick of things.

When interpreting squares, you must come to view them in this dynamic fashion. Too much of astrological literature has labeled them as simply bad news. Most people never stick around long enough to discover the good side of this aspect. Initially, people sense it as an inner struggle between the two archetypes involved. The two archetypes are literally at odds with each other. There is much inner heat, friction and resistance generated from this challenge.

This trait is so obviously reminiscent of the eternal struggle between Osiris and Set. Set initially succeeds in dismembering his brother. As gruesome as this act seems, it is a necessary component in Osiris' ability to later regenerate himself. Squares are ultimately regenerative if one sees the process through. That is the potentiality which they offer us.

Let us say, for example, that a chart contains a square between Mars and Neptune. This creates a truly challenging setup. Mars (the Warrior) is blunt, aggressive and fiery by nature. Neptune is dreamy, ethereal and watery by nature. Here we find a real oil and water mix of archetypal energies struggling, via their square aspect, for position within the psyche.

Each literally wants to dismember the other. The native will be real acutely aware of this friction within himself. Ultimately, these struggles will either make or break us. Squares indicate the areas of greatest inner challenge. The only way to reconcile this challenge is to allow each archetype to periodically slay the other one. As a result of this, they each can also periodically experience regeneration.

What I mean to imply by this is that we should encourage this inner reciprocity because it allows the cyclic energy of the square to be unleashed upon the two archetypes. Returning to our example, Mars will then regenerate Neptune through slaying it. Neptune will also regenerate Mars through extinguishing his flames with her waters. The end result is that they end up empowering each other through this paradoxical form of symbiosis which inseparably links their destinies.

The road to this mastery, of the square's energy, is a rocky one indeed. When one finally surrenders oneself to this inner feeling of perpetual crucifixion, then the experience ceases to feel like death. We will instead start to experience an inner feeling of life and animation. In this scenario, Mars will fuel and turbocharge our Neptunian spiritual beliefs and intuitive imagination. Neptune will empower Mars with a compassionate appreciation for all things living through a sublime feeling of interconnectedness. This will generate a desire to protect and honor these vulnerable creations.

Special attention must be given here to the Grand Square configuration. When this exists, in any chart, the native will be especially attuned to the energy of the Moon. They will be unavoidably aware of the dynamic challenge of Lunar energy. Their lives will seem a constant struggle of endlessly alternating breakthroughs and setbacks. I know from experience. My chart contains an angular Grand Square which includes the Moon within its structure. It is my cross to bear and, at the same time, it is also my salvation.

The Moon also possesses a unique time cycle which correlates to its orbit. This cycle corresponds to the Moon's "nodes." These are the two points where the moon's orbit crosses the Earth's orbit. These two lunar nodes are in a constant state of gradual motion in respect to the Earth's orbit. The whole cycle takes some nineteen years to complete.

When a new or full moon occurs in alignment with one of these two nodes, then an eclipse will occur as a result. The ancient skygazing cultures of the Babylonians and the Mayans both knew of this cycle and were able to predict coming eclipses hundreds of years in advance. The lunar nodes were known in medieval times as the dragon's head (north node) and the dragon's tail (south node).

Beyond their astronomical significance, I believe that this cycle of the nodes corresponds to a larger cycle of Ego regeneration and maturation. This much grander cycle outweighs many of the seemingly insignificant deaths and rebirths we experience under the more fleeting monthly lunations. It therefore signifies crucial times during the human lifespan where the maturing Ego is shedding its skin like a snake or breaking out of its cocoon towards a much greater potential for itself.

These metamorphic phases take place every nineteen years. The whole rich spectrum of what the Moon represents (Ego-eternal child - adapted child-inner child-Wildman), will experience an initiatory rite of passage every time this cycle completes itself. At the age of nineteen, the nodes will begin their second cycle. Each of us yearns to become more objectively aware of our own Ego's potential at this point. We want to spread our wings so to speak.

When we reach 38, the lunar nodes begin their third cycle. This is a time when we start to get a true aesthetic feel for the very nature of our Ego and its regenerative potential. We seek to relate to and harmonize with this wonderful quality of the Wildman within us. This will lead us to a more comfortable acceptance and appreciation for this spontaneous adaptable core of our being.

These nineteen year lunar cycles often manage to coincide with other pertinent planetary lifecycles. At the age of 38, not only are the nodes beginning a new cycle, but frequently people are often experiencing the Opposition of Uranus to its natal position. These two distinct cycles have much to do with the "mid-life crisis" which many of us experience around this time. See Chapters 6 and 8 for more information on these larger planetary cycles.

CHAPTER FIVE

Mars, The Warrior

Spiraling outward from the Earth, we happen upon the red planet, Mars. Here we encounter the last of our personal, human archetypes, the Warrior. Mars becomes incorporated into our experience as it returns to its natal position for the first time. This happens around the age of two in a child's life. The "terrible twos" make their appearance!

During this period, the child begins to set boundaries and say "NO!" This is a time of separation, where he uses the energy of Mars to begin the process of distinguishing himself from others. It takes a lot of energy to separate from our parents. They are very intimidating giants to a two-year-old. Mars supplies the necessary fuel to accomplish this separation.

Mars is connected to the number five and the principle of five-ness. This number represents willpower or adrenalin, the fuel that helps us deliberately forge new links.[1] It helps us to arrange and qualify matter. Mars puts together thought and matter in new ways. Mars combines objective reasoning (2) and form (3). Together, they add up to his number (5). He is like the farmer who arranges the crop in rows so as to increase the yield of his harvest.

The Warrior is, in essence, a laborer, a worker bee. He is devoted to the protection, upkeep and maintenance of the Kingdom. This is why Mars is the outermost *human* archetype, literally encircling and guarding the King's realm!

Mars is associated with the aspect of the Quintile (72°). The Grand Quintile is a rare and little understood structure in the astrological world. That is because the connection between five-ness and Mars has never been stressed enough in astrological literature.

The Pentagon in Washington is actually a Grand Quintile in material form! Here we have a literal temple of the Warrior archetype, a place where the most sacred Warrior planning goes on in secret. Devoutly, the collective minds of Mars gather to worship within its walls! The Pentagon is the actual adrenal gland of the country, a Warrior center. Our symbol for the military is the five- pointed star and the highest rank is that of a five-star general!

Mars rules the medulla (central Yang portion) of the adrenal glands. Venus rules the outer (Yin) cortex of the gland, which produces cortisone. This, cortisone, is one of the body's innate "healing balms." Adrenaline, on the other hand, is the hormone that causes the "fight or flight" response within us, activating the sympathetic nervous system. Blood is diverted from the digestive tract to the muscles. Glycogen (stored fuel) is released from storage and made available. We either stand and fight, or run from harm's way.

Mars has two moons, named after the mythological sons of the Roman god Mars: Phobos (fear) and Deimos (panic). Even though the Warrior can fight, he doesn't always choose to do so. Fear is his wise and constant companion. The true Warrior has a healthy sense of fear. He can wisely assess any situation and determine which response is appropriate, to fight or flee. There is no shame in a wise retreat. Staying alive is the objective, suicide is not. He chooses the path that will minimize damage and casualties.

This is the difference between the mature Warrior and the young, impulsive and immature "Hero" we manifest in childhood. The Hero, according to Moore and Gillette, is the child who is noble in purpose, striving to win the blessing and admiration of his parents.[2] He wants his separateness to be acknowledged. Parents can easily crush our developing Hero/Warrior energy by not allowing us to separate. They admonish and beat the Hero when he starts to show signs of independence and strength. Will-fullness has long been considered a sin and the culture demanded that parents "break the child's will." "Spare the rod and spoil the child," says the Bible. The research of Alice Miller has shown this to be highly destructive to the child. Her case studies of the brutal abuse suffered by Adolf Hitler in his childhood depict the ultimate, horrifying results of the corruption of Warrior energy.[3]

The Hero must, instead, be acknowledged, honored and educated in the true sense. When the Hero is shamed or abused for showing healthy anger energy, he splits off and develops into one of the two bi-polar shadows described by Moore and Gillette: the "Grandstander-Bully" (more than) and the "Coward" (less than).[4]

The Grandstander demands center stage and aggressively competes with others for it. He becomes "king of the hill" by staging an aggressive coup. Many of today's "bad boys" of rock and roll or rap are operating under this infantile shadow.

The Bully usurps the royal throne and, in his arrogant grandiosity, proclaims himself "King." The Warrior can never be the King. His only real place is to serve him. All militant governments, in which the army rules, are examples of "boy heroes" in men's bodies still trying to be King! This comes from woundedness and ignorance. It is usually completely unconscious.

This display of aggression is aimed at hiding the insecurity around his wound. He will assault those who catch a glimpse of his weakness. Nobody gets close to him. The wounded Hero refuses to accept his own mortally. He specializes in denying death, one of life's inescapable limitations. *The Great Santini* is a perfect story of a man with a wounded Hero inside of him.

Mars energy is blunt by nature and a wounded Hero can be crude and obnoxious. He belches and farts with no sense of embarrassment. Mars energy is very physical and he enjoys announcing his presence bodily. A typical Martian greeting might be "Pull my finger!"

The other direction we can go with the wound, is to become "less than" and retreat into the Coward. This is the child who won't stand up for himself at all. He acquiesces to any pressure and caves in easily. Here we have the "doormat syndrome." He's the nice guy who tries to make everybody else happy. Eventually his resentment and rage explode like a pressure cooker. All the repressed anger surrounding his wound finally comes out and becomes apparent to everyone.

This particular shadow pole sets us up for what Robert Bly calls "the naive male."[5] This person has no front door on his house. If you look closely, even the walls are missing! Lacking any sense of boundaries, thieves come in any time they like, taking anything they want. Nobody can truly respect him, because he cannot respect himself. This is the breeding ground of co-dependency.

I believe the Warrior to be an archetype which readily accepts wounding. It is within the nature of the Warrior to sustain injuries during battle. Many veterans will brag as they proudly display the scars of their bloody wounds. This is even traditionally honored by decorating the soldier with medals. He is publicly acknowledged for his sacrifice. Unfortunately this also leaves the Warrior wide open to further attacks of blame from those who fail to see the noble purpose which he seeks to serve.

The image of the Warrior is a highly negative one in our society and little understood, it has even been labeled "evil." Partly it is due to the inability of the shadow Warrior to tolerate any display of anger or strength from other people. The shadow Warrior demands control and lives within a rigid hierarchy, with himself as the King, of course. These shadow Warriors are often the first to condemn the archetype of the healthy Warrior. Ultimately, they fall prey to the very same energy they seek to destroy!

We see this folly played out in the struggle of ultra- conservatives to stamp out the blight of "Satanism" and other assorted "heavy metal" influences. This genre of music, and its fans, have come to be cast in the role of scapegoat. They carry society's ugliness and rage so that the bulk of us don't have to face our own unresolved issues regarding the Warrior within. We simply choose to demonize a select group of people to avoid owning our own rage.

In actuality, these folks do not embody "Satan," merely the shadow of the Warrior archetype. Let us look more closely for proof. All rock and heavy metal music is based upon a "Pentatonic" (5 tone) scale! Because of its very design, the music cannot help but convey the energy of Mars. Even the term "heavy metal" hints of Mar's own metal, iron.

The clothing and paraphernalia, associated with heavy metal, all smack of Martian influence. Black is the predominant color worn (symbolizing the darkness of the shadow Warrior) and this is usually adorned with a whole array of chains (symbolizing the repression of this energy). To top it all off, these folks all identify strongly with the symbol of the inverted five-pointed star (the inverted pentagram).[6] We need to start seeing these people as nothing more than mere humans with a repressed, wounded Warrior archetype, and not the children of Satan.

The negative image of the Warrior is due in greater part to the terrible damage wrought by the shadow Warriors of our history. It is our responsibility as men to overcome this image, and we can only do so first by healing the damaged Warrior, and then by healing the damage he has caused. The eighth and ninth steps of the 12 step programs acknowledge the need for this process of making amends.

Realize that when people, many compassionate men as well as women, attack the archetype of the Warrior, they are reacting to the immature, macho, destructive shadow Warrior. When rape is sanctioned as a weapon of war, it is no wonder that the Warrior is feared and vilified.

The solution, however, is not to try and surgically remove it from our psyche. It is part of our "hard wiring," as Moore and Gillette say.[7] We must instead learn to befriend the Warrior, coax him out into the open and help to heal him. This can be done only through knowledge and initiation. I heard it said once that we can't kill our demons, we can only re-educate them!

I believe this can best be done by going back to the source of the wound in childhood. It is here that we must establish a dialogue with the assorted "family" of children, hiding in our shadows. We may also need to enlist the help of a trained therapist if it gets too overwhelming. But you will be surprised at who shows up, living within you.

There are many wounded children within us. The Trickster is very common. It's hard to get him to sit at the table for any length of time. There is the wounded Lover, usually our most shy and vulnerable inner child. The Divine Child can manifest many forms of woundedness. The wounded Warrior usually shows up as a bully, or brat.

Establishing open cross communication between all these different sub-personalities may seem schizophrenic at first. But we are very complex organisms by nature. We can choose to accept our inner reality and develop a healthy sense of integration and balance. If we choose the alternative of denying our innate complexity, we end up becoming pathologically complex, or schizophrenic. The choice is ours.

As the Warrior begins to heal and mature, we can (for the first time) begin to feel his proper expression in our lives. He faces life head on by engaging it courageously yet respectfully. He is alert and mindful of his environment and his responses to it. A true Warrior lives by a code. It is a total way of life for him.

The Warrior has his code of honor. The samurai, the kamakazi, the martial artist, the knight, even boy scouts all have their particular oath. The true Warrior knows humility well. Moore says, "humility is knowing your limits and getting the help you need."[8] The Warrior does not rush in foolishly without assessing the situation first. He is not afraid to double back or retreat. He knows when to get help. There is no shame in waiting for reinforcements. He is a wise master of strategy. Like the chess player, he can see two or three moves ahead of his opponent and control the outcome.

It is Mars that gives us our passion to engage life. The Warrior knows better than anyone the fragile nature of life. He has been at death's doorstep many times. When engaging in battle, he has the powerful awareness that death can come at any moment. He therefore lives life with conviction, making every act count.

The Shadow Warrior's destructive tendencies towards sadism and masochism are disciplined into honor and respect in the healthy Warrior. The mature Warrior, in order to stay on track, must always bow to the King. He needs to serve a cause "transcendent to himself."[9] Only in this way does he preserve his humility and stay healthy.

The Warrior's word is his honor. He will stake his life upon it. The Warrior honors his code; and his code is honor. It is worth noting that the U.S. Congressional Medal of Honor is none other than a five pointed star! The Warrior knows loyalty to his brethren as well as his sovereign. Loyalty and love for life, for brothers, for family, for sons. The passion and conviction the Warrior feels is evident in every gesture of his life. He has the courage of his convictions. He protects. He nurtures. He serves. You know where he stands, because he takes a stand. He abhors apathy and laziness.

In *Dances with Wolves,* the Warrior—literally, an honored Union cavalry man—finds healing by shedding the shadow Warrior self and being initiated into a tribe. Captured by the brutal army he has rejected, he is to be tried as a deserter. He escapes, rescued by his adopted brothers and fathers. But he kills army men in the process and chooses to leave his adopted tribe, so that the cavalry does not discover their village in the process of tracking him. High up on a cliff sits his warrior friend Wind-In-His-Hair. Wind-In-his-Hair cries out to his departing friend, "I am Wind-In-His-Hair. Can you see that I am your friend? Can you see that you will always be my friend?" These are the kinds of powerful statements that issue forth from a healthy initiated Warrior.

Mars is very similar to Earth. Its axial tilt and length of day are virtually identical to ours. Mars, the red planet, also rules arterial, oxygenated blood. The reason that Mars appears red is because the rocks, on the Martian surface, contain large quantities of iron oxide. Human arterial blood appears red for the same exact reason, due to the presence of the iron and oxygen carried in our hemoglobin.

Mars and Venus share a parallel axis on our Archetypal Tree. They are a bi-polar pair and their energies are always complimentary and inseparable in life. We see their inextricable connectedness in the adrenal glands and the circulatory system. They also represent the phallus and yoni which join together in coitus. Here we see the extremes of the left and right pillars expressed on a purely physical level.

Mars and the Four Angles

Mars in the King Power Zone

When the Warrior archetype is situated just past the midheaven, this often is the primary influence within the charts of career athletes and military personnel. The Gauquelin's research verifies this fact beyond any reasonable doubt. These persons yearn to be publicly acknowledged for their well-developed Warrior.

Often they will choose a public calling which involves some kind of fight or struggle. This will bring out the best in their innate desire to compete against something. Professional sports, the armed services and public service will most strongly appeal to them. Martial arts teachers and security personnel also head the list. Basically any career where they can brandish a weapon and exert their willpower over others is attractive. In the case of athletes, their body suffices as the weapon of choice.

These natives are publicly direct and to the point. They don't beat around the bush when questioned on something. They pride themselves in always telling it like it is, even if another's feeling get hurt in the process. They truly enjoy taking on the noble cause and will fight for those less fortunate than themselves. This is why so many professional athletes also devote part of their time to various charity organizations.

When the shadow manifests itself in these natives, their wound will sour their code of values. They can be quite obnoxious and crude with anyone who disagrees with them. Any resistance to their ideas and beliefs will be met with a full verbal barrage. If provoked far enough, their retaliation will often degenerate into physical violence. The chip on their shoulder can be seen by everyone.

Mars in the Lover Power Zone

This arrangement mellows the flames of Mars somewhat by directing them towards more personal matters. Instead of pursuing public causes, the native directs their quest towards their relationships. They can become fervently involved with their partner instead. They are easily aroused and quite flirtatious, if not downright dominant, by nature. The passion here borders on lust.

Basically, these natives respond ravenously to their sensual nature in an acute manner. They can be easily seduced because of this lustful response nature. Sex and relationship must always be intense for them to remain involved. They will be extremely protective of their loved ones and move quickly to defend them any time a threat arises.

In its shadow form, these natives will also suffer from a soured sense of values. Instead of being protective towards their loved ones, they will seek to control and dominate them in every way possible. They can often resort to physically abusing their spouse or children. A planet situated within the Lover power zone influences the way in which we react when relating to other people. With Mars, the response is usually anger and temper tantrums. (See Bobby Fischer, Chapter 13)

More commonly, they will manifest a vacillation between the Coward and Bully poles of the shadow. This means that often they will stuff their anger and rage deep inside as they seek to be the "nice" person. Months at a time may transpire until suddenly they explode on their spouse or child. These poor innocent victims end up in the wrong place at the wrong time. Without healing, disaster is inevitable.

Mars in the Magician Power Zone

Mars is the most extroverted of planets. When it is found located in this highly introverted zone, difficulties can often arise. In its best scenario, Mars will add tremendous drive and discipline to ones inner spiritual work. These natives can often read or study for long hours deep into the night. They love to plunge energetically into a deep contemplation of their favorite subjects.

Because the Warrior's energy is so completely sublimated into the unconscious, these natives will often struggle to manifest Warrior energy on a conscious level. The result is that much of their anger and rage never gets vented appropriately. They are experts at "cerebralizing" their feelings of anger. The influence of the Magician zone serves to analyze the anger to death. These people can speak very eloquently about how enraged they are over something, while remaining completely calm on the outside!

The result of this Magical detachment, from their feelings of anger, is that they can often become absolute pros in the art of passive-aggressive behavior. They don't like the feeling of being out of control, which comes with anger, so they simply detach and get others to carry their anger for them. They are experts in getting others to take their anger and run with it.

The problem here is that they remain completely unconscious and detached from any access to the full scope of their own Warrior archetype. They can often become experts at procrastination because they can ponder forever when it comes to taking direct action. These natives need to heed the motto: "Just do it!"

They prefer to uphold an image of sophistication as they allow their wounded Warrior to seep out through the cracks of their facade and taint all those around them. They need to shed this image of "coolness" and reclaim the full vitality of their Warrior archetype. Without it, their lives will remain lethargic and uninspired.

Mars in the Warrior Power Zone

Mars is most at home in this power zone. No longer locked in the basement, he is free to manifest himself completely. These people are often like thoroughbred horses fresh out of the starting gate. They are dynamic, forceful and assertive in their approach to life. These natives know what they want and do not hesitate in going after it.

The Mars rising person loves a physical challenge in any form. Adventurers at heart, they love fighting the good fight. Many have tremendous physical strength and endurance. Their pain threshold is unusually high and they seldom will show any signs of fatigue in the course of pursuing their goals. These natives are among the most goal-oriented types alive. They function best when they have a clear objective in mind.

When the Warrior is wounded, in this scenario, he will often spill all of his venom onto anything or anyone in his path. He is always spoiling for a fight. These natives will usually feel frustrated and "penned in". They will often claim that the world simply does not move fast enough for them. Their impatience is more pronounced than with any other placement of Mars.

When wounded, these natives love to get in everybody's face. They are experts at all forms of intimidation, especially physical. Their manner and gestures are overtly "gruff" and will usually serve to keep others slightly "on edge" when near them. People will often feel like they are walking on eggshells whenever they are around them. These natives have a tough time humbling themselves enough to realize that they are wounded and in need of healing.

Persons who have five or more planets occupying the Warrior quadrant will also show many of the personality traits of the Warrior archetype within their overall personality. This holds true regardless of whether Mars is prominent or not. A fully packed Warrior quadrant will add even more spice to a chart which also has Mars angular and/or heavily aspected. They each will serve to reinforce the overall Warrior theme of the chart.

One final factor, which also must be noted, is the presence of two or more Quintile aspects within the chart. Biquintiles (144°) are just as relevant as Quintiles (72°). They each represent a fifth harmonic relationship between the planets involved. This translates to Warrior energy.

Grand Quintiles are a less common phenomenon than Grand Squares, but they can and do occur. One can bet the house on the fact that any chart containing one will be chock full of Warrior development. Any sub-portion of a Grand Quintile is also quite powerful and should be noted. These smaller subsets are more frequently encountered in the everyday delineation of charts. One should therefore become familiar with them.

There is an especially powerful configuration which I have found in quite a few charts. I call it the "spike." It consists of three of the five points needed to form a Grand Quintile. Two of the planets form a Quintile (72°) and the third planet is located 144° (Biquintile) from each of these two. It is visually quite stark, when present in a chart, and resembles a primitive spike or dagger. It possesses tremendous Warrior energy as do any of these sub-portions of the Grand Quintile. (See Hitler's chart, Chapter 13.)

When interpreting Quintiles, view them as a willful and *productively* creative team effort between the archetypes involved. The goal is for them to serve a transcendent cause that will give us purpose and concrete direction in our lives. Quintiles seek to create useful objectives and structures that serve to further our true cause in life.

Quintiles take us a step beyond the cyclic death and rebirth of the square aspect by channeling our energy into a concrete direction of choice. They offer the potentiality for conviction and disciplined resolve between the two planets involved. Taken together, the archetypes will have a definite agenda. They will know that they are in a "working relationship" and that they've got work to do!

Let us say that a chart has a Quintile between Jupiter and Mars. The high ideals of Jupiter will keep the Warrior archetype (Mars) on the straight and narrow. Jupiter willfully imposes his high values onto Mars and seeks to channel the Warrior's tireless spirit into achieving great things. This can often prevent lower shadow forms of Warrior energy from manifesting themselves. Instead, Mars will be constantly trying to improve his usefulness and service to the greater good.

CHAPTER SIX

Jupiter, The Expansive King

♃ Spiraling out, continuing our initiation, beyond Mars, we pass through the veil of the asteroid belt and leave the realm of human archetypes. If our development has been healthy, we are securely centered within Earth and have been initiated into the four aspects of our psyches as we spiraled from the Sun through the early return cycles of Mercury, Venus and Mars.

Jupiter and Saturn are Divine Teachers, Masters that guide us through important phases and initiations. They resemble the Sun in ways that are significant to our understanding of their influence. Each is massive and completely dwarfs all the inner planets. They are primarily gaseous, formed out of the same condensing cloud of hot stellar gases that created the Sun. In truth, all of the four gaseous giants (Jupiter, Saturn, Uranus, Neptune) are literally separate solar systems within our own solar system. If Jupiter were only ten times bigger, it too would have become a star. These solar qualities help explain the immense power of these outer four archetypal generators.

The returns of Jupiter and Saturn, the Great Teachers, are pronounced and significant because they are longer cycles. Jupiter's circuit takes 12 earth years and Saturn's takes 29! When they finally do come to completion, they carry with them a much larger impact than those of the inner planets.

The Jupiterian cycles urge us to expand and grow beyond our limits, to go boldly where we have not yet been. We learn to take risks and keep on trying. Without this teacher, our values would stagnate. He is the white Osiris, who judges the dead. Osiris, in this form, is the purest aspect of our ideals.

Jupiter is the sixth sphere from the Sun, the largest of all the planets. Its configuration is the Sextile aspect (60°) and the presence of six celestial bodies allows for the possibility of the Grand Sextile to exist. Broken into its primaries, six is actually two times three, the number of Venus. So Jupiter truly is a higher evolvement of three-ness, or love.

Jupiter is the love and joy that comes through expansion and growth. There is confidence and optimism present. Jupiter returns to its natal position for the first time around the age of twelve. This is not coincidentally about the time that puberty begins to take place.

Jupiter rules the pituitary gland, or master gland. This gland begins to pump out large quantities of growth hormone, which triggers the process of puberty. Secondary sex characteristics begin to appear and most children at this age, begin to grow.

Jupiter, Fathers, Sons, Initiation

As adolescents, we start to feel confident in our awareness that we are changing. Jupiter is a powerful initiator. But without earthly guides to help teach us of its significance, we may miss the message.

Remember that as each planet returns to its original location in our natal chart, it will have just completed its first cycle. This first cycle is usually experienced as a period of innocence. It resonates with the number one, the Sun, and the Divine Child archetype. As the planet starts into its second cycle, it takes on the qualities of the number two, Mercury, and the Precocious Child archetype.

When we reach the age of twelve and Jupiter begins its second cycle, we will, once again, experience those qualities of two-ness. Suddenly, there is an awareness of separation as our bodies start to expand and grow. We are now leaving childhood, so painfully obvious by the physical changes we are experiencing. There is no turning back, no stopping.

It is important to mark this change by celebrating it ritually and making it conscious. This helps the adolescent to relax, to learn from and even to enjoy the experience, knowing that it is a miraculous part of life. The Jewish culture still celebrates this time of passage with the tradition of Bar-Mitzvah and the Catholic religion with the sacrament of Confirmation. The child is welcomed into the adult world by adults. This is so crucial to the health of our psyches.

Many of today's youth experience puberty alone and uncelebrated. They are not taught, or initiated, by adults as to the serious responsibility attached to their growing awareness of the pleasures of their bodies and their sexuality. Rather, they are drowning and struggling as the powerful flood as expansive hormonal energy, released by Jupiter, washes over them.

The young male sees that something is happening, but still feels completely overwhelmed. Some weather the storms of adolescence, others display rage at their wounding through indulging in promiscuity, substance abuse and violent behavior. They express anger and outrage at the adult world that abandoned them. Their culture and their parents have never acknowledged the Divine Children within them. They have no self-esteem. At this time in their lives, this most wonderful rite of passage could do much to heal them.

The return of Jupiter, its powerful energies and the accompanying of adolescence are a significant time in the development of a man. But most parents are ignorant of its significance and how to handle it. They are terrified of the changes occurring, at the need of their child to expand, grow and individuate. Parents wind up leaving children to their peers.

Today's adolescents are a rejected sub-culture of society, clinging to each other in desperation. They need to separate from their parents on a cognizant Mercurial level. That is the purpose of this emerging second Jupiter cycle. However, separating and acting out are two completely different phenomenon.

Adolescents in tribal cultures were initiated by the elders at this time. They were taught of their passage to the adult world, but they were never abandoned or shunned. Instead, they were blessed and remained an integral part of the community. Their presence was acknowledged and valued.

Jupiter (Zeus) was the father god. The Jupiter return should be a time when a father bonds with his son in a new way, inviting him into his company as a respected peer. Father and son should acknowledge that the son has much to learn, but the father should follow this admission with a vow to support his son in the learning process. Here, the Hero is invited to be Warrior, the Prince to be King.

Associations and Relations with other Planets

Jupiter is traditionally associated with ritual and religion, as is Saturn. This pair of opposites represents the two primary master teachers of life, who usher us into the upper realm of the spiritual trinity, Uranus-Neptune-Pluto. Through a series of trials and tests, we must petition and earn our way through their great portals.

While Saturn represents punishment, Jupiter represents reward. Their Yin-Yang energies are represented by our parents, the first master teachers that most of us encounter in life. They stand for the proverbial "yes" and "no."

Jupiter teaches us to aspire to lofty ideals. It stands for the highest good of all concerned. We expand our pleasure nature to include the joyful concepts of religious beliefs and higher power.

Jupiter imparts to us a sense of class and etiquette. We elevate our standards and strive towards higher and higher achievement. Jupiter helps raise our self-esteem by rewarding us for our good acts. Within this process, however, there is an element of judgment. He compares deeds to the ideal. This energy is, therefore, closely connected to status, rank and royalty. It can be the air of superiority and pomp.

Ronald Reagan is a good example of how these qualities operate in the personality. His cocky manner of speech and swagger are truly Jupiterian. He has Jupiter rising, opposed to the Moon and square the Sun! He was a born actor who portrays himself—and undoubtedly believes himself to be—bigger than life, someone who can do no wrong. These are perfect qualities for both an actor and politician.

Jupiter is associated with the joy of leisure activity, especially the "classy" forms such as yachting, golf, and polo. Anything too laborious is considered undignified in his eyes. He is white collar and, therefore, never allows himself to get dirty.

This teacher shows us that the best way to learn, is to study those you want to be like. Then just do what they do! Emulate and copy. Jupiter has much to do, therefore, with acting, fashions and trends. Herein lies the philosophy, "act as if" and eventually it will become second nature. Without the inner character that Saturn builds, this leads to shallowness.

Jupiter is public and conspicuous. He loves to be seen and admired. Parades and processions are his idea of fun and his sense of self-esteem may come from the eyes of others. He can get so caught up in looking good and conforming to mainstream, that he fails to develop an inner world. He winds up being so status quo, that he lacks originality and true character.

Jupiter has a lot to do with the concepts of abundance, plenty and even waste. He is charitable to a fault and usually gives away too much. The philanthropist and the entrepreneur are his type. Without his type, cultural progress would grind to a halt. Being the largest planet in our solar system, Jupiter naturally tends toward grandiosity. To be loved, in his eyes, is to be admired from his throne as he passively takes in the adoration and applause. He is orally fixated and loves to fill himself as this helps to invoke the feelings of fullness and overinflation. Jupiter prefers to be mothered rather than loved. In fact, Jupiter has as much to do with mothering as with fathering.

Jupiter is literally the "flesh" and Saturn the "bone" of life. This connection to the flesh, of the body, is why Jupiter rules the liver. This master organ regulates and orchestrates the symphony of our flesh.

Jupiter is also the planet of learned optimism and positive thinking. It is the kind of zeal that screams Yes! Yes! Yes! Wisely used, this energy can empower exercises in creative visualization, resulting in vibrant positive attitudes and a continual attraction of positive energy. The lesson here is all beliefs are self-fulfilling prophesies. Jupiter teaches us that we can't afford the false luxury of a negative thought!

This hopeful optimism can also be twisted in this planet's shadow side. We find this principle at work in all forms of gambling and speculation. Jupiter can be guilty of attempting to use this power for personal gain. He gets seduced by the odds, believing he can't lose. There are more prayers uttered in Trump's casino and Belmont racetrack, than in most places of worship!

Within the Jupiterian concept of boldness, we can find many other underlying connections. Many of us comment on the audacity of this type with phrases like, "What gall you have!" The connection to the liver reveals itself unconsciously in common, every day sayings.

When we reach the age of 24, Jupiter returns to its natal position for the second time and begins its third trip around the Sun. Remember here that the number three relates with Venus. It is here that we begin to expand and grow into the feeling and pleasure of maturity. Most people, at this juncture, now feel confidant enough to venture into the world of love. The years from 24 to 36 mark the period where we learn to get the feel of being an adult. We begin to form tastes for specific pleasures: art, music, etc. During this time, we are upgrading and refining our aesthetic values. We strive to form meaningful (Jupiter) love (Venus) relationships, and during this period we seek to find someone to love and with whom we can eventually build a good life.

When we reach the age of 36, Jupiter enters its fourth cycle. We will now strive to manifest all of our accumulated values. There is a desire to bring it all down to Earth. We yearn to be ourselves and to live out and manifest our beliefs and ideals.

The procreative instinct of the Moon urges us to pass on our values and principles by becoming teachers of our beliefs. It means that, even though we may already have children, we now take a deeper more expanding interest in passing on the best of what our belief system can offer them. If we have no offspring, we then express this urge in a growing empathy for all youth. We yearn to pass our beliefs and bountiful experience onto them.

Earlier in this chapter, we mentioned that Jupiter equates with six-ness and the Sextile aspect (60°). It is worth mentioning that Jupiter carries, within its orbital path, two separate groups of Trojan Asteroids. They travel with the planet, one being 60° behind and the other 60° ahead! These asteroid groups each serve to form a constant equilateral triangle between the Sun, their own positions, and that of Jupiter. Within this phenomenon we have physical proof of Jupiter's association with a higher expression of three-ness, or Venus energies. Here we can clearly see two separate trinities that are joined together (2 x 3 = 6; fig. 6a). The connection to six-ness can also be seen revealed in the fact that Zeus (the Greek Jupiter) was the sixth child of Cronos!

Jupiter is the largest planet, and yet it also has the shortest day. The huge giant spins on its axis in just under 10 Earth hours. This speed causes a tremendous centrifugal force which makes the planet bulge and expand tremendously at its equator. Its very physics end up revealing its principle quality!

The equator of this planet is virtually parallel to the plane of the ecliptic. This means that Jupiter stands perfectly "upright" as it spins on its axis. The planet has no seasons (like those of Earth). Because of its alignment with the ecliptic, Jupiter is completely attuned to the solar vibration of the Sun. He truly is the lesser King!

Other well known names for the mythological Jupiter are Zeus and Jove. From the latter we derive the term Jovial, or joyous. In ancient times, the letter "J" was really pronounced like a "Y." In Greece, this letter was called "Iota" and in Hebrew it was known as "Yod". From this, we can follow its pronunciatory migrations. Yessu becomes Jesus and Yah Weh comes down to us as Jehovah.

It is my belief that Jove (pronounced Yo-ve) shares the same ancient roots as the Hebrew god Yah Weh (pronounced Ya-Vey). Zeus (Jove) was the most powerful god in Greek mythology just as Yah Weh was to the Hebrew religion. Zeus killed with lightening bolts and Yah Weh used fire and brimstone.

The Hebrew name of god was called the Tetragrammaton, or the four sacred letters (semi vowels). These letters, Yod-Heh-Vav-Heh, when pronounced, would actually sound like "eeeeeee-aaaaaah-ooooooo-

Figure 6a

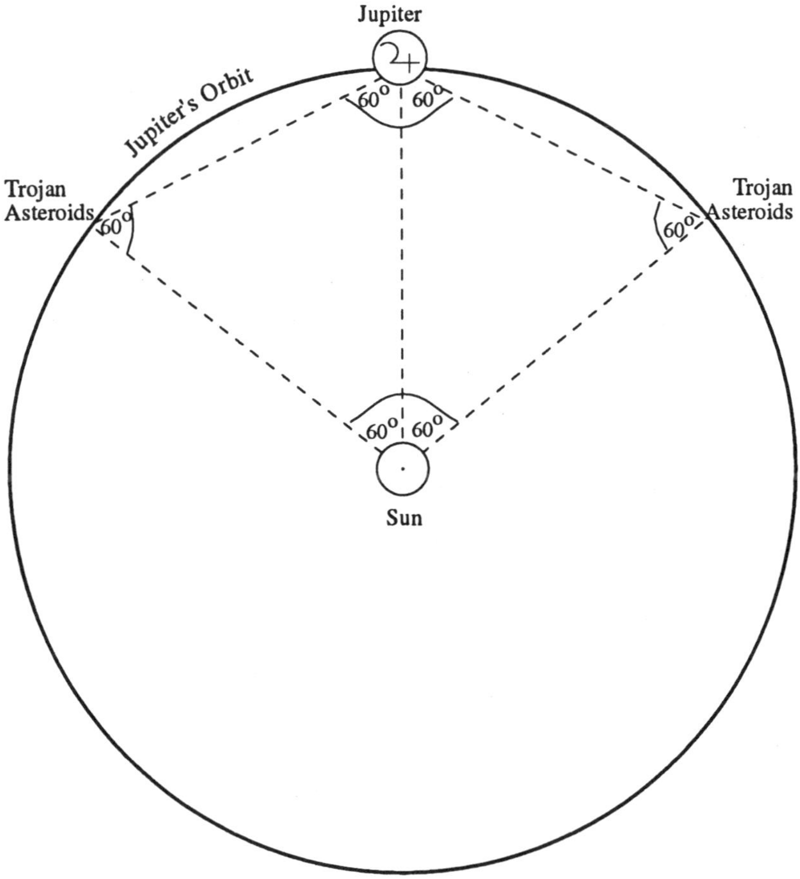
Jupiter
Jupiter's Orbit
Trojan Asteroids
60°
60°
60°
Trojan Asteroids
60°
60°
60°
Sun

aaaaaaaay." In pure vowel form, they reproduce the "acoustics" of an oscillating sound wave. This comes from an Egyptian word (I-A-U-I) which means "one who is exceedingly ancient."

The White Osiris of Egyptian mythology was also associated with resurrection. He was seen as the fully ascended King, with the four "children of Horus" at his command. These were the four cardinal points. There is a strange overlap of four-ness within both the Moon and Jupiter. We see this in the Tetragrammaton and the four children of Horus.

I believe that there is a definite reason for this. The pure crystal clarity of the Egyptian desert was a perfect observatory in ancient times. Stars of very faint magnitude could be easily seen on a Moonless night. It is my theory that these ancient priest-astronomers were aware of Jupiter's four largest moons.

They saw Jupiter/Osiris as simply another manifestation of the principle of four-ness, by equating his four moons (children) with the four directions and the four Lunar phases! These moons were not known by other cultures and were not discovered again until Galileo found them with his simple low power telescope. It is my contention that the Egyptians knew of them in antiquity, just as they probably knew of Uranus, which is also on the fringe of visibility.

Because of the mini solar system design of the gaseous planets, their energies will display a subtle range of variation in the way they manifest. Jupiter will resonate differently, depending upon how its satellites are positioned around it. Many of Jupiter's moons are as large as some of the planets in the Solar system! Their influence must, therefore, be appreciable.

Jupiter always needs to be balanced by Saturn's lessons, in order for it to be a healthy influence. Its place on the Tree is just above Venus on the left pillar. It shares the middle horizontal axis with Saturn, the other Master Teacher who balances his lessons.

Jupiter and the Four Angles

Jupiter in the King Power Zone

When Jupiter is located just past the midheaven, in the King's power zone, we have yet another majestic arrangement. As an archetype, Jupiter represents another source of Kingly energy in addition to the

Sun. He is regal in his own right and when located in this powerful spot, shines magnificently.

Much of the definition which pertains to the Sun in the King zone will also apply to these angular Jupiter types. Jupiter, however, exhibits a much more expansive faith and optimism in his career. At times cocky and confident, these natives are quite sure of their abilities in the public arena. They are flamboyant and charismatic in their dealings with others.

Many of these natives are highly motivated, within their careers, to constantly improve their talents. They are success oriented and always fix their sights on higher ground. The youthful expansive entrepreneurial exuberance of Anthony Robbins is a prime example of this quality. He has Jupiter powerfully involved in a Grand Trine configuration in his chart. This Jupiterian placement is frequently found in the charts of politicians, C.E.O's, and quite significantly in the charts of religious leaders and others who can inspire large groups.

In terms of shadow manifestations, a wounded Jupiter will suffer from what psychologists call "pathological grandiosity." They can be quite conceited and pompous in their opinions of themselves. This stems from an inner sense of insecurity. If we examine the mythological relationship between Zeus and Hera (his wife), we find all sorts of evidence of jealousy and envy. The shadow wound will motivate a Jupiterian type to put up an impressive display of immenseness so as to distract from his inner feelings of envy towards others. Sadly, they doubt their own innate sense of power and are jealous of others who truly possess it.

Jupiter in the Lover Power Zone

When Jupiter is found here, these natives will strive to bring about the highest quality good within their relationships. They seek honesty and fairness in all their dealings of love and intimacy. Ultimately, this person will attempt to constantly expand the quality of intimacy in their lives.

Furthermore, they will yearn for their partner to grow and expand within the relationship as well. They embody the win/win philosophy when it comes to their relationships. Ultimately they are most strongly attracted to persons who possess a solid sense of belief in a higher power. They want a partner who values relationship as much as themselves.

In its shadow variety, these natives will hide their wounds from their partner by attempting to always go "one up" on them. They can be secretly jealous of another's ability to relate their feelings so openly, especially those of weakness and sorrow. They are terrified to be down to earth in relationships.

Jupiter in the Magician Power Zone

This location is a bit of a damper for the normally extroverted Jupiter. Their sense of exuberance and expansion may express itself in a pursuit of inner knowledge through reading and reflection. This arrangement lends itself to the quietly religious life such as that of the monk. These natives seek to privately pursue their higher power in the safety of some hermetic, contained space such as a monastery.

These natives also make excellent therapists because they can extract the highest quality insights from their own lives. They can, in turn, utilize this wisdom in their counseling methods with clients. The result will be a dramatic improvement in the lives of all who take their counseling advice to heart.

In its wounded variety, these natives will be very out of touch with their own power of expansive optimism. Being buried so deeply within the unconscious region of their chart, they will often feel pessimistically weak and envious of others. The wounded Jupiterian type prefers, instead, to hide within their grandiosity. Here they will sit and secretly judge others as being too emotionally weak.

Jupiter in the Warrior Power Zone

These types can be explosively exuberant at times. They are the zealous crusaders of life. Jupiter is quite forceful and dynamic here, seeking to willfully convert others to his beliefs. This arrangement shows up frequently in the charts of charismatic politicians and televangelists. These natives can more effectively sway the belief systems of large groups of people, than any other type that I know.

Gifted with an expanded sense of peripheral vision, these people's minds can behold visions others can only dream of. They have a physical sense of confidence that others pick up on immediately. These natives will take any and all risks to achieve their cause if it is something that they believe strongly enough in. Their quest is always slightly lofty in its purpose.

If we encounter the shadow of Jupiter in this arrangement, we find the person who can fool everybody with their absolutely convincing sense of optimism and confidence. Underneath the surface, however, they secretly doubt their power even in the face of positive feedback from others. They are secretly envious and jealous of anyone who is truly expansive and free. Somehow their wound tells them that they don't have the right to believe in themselves, despite their wonderful influence on all those whose lives they touch.

Another factor which will indicate the existence of Jupiterian influences in the chart is the presence of three or more Sextile aspects. This aspect is slightly weaker and more subtle than those covered so far, and it therefore takes more of them to make themselves known within the chart. A person with a Grand Sextile, or any portion thereof, within their chart will be a powerfully exuberant type by nature.

When interpreting Sextiles within the chart, view the aspect as offering the potential of an expansive opportunity for growth between the two archetypes so connected. The native has the opportunity to bring about the highest quality expression possible between the two archetypes involved. Whether this is actualized or not is up to the native. Remember, an aspect is only a potential. In order to fully actualize this potential, the native must deliberately and consciously invoke it from within himself.

Let us say that a chart contains a Sextile aspect between Mercury and Venus. These natives will possess the potential to realize a high quality relationship between the Magician and Lover archetypes within themselves if they so chose. They can merge feelings and compassion with the ability to communicate wisdom to others. The result might be that they develop the sensitive ability to write exquisite poetry that will powerfully move others. Their ability to powerfully articulate the Lover within them will inspire others to new realizations.

CHAPTER SEVEN

Saturn, The Dark Magician

♄ Saturn is the seventh sphere, which is related to seven-ness and the "Grand Septile." In Greek mythology Cronos (Saturn) was the seventh of the ancient race of Titans. He embodies the "Sabbath" or seventh day of rest, where man was asked to quietly reflect on his life. Seven also has to do with cosmic secrets and fertile imagination.[1] It signifies a powerful form of spirituality.

Saturn is the other Master Teacher who balances and tempers the lessons of Jupiter. Although Jupiter helps us cultivate values and principles, it is Saturn who helps us polish them into gemstones. His influence and lessons start to become painfully aware to us around the age of 29 or 30. It is at this time in life that the second cycle of Saturn begins.

Saturn has been labeled a malefic or bad luck planet. It is neither. However, the lessons of Saturn are life's most difficult and painful. That these lessons are hard learned does not diminish their value. But the lessons have much to do with the changes imposed by death and loss. These inescapable truths are feared more than evil. Many fear Saturn, because they dread the permanent results of his influence.

Even in ancient cultures, Saturn's virtue and value was not understood. In Egypt, he was known as Set. During the earlier dynasties, Set was viewed with reverence and respect. He was believed to offer friendly assistance to the dead. This view changed through time as military invasions of Egypt brought different elements and beliefs into the culture that diluted and distorted Egyptian mythology.

By about the 22nd dynasty, Set came to be seen as the origin of all evil. Almost all of his images and statues were vigorously destroyed. This marked the beginning of a true spiritual dark age that continues to this day. We are only now starting to understand and re-discover the true value of Saturn and the healing principles hidden within its darkness.

Much of the pain of Saturn's lessons arises because it demands we become aware of our separateness, and of our own personal deficiencies and limitations. The time of expansions and boldness— by now we are midway through our 3rd Jupiter cycle—are suddenly stripped away by Saturn. The energy of the first Saturn return is often experienced as a sudden slap in the face, a time when the conditions of life force us to wake up an reassess our lives and attitudes. Saturn returns are often a cosmic "reality check."

The thirties are a time for recognizing our personal limits. The unlimited potential and boldness of Jove gives way to a painful recognition of limits—no, we won't make our first million, write our first bestseller or direct our first movie before we're thirty. We are no longer prodigies, but adults. Our first marriage fails. We lose a parent. We see the first of our peers die—perhaps in an accident, perhaps of cancer or of AIDS. Often our first recognition of our own physical limits and mortality is made apparent at this time.

The thirties are a painfully difficult time for most people. It's a time when we have to adjust to the awakening of Saturn's conscious message. Life starts to become much more serious. Many people get very depressed and suicidal during these years without knowing why. It seems that Saturn came and dropped a big, heavy lead brick in their lap and they are conscious of its presence, but don't know what it means.

Just as we have no Jupiterian initiations, we have no Saturnian teachers or initiators in our culture. Without a teacher to explain what the meaning and purpose of this "brick" is, we end up feeling lost, victimized and depressed.

Poet, teacher and mythologist Robert Bly has provided a model of Saturnian initiation.[2] It is not an easy process, but a necessary one to growth. Bly teaches us about grief, and the importance of learning how to grieve. Instead of "ascending" in the Jupiterian fashion, he explains the importance of "descending" and going "down into our sadness and losses." During the first thirty years of life, we are not completely conscious of the full depth of our sorrow. As we become aware under Saturn's second (Mercurial) cycle, the full scope of our grief starts to emerge. All the ascending techniques, which we have used to escape grief, start to lose their hold. Saturn pulls us down into the lagoon of our unconscious.

The grief and sorrow we feel, triggered through our realization of things permanently lost, serve to awaken all the pain surrounding the psychic wounds we sustained in childhood. All the wounded shadow parts of our disowned and split-off personalities start to re-surface and demand our attention. Our demons come knocking on our door.

Most of our cultural and social upbringing tells us not to answer that knock, just to ignore them and they'll go away. But we cannot and should not avoid them. They will not only become worse, they will kill us if we neglect them. But, facing them will free us. The true lesson of Saturn is painfully beautiful. These scary, ugly, dark, smelly parts of ourself can actually be the most beautiful!

Saturn is the "psychic recycler." He teaches us how to descend down into the shadowy pit. It is here that we salvage the gems of our psychic archetypes from amidst the shame and abuse that was originally cast onto them. He helps us to sort through the shit of our lives by descending into the bowels of our psyche.

Jupiter rules the upper end of the gastrointestinal tract. It is orally focused on the mouth, stomach and ingestion. Saturn represents the lower functions, and is anally focused on the bowel and elimination.

Saturn is the bowel, that place where the unprocessed and rejected parts of our food wind up. Even within this so-called waste, our bodies continue to absorb and make use of the valuable nutrients still contained therein.

Holistic health professionals seem to agree on one unavoidable fact: all dis-ease originates in the bowel! We have a silent epidemic of bowel dysfunction and cancer in this country. I believe this is a reflection on the physical level of the toxic state of our "psychic bowel," or unconscious mind! We have massive shame and secrecy around our bowels and their excretory functions. It is a subject that no one dares talk about. We deny its significance and beauty.

The word Saturn literally means "urn of the soul." It is the container, or bowel, where the shamed and rejected parts of our psyche go after they split off. The Saturnian process of grieving is one of going down into the pain and finding the valuable nutrients still locked within. These nutrients are the very food of our soul! They actually are some of the fragments and pieces of our original Great Self with which we came into the world. Through the Saturnian process of grieving, we re-discover the joy of being whole and integrated!

Saturn is said to build character because he truly does. It takes place through a very slow and almost imperceptible process of transformation and resurrection. Have you ever noticed the changes in the face of someone who has just had a good cry? Their countenance lightens, the creases in their brow vanish and the eyes glow with the spark of new found soul!

In the classic myths and stories of antiquity, the hero must often go through a period of time where he suffers alone. This significant phase of his growth and initiation is very often seven years in length. The most obvious example is the myth of Percival and the quest for the holy grail.

There are no easy shortcuts with Saturn and no back alleys. The only way out is to go through the pain. The path to spiritual resurrection entails picking up our cross and descending into the pit of hell. It smells foul down there and we can think of a million reasons not to go. Many of us never get around to the real work we need to do: that of finishing our unfinished business. This is scary work and we need all the help and support we can find! We need teachers to educate us of the value that's in it for us when we actually do this work. We're not going to get dirty sorting through our shit if we can't see the purpose behind it all.

Excrement is actually full of rich nutrients, as we have already mentioned. This is the source of most fertilizers. Manure and feces are a fertile gold mine, out of which vibrant plant life grows. The most beautiful flowers thrive on shit, roses require lots of it! The lesson is so simple that we overlook its wisdom.

Garth Allen sheds some interesting light on this point. Try to remember way, way back to when you were a young child. Back before the shame surrounding your eliminative functions had fully set in. Most children that young actually find the earthy, pungent smell of feces to be somewhat pleasant![3] Anyone who has ever known small children has experienced how creative kids can get with their shit!

Saturn rules the process of decay and destruction. This is reflected in its very physics. We find the most noticeable feature of this planet is its beautiful and mysterious ring system. The other giant planets also have rings, but none approach the massiveness of Saturn's.

The rings are actually a collection of billions of ice fragments that are caught within its gravitational field. These pieces are probably continuously colliding, and breaking into smaller and smaller fragments as they circle the planet. Saturn is, in effect, a huge gristmill. It rules the process of breaking down and destroying useless objects that have become obstacles to life itself. It is the grim reaper who separates the wheat from the chaff. This process of being ground down between the stone wheels of his mill is both painful and terrifying.

We fear that we will die, so we run when he comes. He's too horrible to look at. In truth, Saturn only represents the death of denial and the falsehoods of life. He comes to "break the spell" and destroy the lies that keep us from our Great Self.

The actual fear of Saturn and death is so beautifully portrayed in the movie, *The Fisher King*. Robin Williams plays a psychotic schizophrenic man; his illness is rooted in his inability to connect with his pain and grief.

He was a college professor whose wife was brutally shot and killed while they were dining in a restaurant. She died right in front of him, her blood splattering all over him. In order for him to defend his conscious mind from the pain, he had to split off every aspect of himself and bury his whole identity in the unconscious. This way nothing could possibly trigger the experience to resurface again.

He develops a new, false, personality to replace it with by becoming, in is mind, a knight who believes he is on a quest for the Holy Grail! His old, true, personality, with all its unresolved pain, starts to follow him around.

We see it symbolically represented by a fire breathing knight on a huge, ominous horse, that begins to chase and stalk him. He flees down the street in fear, trying desperately to outrun the Dark Knight. As the rider draws closer and closer to him, he starts to have flashes of his real self and the trauma he locked away so long ago. He collapses in the street, writhing in agony and grief.

The dark horseman is Saturn himself, coming to drop his brick. Our split-off pain and un-grieved losses chase us, relentlessly, like a pack of hungry dogs nipping at our heals. We are terrified for our very life.

What Saturn delivers is death of the false self so that our true Great Self can re-emerge from the prison of the unconscious. He seeks the death of the old order, crushing that which is useless to our evolution and progress.

The false self, or "adapted child," is actually created to take the place of those parts that we split off from our Divine Child and banish into the unconscious. It is a defense mechanism, needed to actually survive childhood abuse and shaming.

As we reach adulthood, it now becomes an obstacle in our own path towards self-actualization. Saturn comes along to chisel away the grandiose adapted child and bring us back down into our bodies where all the painful wounds are stored.

It is through body-work, psycho-drama and other techniques that we can begin to access these unconscious "body memories" and finally reconnect with them. When we connect with our grief, we are actually rediscovering long lost parts of our beautiful, divine nature. In befriending our demons, they lose their ominousness. They then begin to shine with beauty!

In *Iron John*, Robert Bly retells the story of the young boy who dips his wound into a pond.[4] It then turns to gold. By dipping down into the dungeon of our demons, we find the true gold of our soul. Saturn represents the medieval Alchemist, who magically turns lead, Saturn's metal, into gold. This is the process by which he imparts his lesson and Master teaching.

Our un-grieved losses are the lead brick that weighs heavy in our lap. As we connect with them, through the alchemical process of Saturn, they start turning back into gold. This is the shining inner gold that we entered the world with. Our divine nature has been resurrected. We can now, for the first time, fully appreciate its gifts.

Not understanding this vital process of initiation and its true value leads us to fear and slander Saturn in our ignorance. This planet has been labeled evil, bad luck, ugly, cruel, cold. He has come to be seen as Satan, the fallen angel.

The beauty of this is that Saturn is really the falling angel. He causes us to fall out of our grandiosity and come back down to Earth. We learn to accept our limits. He is also known as Cronos, Father Time, and teaches us the limitations of human life, the limitations of space and time.

Our spiritual essence can pass through his filter, but our limited physical containers cannot. These disposable vessels, called bodies, are finite. Saturn teaches us to find and connect with our gold before we die. He may seem foreboding on the outside, but the inside of his house is incredibly beautiful.

As we reach the age of approximately 59 or so, Saturn will begin its third cycle for us. If we have adjusted well to his presence, then we begin to get a true "feel" for his purpose. During this third cycle, we will gain a Venusian acceptance of his unavoidable influence in our lives. We can feel it creeping into our very bones!

Most senior citizens have no choice but to now develop a permanent relationship with him. They have grown wise enough to realize the precious fragile beauty of life. If we fail to make this quantum leap in our gratitude, we succumb to bitterness and cynicism in our final years. Let us all embrace the mystery of our own mortality. The only purpose of death is to urge us to live our lives now, in the fleeting temporal moment. Let us be both dignified and graceful in our aging.

Saturn adds the qualities of true inner worth that Jupiter lacks. These two great Master Teachers provide the grounding from which we can enter into the spiritual realm of the Outer Trinity which lies beyond.

Since Saturn has to do with the principle of breaking down and salvaging, it has rulership over the spleen. This organ is a processing station for old tired blood. It breaks down the blood corpuscles and salvages whatever parts can be reused. I have even seen it referred to, in medical texts, as a graveyard for old blood.

We mentioned in the previous chapter that Saturn rules bone and Jupiter flesh. It for this reason that Saturn rules the parathyroid glands. Saturn regulates the secretion of calcitonin. This hormone acts to retain calcium within the bones. Jupiter regulates the secretion of parathormone. This hormone acts to mobilize calcium, from bone mass, to enter the bloodstream where it can nourish the flesh.

Saturn also co-rules the pituitary gland, along with Jupiter, much the same way Mars and Venus co-rule the adrenal gland. Jupiter rules the anterior, or front, portion, which controls the secretion of growth hormone. Saturn regulates the posterior lobe, which restricts water loss in the body.

Consider Saturn and its relation to seven in the curious fact that the human body completely renews itself every seven years. In the course of any given seven year period, every single cell of our body has died and been replaced. As with the body, so with the soul.

Saturn and the Four Angles

Saturn in the King Power Zone

When Saturn is perched on high, just past the midheaven, the native will have a strong desire to always appear conservative and uphold the status quo when it comes to his public image and career. They are often scientists and researchers. Lawyers, clinical statisticians and lab technicians also top the list. These people like to appear steady and reliable in their work.

Saturnian types are career people. Others will often refer to them affectionately: "Oh that's old George, he's been here forever. A real company man!" They enjoy the type of work where they can grind away at it, bit by bit. Patience is a strong virtue amongst these types. They have all the time in the world and take pride in their workmanship.

In its shadow form, these natives fear any loss of hard earned status or reputation. These things are sacred to them and they will devour anyone who even appears to threaten them. Their fears, in this area, can lead them to eat others alive much like Cronos did in myth. They don't like competition because they want their works to stand unchallenged. They crave the illusory image of permanence because deep down inside they know that there is really no such thing. They seek to immortalize themselves through their works.

Saturn in the Lover Power Zone

Saturn here seeks permanence in relationship. These natives will seek the ideal image of the totally reliable and faithful spouse. They are slow to warm up to someone because of their innate mistrust of others. Once they have committed to someone, however, they are committed for life. They make the most solid and dependable of partners and they desire the same in return.

These natives deplore risk in relationship. They will therefore avoid mates who are too wild and unpredictable in nature. Stability is what appeals most to them. They fear the spontaneity of human emotions in general. These natives are excellent observers of people. Many will carefully select only emotionally predictable people as their friends. In this way they attempt to screen out the possibility of being hit with an emotional "curve ball."

The shadow form of this arrangement fears abandonment and loss of those he loves. He will obsessively control those around him in a desperate attempt to hold on to them. Mates, to these types, can end up feeling imprisoned by this oppressive strangle hold of their Saturnian partner. They can ultimately suffocate that which they seek to preserve.

Saturn in the Magician Power Zone

Saturn is quite comfortable in this location of the chart. These natives are solidly grounded within themselves. They yearn for, and will create, "sacred space" within their lives so as to firmly root their psychic security. These folks absolutely need a foundational sanctuary to which they can retreat for inner security. This is from where their inner stability issues forth.

These types can be hermit-like by nature. They can sense the grief and sorrow that lies deep within their unconscious. Most desire to get in conscious touch with it but require the uninterrupted solitude of private lifestyle. Many will lean towards celibacy and possibly even fear intimacy and relationship on all levels.

The shadow of this Saturnian arrangement will bias the native towards secrecy fueled by a morose sense of deep inner shame and fear about themselves. Their self esteem is faint and quite fragile as well. As a result, they will often resort to a whole array of secret manipulative tactics designed to control their world and keep others out. Like the mole, they prefer to burrow deep down into the Earth and hibernate from life as they secretly observe it.

Saturn in the Warrior Power Zone

Saturn occupies this zone reluctantly. He does not like the idea of having to leave his safe burrow and be thrust into the light of day. These natives are usually quite reserved in their physical gestures and mannerisms. They don't like to draw attention to themselves and prefer keeping a low profile. They are therefore not likely to dress or behave in a manner that will draw attention to themselves in any way.

These natives are physical work horses with a surprising amount of physical power. Their frames can often be large and bony. Although quite powerful, they tend to pace themselves in expending their energy. They are physically cautious and reserved. Any action initiated by them is long thought out and very deliberate in its intent. These people are anything but hasty in the way they direct their lives.

The shadow manifestation of this placement can predispose the native towards a seemingly cold foreboding exterior. They are quick to cut others short and control them through putting them in their place. They can be quite stoic and heavy in the way they express themselves, seeking to drag others down and depress them just for the hell of it. Their normally healthy quest to explore their own grief can be replaced by a ruthless desire to negate everyone and everything. These persons can become active "deconstructionists," seeking to invalidate all purpose and meaning in life.

The Septile aspect (51.4°) is one-seventh of the circle. It resonates with the archetype of Saturn and is therefore another indicator of Saturnian energy. We also have the Biseptile (102.8°) and Triseptile (154.3°) to consider as well. In discussing the Septile, Octile, Novile and Decile, we will encounter these multiples of each and must take note of them. In terms of the Septile, any one of its multiples will connect the two planets along a seventh harmonic.

As we move up into interpreting these higher harmonics, we must realize that their presence is less conscious, less physical and therefore less detectable to most people. Each progressive harmonic becomes more subtle and spiritual as we move higher. Septiles (seventh harmonics) are more difficult to sense than Sextiles (sixth harmonics). Noviles (ninth harmonics) are even more subtle for the conscious mind to sense. In order to get in touch with these higher harmonics, we must have achieved some level of inner spiritual development already.

When interpreting Septile aspects, we must come to see them as offering lessons and training in the area of grief and loss. When two planetary archetypes are connected via a Septile, they will each have the potential to learn from the innate limitations of the other. It is a pathway to eventual wisdom that evolves from this inner grief process and working within whatever limitations exist between the archetypes so connected.

Let us say for example that a young man's chart contains a Septile between the Sun and Mars. This indicates that his Father (Sun) most likely had a wounded Warrior (Mars) that was never dealt with. This wound (limitation) was never healed, by the father, so he has passed it on to his son who is now the direct multi- generational recipient of this neglected wound. The son must now do the work of grieving this loss and salvaging what he can of it, otherwise he will simply go through life carrying the rage of his father's shadow Warrior. A person with a multitude of Septiles most likely has considerable grief work to do.

Without being conscious of the Septiles in our own chart, we have no idea where our unresolved grief issues lie. Many people never get deep enough into their own personal development to deal with issues of grief and inner wounding. They are kept too busy, on a conscious level, by the dominant energy of the major aspects within their charts (Squares, Oppositions, etc.). Most of us never get past all this surface noise to what's really going on under the surface.

CHAPTER EIGHT

Uranus, The Spiritual Rebel

♅ We are now entering the realm of the spiritual trinity, beginning with the eighth sphere, Uranus. Uranus has to do with the concept of eight-ness, and the Grand Octile. This aspect, the Octile, is better known as the semi-square (45^{0}). Here we have the combining of Mercury's two-ness and the four-ness of Earth or 2 x 4. A straight-forward interpretation of this would simply mean: awareness of separation from Earth! The Earth signifies both time and space, as well as our bodies.

Uranus is the spiritual crisis or trauma involved with disembodying, or death. It signifies the liberation and freedom experienced through not being limited by time and space. This planet represents that in-between or in-transit stage of the death and birth experiences. It marks the transition between worlds. Uranus is the rest stop between leaving the limited body, Saturn, and merging back into the great feminine absolute, Neptune.

In representing birth, the direction is reversed. Upon our entering the world it denotes the birth trauma. This time, we are separating from the womb, Neptune, of our Earthly mother, and entering into our own finite, limited, Saturn bodies. In either case, Uranus represents change. We have a chance for a new start, as we pass from one world to another.

In a true sense, it represents the black holes and white holes of our inner universe. These are the windows that transport us to the other side and back. Birth and death are the passage ways through the time-space continuum.

Uranus behaves unlike any other planet, and its behavior accounts for some of its special and unique energies. The other planets all spin fairly upright, like a top. Uranus, however, spins on its side! Its axis of orientation is very different from the rest of the solar system (fig. 8a).

Figure 8a

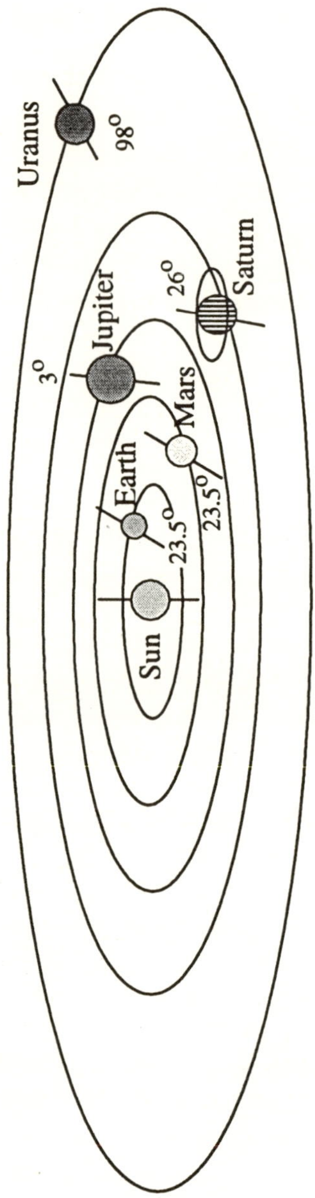

The Voyager probe discovered that the magnetic field of Uranus is some 55^0 off from its axis of rotation. All other planets with measurable magnetic fields, tend to have them somewhat closely aligned with their axis. (For instance, our Earth spins around the imaginary pole from North to South, with a strong magnetic field emanating from its axis of rotation, the North Pole.)

This unusual arrangement, where the magnetic field of Uranus emanates from a separate location than its poles, causes the magnetic field of Uranus to wobble in relation to its poles during the course of its 17 hour day. This simply means that the Magnetic field of Uranus is in a constant state of flux, always changing, relative to the poles. Within the very physics of this planet's unusual behavior, we have proof of its rebellious non-conformist reputation. There is now concrete physical proof to validate what astrologers have known for years!

It's interesting to note that in mythology, Uranus was castrated by Saturn. Could this have been the ancient's way of relating cosmology through myth? Might they have known of a prehistoric celestial near miss where Saturn, or its huge moon Titan, set Uranus on its side?

Uranus is a very disoriented world from our perspective. From his perspective, however, it is everyone else who is weird! Recall the English professor of *Dead Poet's Society*, who encourages his students to come up, one at a time, and stand on top of his desk. In doing so, he is challenging them to look at the world from a different perspective. They are learning the value of Uranian principles.

Uranus is the planet of pure genius. His insights are fresh, new, unheard of, and seemingly crazy. They often appear to come from out of nowhere, usually arriving like a flash. Uranian types are often accused of being off the wall, or out in left field— phrases that suggest the same out-of-kilter nature as Uranus's rotation and magnetic field. As crazy as Uranian energies might seem, there is this excitement within us that says, "Hey, you know this just might work!"

The chess master Bobby Fischer is a good example of a Uranian type. In a classic match with Boris Spassky, Fischer had been backed into a corner and was obviously losing. According to the textbooks there were no possible winning moves available to him. In typical Uranian brilliance, Bobby shocked Boris with a totally original move and took him unaware. Spassky never recovered and Fischer went on to win the championship.

Fischer is a true Uranian prodigy. His chart contains the most partile (exact) Grand Trine I have ever encountered in all my years as an astrologer. The Trine is composed of Uranus, Neptune and Mars! Aside from the Grand Trine, Uranus is also connected to every other planet in his chart.

All four of Fischer's central archetypes are powerfully aspected to Uranus. There is a Quintile to the Sun, a Square to Mercury, an Octile to Venus, and the previously mentioned Trine to Mars. Add an Octile to Jupiter and a conjunction with Saturn for good measure! More on this later when we will analyze his chart more completely. Needless to say, his life has been both brilliant and bizarre. After winning that infamous match in 1972, he retired from competition. Just as suddenly as he flashed the move on Spassky, Fischer disappeared from the chess world.

The brilliant comedian Robin Williams is another typically Uranian character. While performing, Williams seems to come at you from twenty different directions! Uranian energy is that of the original thinker, the non-conformist, and the true rebel. Often he is accused of being in a world all his own.

Saturn slowly grinds away at our internal obstacles. If we resist this Saturnian process, Uranus will step in and totally shatter them! He shouts out with excitement, he is in your face. The energy of this planet is very impatient. He wants us to step up on top of the desk, RIGHT NOW! His passion to liberate us is sincere.

The intense Uranian desire for liberation is due to the fact that he represents a higher evolvement of Warrior energy. He is the spiritual Warrior whose causes and quests are beyond the scope of vision typified by Mars. In fact, one of the symbols for Uranus (other than the more common one used in this book) is virtually identical to that of Mars! (fig. 8b)

The word Uranus means heaven in Greek. There is even an interesting Egyptian parallel found in the word Ur-Annu. Ur in Egyptian means great. Annu was the name of Heliopolis. This translates to "the city of the Sun," which is another way of saying heaven. The Sun's dwelling place, or city, is literally the "great vault of heaven!"

In Egyptian mythology, Uranus was represented by the cosmic god PTaH. He opened the mouth of the dead with his special tool, so they could leave the body and enter the next world. The word PTaH literally means a doorway, or an opening.

It is worth noting that if we reverse the word PTaH, we get the word HoTeP. HoTeP means peace, closing, or enclosing, as in the protective embrace of the sky goddess Nut. The womb of Nut represents Neptune, which is the polar opposite of Uranus.

Figure 8b

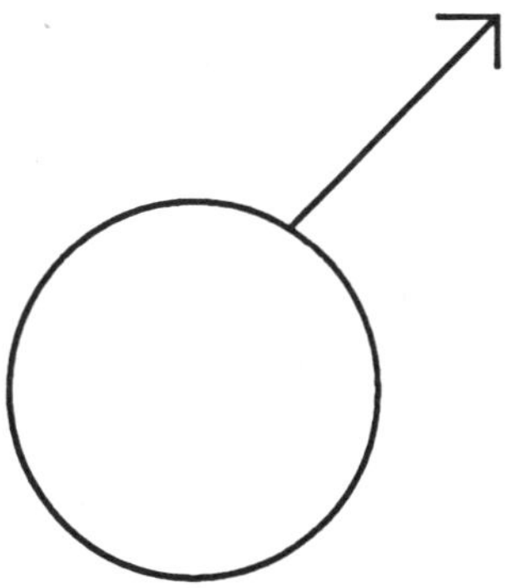

Mars
(The Warrior)

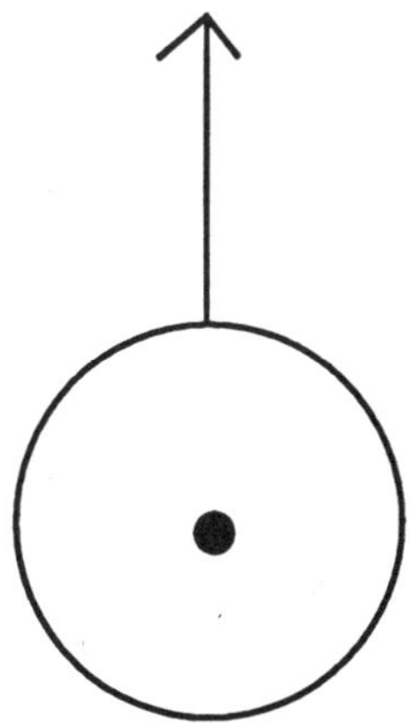

Uranus
(The Spiritual Warrior
or Liberator)

Uranus represents all leading edge technology and creativity. Anything that is state of the art comes from his inspirational mind. Robert Moore says these are the creative type who "fly real close to the edge of the envelope!"[1] Uranian types can be accused of being crazy or eccentric. It comes with the territory.

The late Frank Zappa was another classic example of a Uranian type. His chart contains a powerful Opposition of Mars and Uranus. The fiery energy of the Warrior archetype served to fuel his rebellious need for total freedom of expression in terms of his creative juices. Zappa was a major opponent to all the attempts at censoring music lyrics.

His own style of music has always been viewed as avant garde and highly unconventional. Zappa was a true pioneer of improvisational composition and deliberate dissonance. Zappa summed up his approach in an interview, "I like carrying things to their most ridiculous extreme because out there on the fringe is where my type of entertainment lies. Once I've gone out there and dabbled on that fringe, I feel as if I may as well bring some artifacts back, in case anybody else is interested. That's what I do. I come back and go."[2]

On many levels, Uranus stands for progress through shock. Most humans tend to disguise life, rather than discover it.[3] Uranus pulls the covers off of us, and exposes us to reality in one fell swoop. He catches us with our pants down, and ruptures all our attempts at secrecy.

It is a great cosmic truth that the only constant in life is change. Uranus represents all change. He is unconcerned with the world of human morality. His job requires him to answer to a higher authority. We fight his attempts to free us up, because we perceive change to be threatening or bad.

This is inherent within the human condition of limitation. We fear change because we dread ending up worse off after the change, than before it. Uranus-Neptune-Pluto represent divine spiritual principles that we limited humans cannot fully understand. The master teachers Jupiter and Saturn try their best to prepare us for this divine world during life so that the transition of death might be less traumatic.

The very mechanics of Uranus are designed to produce the energy necessary for personal growth. All planets are electro-magnetic generators that release their energies to the human psyche in a fairly steady and continuous flow. Uranus, however, tends to store up his energy and release it via intensive shocking bursts. He functions much like a coil in an automobile engine. An ignition coil stores up the car's twelve volt current by creating a huge magnetic field within its copper windings.

When the influx of twelve volt current is stopped, this magnetic field collapses creating a powerful surge of 20,000 volts which supplies the energy needed to jump the gap of the spark plugs.

Because Uranus has his rotational axis oriented in a completely different direction than the other planets, his energy tends to accumulate within the collective unconscious. He is busy charging his coils while we are obsessed with trying to exclude all change—Uranian energy—from our lives. When the situation gets out of hand, he transits back into our world and delivers his shocking blow. The purpose is to restore us to a balanced reality.

Our fear of change can be traced all the way back to our unconscious memories of the trauma of being born. We spend nine months in this perfect environment where all our needs are met, floating in a sea of warmth and contentment. Then the water breaks, literally, and we are powerfully propelled through a passage-way into another very different and alien world.

Einstein on his death bed said, "There is only one important question... Is the universe friendly?" The Uranian brilliance of this statement is very obvious. This is probably the first question we all asked ourselves as we emerged from the birth canal!

Our answers are probably very different. Some of us were allowed to lay on the warm body of our mother and bond with her. We might have even started breathing on our own, and been allowed to just decompress and given time to make the adjustment somewhat smoothly.

Others of us were wrenched forth with cold metal forceps, slapped on the ass, and quickly dumped into the incubator. If you had a choice, which would you have preferred?

I believe that these first primal thoughts and impressions deeply affect the way we approach and respond to life as we grow. It's definitely part of our reality map, and it is a continuing process. The trauma of our birth experience will color our attitude towards all changes we experience in our lifetime. This will include the death experience as well. Those of us who really fear change and death probably did not have the most pleasant of birth experiences.

Uranus is linked to transportation and the wheel. Its number, eight, is represented by the Grand Octile, which is a circle cut into eight pieces. This symbol is very reminiscent of a wheel and its spokes. It has been said to be the planet of astrology, which represents another type of wheel, the chart. It was probably for this very reason that Cyril Fagan tried to revive an ancient Egyptian "eightfold" house system called the Octotopos (eight places).

Uranus represents the circular or cyclic motion that propels us rhythmically and spasmodically through the birth canal. This is the same power that propels atoms within the cyclotron to a fast enough velocity to split apart. This splitting or separating principle is why Uranus rules the process of mitosis, or cell division. One cell becomes two, two becomes four, and four becomes eight.

Although we are all aware of our separateness in body from our mother, many of us never outgrow the desire to return to the bliss of the womb. Emotionally we crave the memories of those nine months of nirvana, and we desperately try to find it in this world.

Uranus pushes us on towards independence and diversity. It teaches us to enjoy our new found freedom, and cherish it. This is the surgeon's cutting of the umbilical cord. We learn to break the umbilical connection to the other world and live in this world while preparing for our return to that other place.

On a physical level, this planet rules the thyroid gland. It is no coincidence that this endocrine gland is the one most likely to be hyperactive. The thyroid's functioning can reflect the erratic nature of its ruler. Uranus also regulates the nerve synapses, where signals are transported between neurons. This planet sits on top of the right pillar of the Tree.

Uranus and the Four Angles

Uranus in the King Power Zone

When Uranus is found manifesting here, the native will have difficulty working for others. Their powerful rebelliousness leads them into constant difficulties with authority figures. These natives need plenty of elbow room and will simply not tolerate a restrictive job setting.

Many of these people are highly original in the ways that they manifest their gift to the world. Because of this fact, self employment is usually the best route for them to take. They are happiest when they are their own bosses. Most lack the patience of being held back by endless corporate rules and policy. They prefer instead to shatter all restraints and put the pedal to the metal in terms of their creativity. Many of their greatest creations come about in this manner.

People who have made a career out of their unconventional creativity will often have this setup. These folks make excellent inventors because of their lightening fast ability to conceptualize complicated ideas. What might take someone else years to envision, they will produce in a matter of weeks or days! This ability comes from their refusal to limit their imaginations.

In its shadow form these people can often be loose cannons. They are so hot-headed and rebellious that nobody can stand dealing with them. They can often be labeled a rebel without a cause. In these cases, their kneejerk reactions to everyone and everything around them make it difficult for them to manifest any of their brilliance. They can be their own worst enemies, sabotaging their own progress.

Uranus in the Lover Power Zone

These natives love diversity in their relationships. They enjoy relating to all kinds of interesting people. Their openmindedness allows them to experience a wide variety of human personalities. As a result, they will often be highly tolerant, and even supportive, of other's rights towards individual expression.

These natives will usually only be attracted to partners who are highly liberated in their outlook of life. They want a mate who will live and let live. Anything short of this is intolerable to them and will cause them to bolt for their freedom. They may often marry more than once before finding this type of liberated mate. Many choose to simply give up on the idea of settling down with any one person. They will often refuse to deal with the restrictive compromise of relationships at all. The "no strings attached" lifestyle appeals to them.

When the shadow manifests, these natives can often "use" their partners for instant gratification of their sensual needs and then hit the road. When they grow tired or bored in their relationship, they simply move on to someone new and exciting. They crave a thrill a minute and will use anyone or anything at their disposal to maintain that intensity.

Uranus in the Magician Power Zone

When Uranus is found here, the creative pioneering spirit turns inward into oneself. These natives always feel excitable or anxious deep inside. They struggle with an inner restlessness that may cause them to move and relocate often during their lives. Their concept of sacred space is constantly changing. If they don't move often, they may frequently redecorate their home or apartment to reflect this inner changeability.

They are inner psychic daredevils who love the excitement of exploring the very edges of their own psyche. They will also indulge in reading science fiction and other cutting edge speculation. In their ravenous consumption of this data, they can often leave an endless trail of wrappers in their wake!

In its shadow form, these people will live unraveled lives. Their home environment will often look like a bomb hit it. They have extreme difficulty in organizing their private lives into anything resembling sanity. They are so busy with the exciting pursuit of inner truth, that they forget to pick up the pieces. Their personal lives can often be in a complete shambles.

Uranus in the Warrior Power Zone

These natives are the most active of rebels. They assertively refuse to conform with anything. They can feel claustrophobic and frustrated when confined physically in any way. These people love the explosive thrill of speed and acceleration. This powerful inner urge causes them to take many risks in their lives. They are impulsive by nature and predictably unpredictable!

Many of these natives go through life on the seat of their pants, living life like an amusement ride. They would love to be able to plug into some cosmic electric socket so that they never have to sleep. They are drawn to coffee and other "buzz" accelerators like cocaine. These people simply do not want to take their foot off the gas pedal! This inner urgency can drive them to become workaholics if their work is a source of excitement for them.

In its shadow variety, these natives are prime candidates for burn out. In driving themselves in such a ruthless manner, they frequently can, and do, ignore physical warning symptoms of fatigue or pain. The end result is that they run a high risk of some serious illness showing up after countless years of ignoring symptoms. They can also alienate others with their extreme individuality and refusal to compromise. (See Hitler's chart, Chapter 13.)

The Octile aspect is another place to look for Uranian energy in the chart. Take note of any chart where you discover a large preponderance of

Octiles. We must include the Trioctile as well (135^0) because this aspect will also connect planetary archetypes along the eighth harmonic, being that it is a multiple of 45^0.

When interpreting Octiles, view them as offering the potential for exciting change and liberation between the two archetypes so connected. Few people seek to actualize these kinds of potentials within themselves because few of us have a completely positive outlook about change. Most of us are therefore more likely to ignore these potentials even when they exist within us. It takes an unusual person to respond to, and consciously activate the potential of an Octile within their chart.

Let us say that a person has an Octile aspect between Mercury and Neptune. This means that they have the potential to liberate their thinking processes (Mercury) through venturing into the sublime world of mysticism (Neptune). The freedom experienced through this connection, if consciously realized, will change their life for the better. The energy potential contained within Octiles should be consciously activated whenever we feel stuck.

Not everyone lives to experience the return of Uranus to its natal position in their chart. This takes some 84 years to complete because this planet is so far away from the Sun. Most of us will, however, experience the halfway point of this return when Uranus will be in Opposition to its natal position in our birthchart. This happens between the ages of 38 and 42. The timing varies for each person.

This Uranus Opposition is the obvious precipitator of the infamous "mid-life crisis." If by the time we reach the age of 40, we are stuck in a career or relationship which is toxic to our true nature, Uranus transits into our life and shatters the shackles.

Many people will realize that they answered the wrong calling in life and will simply quit their lifelong career and go back to school. Others may end a 20 year marriage because they finally wake up and realize that they no longer love their spouse. The Uranus Opposition is like a conductor who steps into our car and announces: "This is the 8:32 to Chicago, if you're in the wrong place now is the time to change trains!" It offers us a chance to get back on track with our lives.

CHAPTER NINE

Neptune, The Blissful Mystic

♆ Neptune is the last of the gaseous giants, and the ninth planet in our outwardly spiraling journey. It represents nine-ness and the Grand Novile, which are both symbols of completeness. Nine is actually 3 x 3, which is the highest essence and expression of three-ness (love). Venus and Neptune have the two most circular and balanced orbits of all the planets!

Here we have the planet of absolute serenity and peace, HoTeP, the Egyptian goddess Nut. All the stars were said to be afloat in her great cosmic ocean. Nut was depicted as a woman with her body arched over the Earth, in a protective nurturing embrace. The orbit of Neptune protectively embraces all the other planets within it.

All of creation was believed to have arisen out of her waters. Neptune (the Greek Poseidon) represents this primordial ocean, from which all of the myriads of forms were brought forth. It is the principle of ether, that misty vapor-like substance that obscures and protects the secrets of life.

Neptune represents the heavy fog covered sea that ships fear to enter because of its unfathomable depths. From deep within its mysteries spring the whispers that draw the spiritual mystic to its doorway. Just like the sailor who responds to the call of the sea, we intuitively know when to return.

On a spiritual level, Neptune represents nirvana and the feelings of bliss or oceanic oneness. Everything dissolves back into the absolute, celestial mother. This imparts humility through passive understanding of universal truth.

Neptune stands for the paradise out of which we were cast at birth. The creation myths of Genesis and others depict this beautifully. None of us, no matter how together we are, ever forgets those nine glorious months we spend in paradise. The connection of Neptune and the womb is further reinforced by its number, nine.

Many of us are driven by this unconscious yearning to return to the womb. As Robin Williams joked, "We spend nine months trying to get out, and the rest of our lives trying to get right back in!" This powerful primordial urge is what drives us to seek out bliss, in whatever form we can find it.

Badly used, this energy is the driving force behind all addictions and substance abuse. We express our dependence on the great mother, by becoming chemically dependent instead. The seductive nature of drugs and alcohol is very powerful. The more pain and grief we have locked in the unconscious, the stronger is the urge to use drugs to escape it all.

All drugs, from heroin and crack to nembutal and alcohol are powerful agents for numbing the body and the mind and escaping their stored pain. Drugs offer a back door into the worlds of Neptune and Uranus. Cocaine is a very cerebral Uranian drug. Once the user experiences the bliss of the upper kingdom, he very easily becomes hooked.

The problem lies in the dishonesty with which we gain entry. Drugs are a short cut that causes serious psychological problems. They allow the user to bypass the teachings and initiations of Jupiter and Saturn. We slip undetected past their portals, directly into the upper kingdom. It's rather like cheating at Monopoly: we pass "go" and collect $200. When we're caught, we don't want to give the $200 back. Eventually, we are thrown out of the game, ejected from the garden as the drug wears off. The Addictive-Compulsive personality starts to develop, as we become obsessed with getting back up there again.

The truth of the matter is that the real world of Neptune can only be fully experienced after death. Falling prey to its seduction on Earth leads to the risk of drowning in the sea of illusion. These upper worlds have built in protection mechanisms to keep out unwelcome visitors. We must earn our access into Neptune's waters.

Neptune's link to protection against unhealthy invasions is why it is said to rule the lymphatic system which guards us from infection. This watery planet controls the lymphatic ocean that carries the immune factors throughout our body. The lymphatic fluid has this wonderfully Neptunian quality of being able to pass right through the walls of our cells, and literally bathe them.

This bathing process breaks up, disperses and carries away harmful invaders. In this way, they can be destroyed in the lymph nodes by antibodies, T-cells and macrophages. The dispersing quality of Neptune, actually prevents the enemy cells from organizing an attack.

We mentioned earlier that Venus rules the thymus gland, which is the central core-regulator on the physical level. Neptune corresponds to the diffused periphery of the immune system, represented by the sporadic nodes and vessels. Neptune also rules the islets of Langerhans, which secrete insulin. These glands are sporadically dispersed throughout the pancreas in a typically Neptunian fashion. Venus rules the pancreatic *enzymes* that physically break down carbohydrates into simple sugars. Neptune rules the *hormones* that help regulate their passage into and out of the cells. Again, the concepts of osmosis, fluidity and water are present.

The essence of Neptune is best expressed through the eastern beliefs of Taoism. The Taoist philosophy is very closely associated with the qualities of water. Water has always been associated with baptism into the spiritual world and, being the most prominent compound on Earth, will forever dissolve us in its wake.

Taoists point to the profound and sublime reality that, in nature, the soft always triumphs over the hard. Through taking the path of least resistance, water will choose to go around a large granite rock placed in a stream. Yet over the years it will slowly wear away this seemingly immovable object! The old rigid tree comes down in the storm, yet a young, supple, green shoot will survive through bending and giving way to the storm's fury.

There are many concepts and words that convey this connection between Neptune and water, terms like mist, mystic, nebulous, cloudy, foggy and hazy. They all convey the spacey nature of water, when it is dispersed into a fine etheric mist. Neptunian awareness, or consciousness, has this very nature inherent within it. We have the qualities of Water (feeling and emotion) finely dispersed and intermixed with Air (intellect and thought). This leads to the Neptunian world of felt thought or intuition.

This form of consciousness is really just a higher vibration of Jupiterian ideals, taken from the religious level to the more refined spiritual level. Neptune's symbol, the Trident, is testimony to his attunement to the three-fold world of Love. At the top of each of its three prongs is a triangle shaped point. This symbol thus reveals Neptune's number, through its three triangular points or trinities: 3 x 3 = 9!

Venus-Jupiter-Neptune (3-6-9) all represent different multi-level, facets of the torrid, passionate nature of love and spirituality. Neptunian mystical thinking can produce the ecstatic poetry of great minds such as Walt Whitman, Kabir, Rumi, and Gibran. Neptune energy elevates the mind into a state of spiritual ecstasy.

It is critical that we examine our motives when we invoke Neptune's powers. If we seek to use it to escape something, we shall become lost within its cloudy depths. Yet if we approach it with discipline and awareness, we can open ourselves to new and higher levels of spirituality and lovingness.

Neptune rules denial and delusion. If we use its energy dishonestly, we may start to believe that we can actually obscure others from seeing our true motives and thoughts. If we choose to hide, we certainly can. Yet we will fall prey to the very influence that we try to control. We become capable of convincing ourselves that our lies are in fact truths. In doing so, we drowns in our own personal quicksand.

Ronald Reagan has Neptune opposed to Mercury in his birth chart. I believe this gave him a very conscious awareness of Neptune's deceptive powers. We might think back to his infamous case of amnesia surrounding the Iran-Contra scandal. This was simply the Dummy shadow of Mercury pulling the strings from behind the Neptunian wall of denial.

The shadow side of Neptune leads us to believe we can create a safe womb inside our minds, where we can reorganize the world to suit ourselves. The thing to look out for here is the telltale signs of grandiosity. Are we trying to escape the pain of something by encapsulating ourself within this psychic sanctuary? We all need to take a break now and then, but we should not lock the door behind us. We then run the risk of losing the key! It is important to avoid "-osophies," and "-isms," absolute belief systems which lock us into closed psychic loops that are difficult to escape from.

Neptune's nature is ephemeral, non-physical. It cannot be grasped. It is a high spiritual vibration, and can only be accessed by disciplined search and meditation. It cannot be physically seized, maintained through drugs, or controlled and grasped in any mundane way.

While Neptune energy is bliss, shadow Neptune is the ultimate seduction. He can deceive and betray. When we try to grasp his uncontrollable nature, he rises up like a cobra and strikes out at us. Yet he is only acting as a psychic mirror, to show us the reflection of our true underlying motives. We cannot control, manipulate, or dominate this power. We can only use it respectfully.

When Neptunian energy is used wisely and spiritually for growth, we can alter the energy around us and bring forth conditions that nourish and sustain our growth and our daily lives. We must have simple faith and strong ethics to do this well. We must be self aware, and use the wisdom imparted by the Master teachers, especially Saturn. Before we can use Neptune's energy safely and well, we must heal the deep wounds in our guts, and mine the golden rich nutrients from our unconscious.

Neptune is the place of our deepest vulnerability and naivete. Our fear of being wounded or betrayed leads us to become distrustful and paranoid. Sometimes we may go so far as to start imagining and projecting various troubles and catastrophe where there actually are none. We wind up sealing our own fate by creating self-fulfilling prophesies. In a sense, we invite the very betrayal we fear.

These rippling waves of fear, that we start in motion, eventually become tidal waves that carry us away in a full blown anxiety attack. The waters of Neptune are powerful and run deep. We must be very mind-full of the types of thoughts we cast upon its waters. This brings to mind the old saying, "be careful what you ask for, you may get it!"

It doesn't take much to taint a body of pure water and turn it toxic. Testimony to this is in the fact that water borne toxins are measured in *parts per billion*. We are in the midst of a critical Neptunian crisis. I don't know which is being destroyed faster, our oceans or our immune systems! Our flagrant disrespect and ignorance of Neptune, have led to the poisoning of both.

It seems to me, that in this increasingly violent culture of domination and fear, all of the archetypes are gradually becoming more and more toxic. The cause of all this, is based on a simple fundamental error in thinking. We have consciously chosen to split the Tree apart into its lesser components. We are clinging to the lifestyle of the left pillar.

Most of the world has chosen the coziness of Venus, the Jupiterian shallowness of looking good, and the blissful Neptunian seduction of the left pillar. This is like severing the roots from the trunk, and expecting the Tree to keep on living. We need to accept responsibility for both halves of our makeup.

The emerging picture is one in which the energies of both pillars are turning toxic and fermenting within the collective unconscious. They are rising in demonic proportion, to signal that something is seriously wrong. The result is obvious. The pillar we own, *and* the pillar we disown both start to wither and die. We are now starting to suffer the noticeable consequences of this ignorant choice.

Toxic Mars = rage and crime, toxic Saturn = depression and suicide, and toxic Uranus = addiction to all forms of excitement. The left pillar ferments as well. Toxic Venus = sex and love addiction, toxic Jupiter = rapacious materialism and consumerism, and toxic Neptune = substance abuse and co-dependency.

We cannot simply perceive planets and their energies as malefic or benefic. Neptune teaches us to approach these energies with humility and intuitive awareness, to seek a vision of unity for ourselves and to nurture it. All energy must be honored and valued. When we do so, we can make balanced judgments and avoid falling into harm. Through respecting and nourishing the whole Tree, it will begin to heal and grow. It is only though this that we can heal human society, the Earth, and all of her incredible life forms.

Neptune and the Four Angles

Neptune in the King Power Zone

Neptune is frequently found here in the charts of people who choose careers in art, dance, spirituality and dramatic acting. These natives are highly sensitive. They often feel extremely vulnerable and naked in public settings. They seek the limelight but yet are quite emotionally anxious about feeling exposed in the process.

These people crave recognition of their dreamy idealism. This naive predisposition can make them a perfect sucker in the public world of dog eat dog business tactics. They often throw their pearls before swine and get taken by some shark lawyer or agent. They need to protect their vulnerable creative assets.

In its shadow form these natives are easily flustered by the harsh reality of the business world. Their dreamy, ethereal nature makes it difficult to manage their own careers well. They often drift for years and never seem to get anywhere. Their innate sense of denial, about their ineptitude in this area, leads them into a sort of perpetual procrastination regarding career moves and decisions.

Neptune in the Lover Power Zone

Found here, Neptune is quite cozy and thoroughly within its element. These natives simply love togetherness in any form. They will seek ecstasy through relationship. They can powerfully embody the 60's philosophy of peace, love and happiness. They want all stories to have a happy ending and everybody to live happily ever after!

These natives are ultimately searching for a soulmate. They seek an eternal partner who embodies all of their dreams and fantasies. They love reading romance novels and imagining themselves in the leading role of the one desired. Relationship fills the sails of their ship and gives them direction and purpose. Otherwise they simply dream and drift through life.

In its shadow form, these natives can be among the most codependent of people. They can't live without their partner and will often feel empty and directionless without them. This scenario makes for people who live in constant fear of betrayal and abandonment. They will sell their very soul in order to secure the future of their relationship. The result is an ostrich mentality that buries its head in the sand and is afraid to examine their partner honestly. They prefer, instead, to live in a fantasy world regarding love.

Neptune in the Magician Power Zone

These natives are highly sensitive to the inner world of dreams and impressions from the unconscious. They enjoy following these whispers in the safety of their sacred space. Meditating on their dreams and keeping a journal will appeal to them. They value this information greatly.

This arrangement is frequently found in the charts of spiritualists and sensitive psychotherapists (see Carl Jung's chart). They enjoy using creative mediums to convey this information such as drawing, sculpting, writing poetry and chanting, etc. These people are extremely vulnerable at their deepest core. They will often seek to create a sense of security through decorating their home in such a way as to convey a cozy feeling reminiscent of the womb.

The shadow manifestation of this arrangement can burden the native with powerful emotional upwellings that quite possibly may bloom into full blown anxiety attacks. Whenever they are not consciously occupied with other things, they can often sense a deep uneasiness and restless imagination that may also vent itself through nightmares.

Neptune in the Warrior Power Zone

When Neptune is found rising, these natives can be extremely sensitive to their environment. Like sponges they will soak up all the impressions from around them. This oversensitivity causes them to be impressionable and naive in the way they approach life. Like Percival, on his quest for the holy Grail, they can expend much energy in the pursuit of their ideals.

These natives can often feel drained by negative people. They may also develop allergies to things in their environment. They actively absorb everything in their vicinity, good or bad. This makes it imperative for them to choose their surroundings wisely. I once heard it said that: "If you sleep with dogs, you wake up with fleas!"

These natives have a strong drive to pursue spiritual causes and dive, headlong, into the mysteries of life. They prefer to be surrounded by nature and the universe rather than shopping malls and city streets. They are acutely sensitive to harsh artificial settings. Their sense of intuition is keenly developed, but sometimes they can be overloaded by a flood of too many impressions at once.

In its shadow form, these natives will often smokescreen others with their chameleon-like ability to blend with their environment. They will actively change colors to suit the mood of their environment. The problem is that they very rarely reveal their true colors to anybody. They actually may fear that inwardly they are colorless and if others discovered this, they would abandon them. They desperately want to feel like they fit in and will actively takes steps to insure this. The problem lies in going overboard.

A final indication of the presence of Neptune's energy can be found if the chart contains a surplus of Novile aspects (40°) The multiples of this must also be noted: the Binovile (80°) and the Quadranovile (160°). If there is a total of four or more of these Novile aspects, then this will indicate a strong potential for the development of Neptunian energy within the native's personality.

When interpreting Noviles, it is important to view them as a potential pathway towards a possible spiritual development between the two archetypes so connected. These two planets will have the opportunity to cooperate in the pursuit of spiritual development as a result of mystical insights. Whether this is activated or not is up to the native. These subtle aspects will lie dormant unless consciously invoked by the native.

Let us say, for example, that a birthchart contains a Novile aspect between Mercury and Uranus. This means that these two planets are attuned to the vibration of the ninth harmonic and will contribute to our growth within that realm. When it comes to our spiritual development, the unique and brilliant nature (Uranus) of our intellect (Mercury) will play a major role.

CHAPTER TEN

Pluto, Charon and Persephone

P Astronomically, Pluto is an enigmatic little object with a bizarre nature unlike anything else in the solar system. Pluto is the tenth sphere and its aspect is the Decile (36°). The number ten contains all other numbers.

This in itself proves to be a helpful clue. Pluto is in actuality a double planet—it has a moon that is roughly of half its size. This moon, named Charon, and Pluto revolve around a common center somewhere between them in space. In a sense, they are both satellites of each other. They are icy, methane snowballs, performing a unique and mysterious dance.

Pluto was the God of the underworld and Charon the ferryman who helped transport souls to the land of Hades. These two represent the miracle of conception and genesis. They symbolize the creation of order (life) from chaos (the underworld).

The Plutonian forces at work in the story of creation are the same as those present during procreation. Out of darkness and chaos came the light. This was seen as good. Conception takes place as the end result of the frenzied, chaotic, emotional and physical cyclone we call making love. The life we create is also miraculous.

Pluto is placed at the top of the Archtypal Tree for good reason. He is the Crown or Kether, the very Logos or God-head. Our ability to conceive and create life, is what makes us most like gods. It is our god-likeness. We are only co-creators at best. This is important to realize, and completely accept.

If you rise to the throne of Pluto with even an ounce of grandiosity hiding in your soul, he will utterly destroy you. He is the highest octave of Mercury, The Magician, and he possesses the powers of the whole universe. One of the symbols of Pluto (Hades) was the cornucopia or "horn of plenty" out of which flowed endless creativity.

It is my own personal belief that Pluto's Moon should actually be viewed as Persephone, Demeter's daughter. In late Greek mythology, Pluto abducted Persephone so he could have her as his eternal wife and consort. In the earliest myths, Persephone voluntarily descended into the underworld, to guide the souls of the dead towards peace and rebirth. The story of Persephone better depicts the Yin-Yang relationship between Pluto and its Moon, between masculine and feminine, and the two genders needed for procreation. For our purposes, I will call the Moon Persephone.

Pluto is the power of the collective unconscious, and the wealth of all creativity that is contained therein. Pluto/Persephone represent the forces of Yin and Yang, taken beyond the tangible mundane realm of these energies. They are the ida and the pingala entwining around each other in cosmic union, the perfect crowning star for our Tree. This is the place where the polarities of the left and right pillars are balanced.

Within the walls of its temple, the most sacred of marriages takes place. The cosmic couple comes together in their secret tantric union and are joined as one. The center, between their orbits, is the sushumna, through which the cosmic fire of creation-conception does flow.

This represents the open window beyond time and space, a void where anything is possible. Pluto/Persephone represent our true way out of limitations and opposition. This bi-planet represents the creation-transformation process by which all opposites are ultimately transcended. This is what Buddha meant by the Middle Path. It's the same as the road of the Middle Pillar of our Tree.

Pluto and Persephone are the re-evolutionary couple. They cannot explain their mystery to the mundane and profane. Instead they choose to stay far away from the crowd, where they can remain undisturbed in continuous cosmic union.

Charon, the ferryman, is more accurately representative of the orbital point of balance between these two celestial bodies. He is the sushumna that acts to ferry, or transport our consciousness into the realm of the collective unconscious. Pluto and Persephone create the energy necessary to activate this transformative ferrying process.

They are the magical alchemical couple, involved in the most sacred and intimate act of union. The mundane see this as socially taboo. Here we have a reclusive couple, who truly cannot relate what they have. Pluto and Persephone are beyond the physical, because they have lost awareness of themselves as separate bodies and are fused together in cosmic ecstasy.

Their's is the spiral dance of life. It is symbolized by the ida-pingala, and also the two snakes wrapped around the cadusus. This spiral is actually the true spiral of life, the DNA molecule. Without this invisible microscopic gem, life and conception would simply not exist.

This bi-planet regulates the process of actual conception. During conception one sperm out of millions and one egg fuse together, creating an entirely new single entity. As a result of this process, the sperm and the egg appear to disintegrate. They have merely undergone the miraculous Plutonian experience of transformation. Conception is the very miracle upon which all life depends for its perpetuation.

Pluto/Persephone is the fusion of two into one, at all costs! It is ruthless and amoral in achieving this end. This fusion process is the same power-source that fuels our Sun. Two hydrogen atoms fuse together to form one atom of helium. The Sun and Pluto are on opposite ends of the middle pillar for good reason. Pluto rules mass-movements, and revolutionary frenzy. Watching through the microscope as millions of sperm frantically try to gain entrance into the egg, is much the same as witnessing the storming of the Bastille. The very same Plutonian energy is at work. A miracle is described as a one in a million occurrence, or something with incredible odds working against it. As these millions and millions of sperm are desperately trying to fertilize the egg, only one will succeed. The meaning of this is exquisitely beautiful. At that exact moment in time and space, a sacred wisdom within the ovum knows and recognizes exactly which sperm is a perfect reflection of that very instant. This is the lucky one who gets to enter in. Here we have the epitome of Jungian synchronicity.

The sperm and egg both know that they must offer themselves up in sacrifice so that new life may come into being. This is done without fear because the amoral objective is the continuing of evolution. The genetic code is being refined and perfected through this microscopic process of natural selection. I am in total agreement with Garth Allen when he refers to Pluto as the maligned planet of miracles.[1]

Pluto/Persephone are the coming together of the two pillars of extremes. They represent the merging of PTaH (Uranus), and HoTeP (Neptune) into one principle (PTaH-HoTeP). This is an Egyptian word that symbolizes the breathing in, and breathing out of life-energy.

It is for this reason that I believe Pluto rules and regulates the process of cellular respiration. This is technically called the Kreb's cycle or citric acid cycle. Here is the process by which each tiny cellular furnace generates its energy. The source of this energy is located within the mitochondrion of each and every cell.

Pluto does have a dark side just like any other archetype. The central pillar, as a whole, is a huge magic wand of power. Those with grandiose motives will be drawn to it just like moths to a bug-zapper. We can expect much the same result.

Here we come upon very ironic proof. The most noxious and destructive element known to mankind is called Plutonium. This is appropriate, because a mere gram of this substance is enough to destroy all life on Earth. Here is a testimony as to the sheer awesome power of Pluto for good or bad.

It is worth noting that Plutonium is not a naturally occurring element. It was created by men who, acting out of their infantile grandiosity, were trying to play God. Through direct misuse of the Plutonian principles, they have created isotopes that we have no idea how to safely store or destroy.

Pluto's power for good or evil is in direct proportion to the motives of the user. This planet flashes a hands off warning to the selfish grandiose person. He requires a proper relationship before you can engage him.

Garth Allen expands nicely on this concept within his book. He refers to the philosophy of Martin Buber whose theory of I-Thou is brilliantly Plutonian.[2] Buber states that all relationships are either "I-it," or "I-Thou." Most of us go through life experiencing our existence as a series of "its." We get stuck in a rut of viewing people as nouns, things or its, objective others. Some of us even view God as an "it." The truth of Pluto's teaching, is that both God and Goddess are verbs. All living beings are verbs. Seeing people as nouns or "its" only serves to de-humanize them.

The word "Thou" respectfully acknowledges the presence of another being. I-Thou recognizes both parties as separate, yet essential and equal. We must stand facing each other and learn to accept each other's humanity, even if we are very different. I-Thou represents the Sanscrit word namaste, meaning "I honor that place within you that...when you are in yours and I am in mine, we are one."

Robert Moore describes this as the need to transcend and move beyond our separate tribal and cultural differences towards a more global, humanistic view.[3] This is a necessary change, critical to our survival, and it is already beginning. The world grows smaller every day and we are moving closer and closer towards an understanding of the Earth as a global community. We laughed at the Soviets because they destroyed their economy in an attempt to keep their military machine afloat. The truth is, that the United States did much the same. As oceans die and the sky is destroyed above us, as the ozone is depleted by our toxic waste, we recognize that environmental concerns transcend territorial boundaries.

Our expanding visions makes our Earth smaller, and links it to the cosmos around us. The Hubble space telescope and the two Voyager missions have radically expanded our conscious peephole into space. The worlds of Uranus and Neptune have been brought more powerfully into our collective conscious experience through the data we have gathered.

Pluto has just completed its perihelion in 1989. This is the point of its closest approach to the Sun and Earth. It will actually remain within the orbit of Neptune until 1999. Pluto's transformative influence has been powerfully effecting us since 1979 when it began this close pass of the Sun.

This explains many of the inexplicable phenomenon that are occurring at a faster and faster pace. Those of us—all Baby Boomers—who grew up in the shadow of the cold war never believed that we'd live to see the dissolution of the U.S.S.R. and the dismantling of the Berlin wall! The mid-east peace talks have just succeeded in facilitating the release of many hostages. Two bitter enemies, the PLO and Israel, have just recognized the right of the other to exist.

Yet Pluto's shadow is strong, the Shadow Magician and his powerful wand seeking power and domination. The real threat to world peace and stability are the terrorist nations and many of these countries may attain nuclear capability in the near future.

The karmic outer trinity is bringing us closer to a day of reckoning where we must all learn to live in an I-Thou world, or suffer the alternatives. There are many paths to destruction, but only one towards salvation and peace.

Pluto and the Four Angles

Pluto in the King Power Zone

When Pluto is found in this position, the native can express two different scenarios. Because of the dualistic, Yin/Yang nature of Pluto/Persephone, they may choose to express either the active (dominant) or passive (submissive) half of this archetype in terms of their public persona. Choosing the dominant half will usually cause them to seek careers of raw power. Any career where they can dictate the flow and sit in the driver's seat will appeal to them.

Some, who identify with the submissive traits, will have strong empathy for social underdogs and may choose a career where they can fight for social justice in some form or other, or volunteer for organizations such as Greenpeace, the Sierra club, or the Peace Corps. Others may volunteer for a rape crisis hotline or become counselors at a rape center. They seek to comfort and uplift those who have been trodden down by society.

In its shadow form, these folks can become overtly intimidating and manipulative. They may seek to blackmail others through any means at their disposal. They seek control at all cost. No other archetype can be as shadowy and secretive as Pluto. These natives are power mongers who will stop at nothing to achieve their ends. They are ruthless. The submissive shadow type will often fall prey to public domination and control. They surrender control of their career into the hands of others.

Pluto in the Lover Power Zone

Pluto/Persephone is the most passive/aggressive archetype by nature. This phenomenon will often have a field day when the planet is located in this region of the chart. These natives often gravitate towards a relationship that is rich in emotional intensity and power struggles. They thrive on this dynamic dance of the sexes. Many love to fight and then make up!

These natives are often in search of an eternal consort just like Pluto himself. If they identify with the dominant traits of the archetype, they may resort to any means of manipulation and control to achieve this end. Because of the passive influence of the Lover zone, most will probably identify with the submissive Persephone, and will attract a partner through their tenderness and innocence. They secretly dream of being swept away and ravished by their mate.

Because this archetype represents the shadowy realm of the underworld, it can easily slip into its shadow expressions. These natives, if wounded, will often drift into destructive passive/aggressive games with their partners. Sadomasochistic tendencies may arise and the relationship will often regress into an endless struggle of domination and submission, where each partner gets locked into a predetermined role. Others will degenerate even further, drifting into the world of bondage and discipline.

Pluto in the Magician Power Zone

Pluto is completely at home in this subterranean region of the chart. As a result, these natives can be deep soul searchers and seekers of inner wisdom. They are also usually quite sensitive and introverted preferring to keep to themselves. These folks can make excellent therapists and counselors if they can bring their inner talents up into the conscious world and manifest them. This would require their Pluto to be tied in, via aspects, to some other archetype which is above ground and preferably angular.

If this is not the case, and Pluto is isolated from other archetypes, they can be completely unconscious of its presence within their lives. They may occasionally be bothered by disturbing dreams, but other than that they will be unaware of its influence. That does not mean, however, that Pluto ceases to influence their lives. He simply goes underground and works on the unconscious level where he is comfortable.

This will often set the native up for a whole mess of shadow manifestations. Pluto is so underhanded and secretive by nature that the evidence of his actions is difficult to clearly see. He will cause us to act out in subversive, manipulative and controlling ways. These natives may drift into the underworld of crime and street life. They will often commit acts and offenses that others are shocked by. Neighbors may say: "Mike was never like that. I don't know what has become of him. He was always a quiet guy, kept mostly to himself. He never bothered anybody!"

Pluto in the Warrior Power Zone

Pluto tends to manifest more of its dominant tendencies when located in this power zone. The assertive influence of the Warrior archetype sends them on an eternal quest for the ultimate power. If they are unwounded within this archetype, they may take up after social causes. They will choose to use their power in the tradition of a noble Warrior, protecting and serving the rights of the weaker and less fortunate. The key to understanding the Pluto/Persephone archetype is that it contains both an aggressor and a victim of sorts. We must consciously own both halves or else shadows will instantly manifest in our lives. Because of the strong Warrior flavor of this location, These natives will frequently fall prey to identifying with the aggressor role. This sets them up to pursue power and prey on the weak.

Shadow opportunities abound with this setup. These natives may secretly love the feeling of overpowering others. They will seek to accomplish this through any means possible. Many of their methods will be quite sly and surreptitious. Most of their victims will not know they've been had until it's too late. They will justify their behavior through depersonalizing their victims into "its."

The Decile aspect (36°) is also an indicator of Plutonian energy. The problem is that their influence is rarely if ever felt. There are so many other more dominant harmonics vying for position within our psyche that they usually won't stand a chance of manifesting. The only exceptions would be if a Decile connected to a planet that was located in one of the four power zones. The other instance is if Pluto is angular, or prominently aspected, and the chart contains a rather large amount of Deciles (five or more).

When interpreting Deciles, one can view them as a potential pathway for the two archetypes involved to do business within the realm of the collective unconscious. If one had, for example, a Decile aspect between the Sun and Jupiter, they would have the potential to experience the full expanse of their King archetype through inner dialoguing, creative visualization and dream interpretation. These methods tap us directly into the riches of the Plutonian realm.

Number	Planet	Aspect	Key Words & Phrases
1	Sun (King)	Conjunction 0°	Fusion - Subjective Unity Blessing - Radiating Power Source - Sovereignty Creativity - Benediction Sacrifice
2	Mercury (Magician)	Opposition 180°	Awareness of Separation .Objective - Clarity - Tension of the Opposites - Magic Opportunity for Realization and Fruition
3	Venus (Lover)	Trine 120°	Harmony - Ease - Cooperation Relatedness - Flow Reconciliation - Healing Beauty - Yearning for Comfort Love - Nurturing
4	Earth-Moon (Wild-Child)	Square 90°	Procreative - Regenerative Manifestation of Energy Heat - Friction - Challenge Dynamic Crisis - Acute Awareness of Pathos
5	Mars (Warrior)	Quintile 72°	Application of Will Productively Creative - "Worker Bee" - Focused Energy Commitment - Conscious Manifestation of Form Servicing
6	Jupiter	Sextile 60°	Expansion - Growth - Optimism Faith - Prayer - Positive "Quality Thinking" - Salvation through Joy - Higher Power
7	Saturn	Septile 51.428°	Contraction - Death - Loss Elimination of Useless Forms Reclaiming - Reaping Salvation through Grief Work Lower Power

Number	Planet	Aspect	Key Words & Phrases
8	Uranus	Octile	Liberation - Progress through Shock - Freedom - Exhilaration Shattering Forms - Genious Manifesting - Healthy Trickster
9	Neptune	Novile 40°	Spirituality - Nirvana Yearning for Bliss - Psychic Womb - Mystical Peace - Dream Like Ecstasy - Creative Impregnated Matrix
10	Pluto	Decile 36°	Conception - Creativity - Tantric Power - Re-Evolution Becoming - Transformation Cyclic - Death & Rebirth Alpha & Omega
12	Lunar-Like	Semi-Sextile 30°	Organic Soup - Vital - Potential Renewal - All the Ingredients for a New Life - Youthful Spontaneous - Ready - Tender - Vulnerable - A Process of Initiation , Which Pushes One Forward, Out of One's Own "Comfort Zone"
	Chiron-Like	Quincunx (Pre-Opposition 150°	Towards Complete Conscious Realization. Growth and Set backs Alternate as One is Forced to Approach the Altar of Supreme Sacrifice. The Ego's Last Hurrah.
		Sinister Quincunx (Post-Opposition) 210°	A Process of Transformation where One is Still "Raw" from the Experience of the Preceding sacrificial Initiation. One Needs Time to Reintegrate and Re-forge the Ego, Which has Just been Consumed in the Sacrificial Fire. Continuation of Learning Spiritualization of the Ego. Post-Grad Work.

CHAPTER ELEVEN

The Archetypal Tree

Each of the previous chapters has dealt with a single archetype in great detail. We shall now begin the task of showing how all these separate sub-worlds tie in together to form an actual living organism. I like the term "Archetypal Tree" for just this reason, because it reflects the idea of the life contained therein.

At first glance, the Tree looks organized, structured and symmetrical. It bears a close visual resemblance to the Kabalic tree of life. I believe they both represent a primal archetypal "shape." As we explore it further, the mystery will begin to unfold more clearly (fig. 11a).

The most immediately apparent feature of the Tree is its three vertical pillars. We have the Yin pillar, Venus, Jupiter and Neptune on the left. The central pillar represents impartial clarity and contains the Sun, Mercury, the Moon and Pluto. On the right we have the Yang pillar, Mars, Saturn and Uranus.

What I am attempting to do, by separating the planets into three distinct vertical groups, is to show how certain planets are more predominantly Yin (passive-receptive) or Yang (active-assertive) in their expression. Certain others fall in the grey zone between these two extremes. Some folks may have difficulty in seeing the energy of Jupiter/Zeus as being Yin in nature. This is due to the limitations and patriarchal distortions of mythology we have inherited. Zeus was always viewed, in ancient times, as part of a diad which consisted of his wife, Hera, and himself. We have lost sight of this ancient truth and have instead obliterated all references to his feminine, Yin side.

The modern planetary names have all come from the mythological gods of the Roman culture which trace back to ancient Greece. These mythological gods were always viewed as part of a seemingly incestuous relationship. Every great god was usually paired up with or married to his sister. All that was implied by this pairing was an emphasis on the bi-sexual nature of every god/goddess. They were seen as inseparable.

Figure 11a

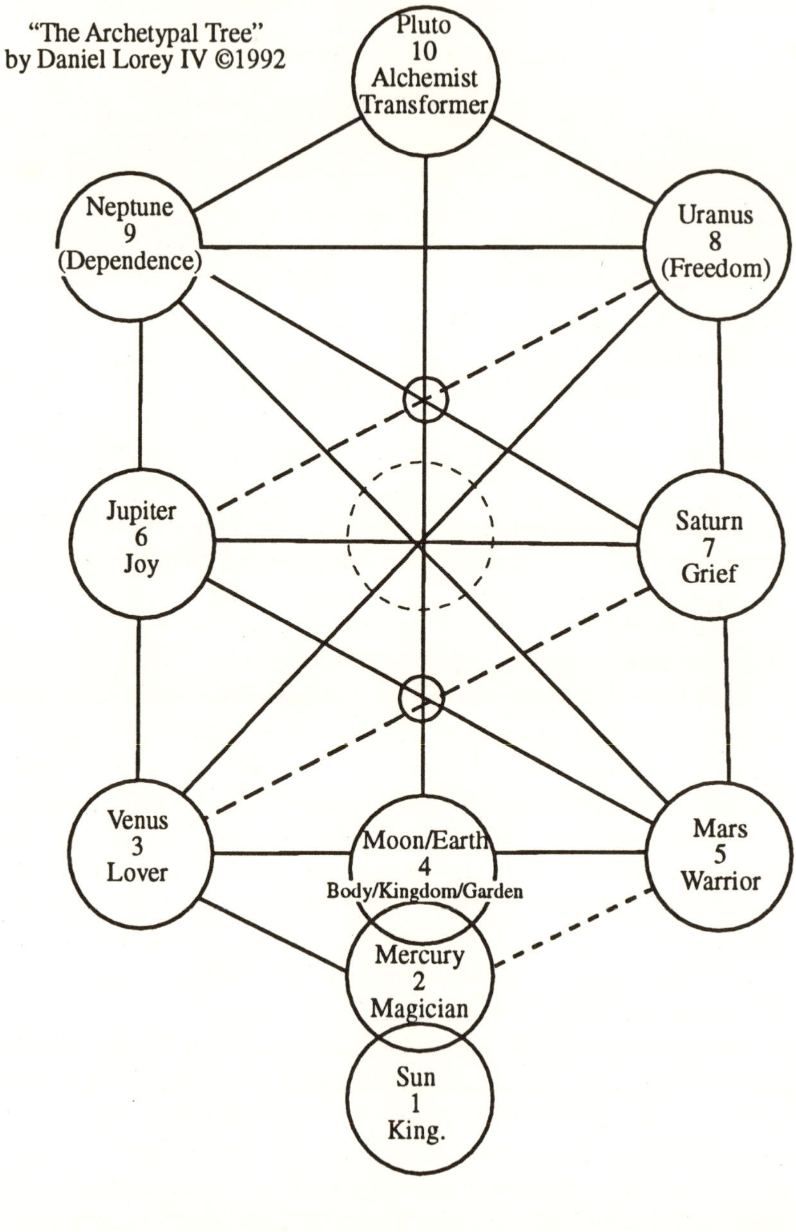
"The Archetypal Tree"
by Daniel Lorey IV ©1992
Pluto
10
Alchemist
Transformer
Neptune
9
(Dependence)
Uranus
8
(Freedom)
Jupiter
6
Joy
Saturn
7
Grief
Venus
3
Lover
Moon/Earth
4
Body/Kingdom/Garden
Mars
5
Warrior
Mercury
2
Magician
Sun
1
King.

In this sense, Zeus / Jupiter can just as easily be seen as Hera / Juno. These goddesses have just as much claim to the influence of this planetary body.

Although all planets ultimately contain both feminine and masculine components, Yin and Yang, some more easily display a predominance of one or the other. The third group, of the central pillar, can vacillate and are more readily bi-sexual in their manifestation. The design of the Tree simply attempts to represent this "bell curve" phenomenon of planetary expression when it comes to the forces of Yin and Yang.

The problem in representing the Tree as containing certain Yin and Yang components is that we are limited by two-dimensional thinking. The Tree cannot achieve a dynamic balance when limited to the linear, rigid, black and white world of Mercury. To explain what we mean by balance, it is necessary to elaborate on the eastern philosophy of the I-Ching.

When casting the three lines of an I-Ching tri-gram, there is a basic fundamental law to follow. A line that is all Yin, must ultimately become old and change to Yang. The reverse is also true of an old Yang line. We change it to Yin. The energy flip-flops to maintain balance within the system. We can view this as the "edge" of the coin that separates heads from tails. Failure to acknowledge this edge will keep us limited to one side of the coin. We see only its width and height, which give no hint of its other side. This law must be obeyed by our Tree as well. This will occur, quite naturally, when we add the third dimension of depth. It is this depth which allows us to freely move from one side to the other.

Upon entering the three-dimensional Venusian world of form, we find that our Tree can now retain the purity of the Yin and Yang strands, while still maintaining dynamic balance. This is achieved by alternating each consecutive horizontal axis. The result of this modification transports the Tree out of the rigid two-dimensional realm and into a fluidic relationship reminiscent of the third dimension. We can best depict this phenomenon through a series of illustrations.

First we take the two-dimensional Tree as we are familiar with it (fig. 11b). Now we begin by twisting the middle horizontal axis 180° (fig. 11c). This process must be followed through on the top horizontal axis as well. We continue twisting until Uranus and Neptune have also flipped 180°, ultimately ending up right back where they began (fig. 11d).

After all is said and done, the only two planets which are in different locations are those of the middle horizontal rung, Jupiter and Saturn. This simple mid-structure flip cancels out the imbalances between the

Figure 11b

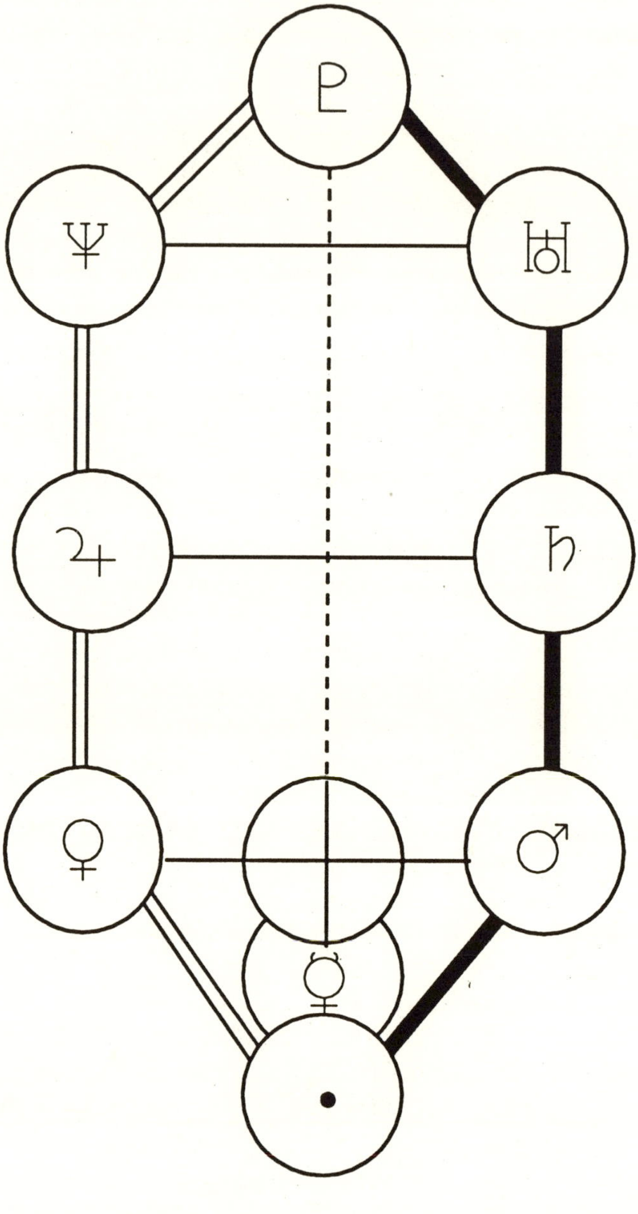

Figure 11c

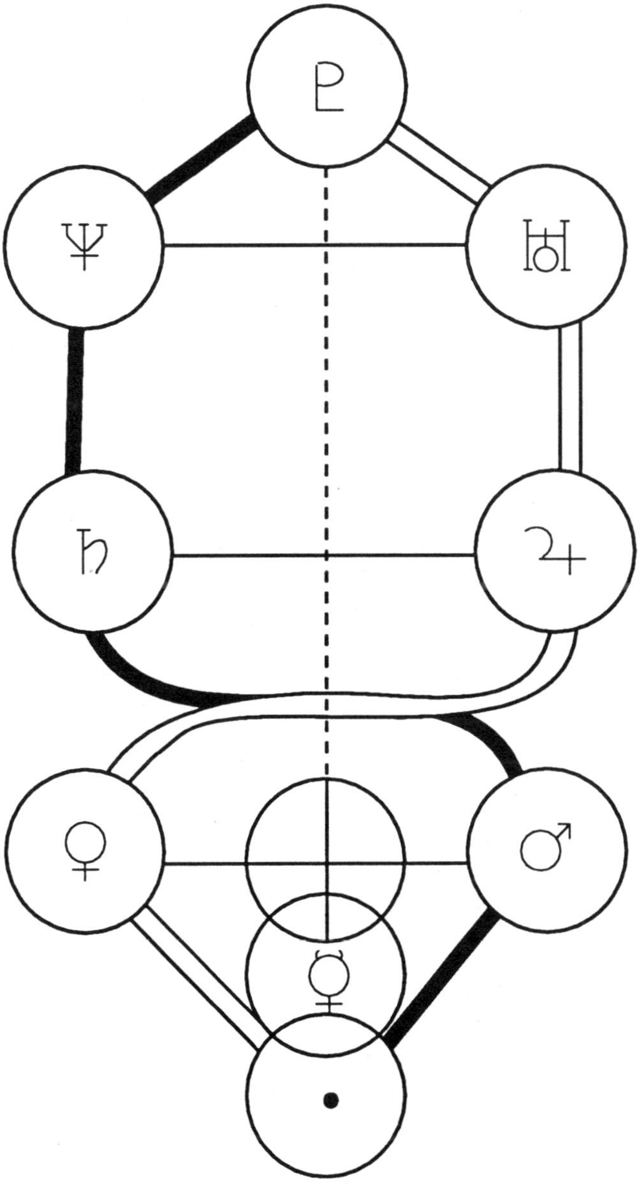

Figure 11d

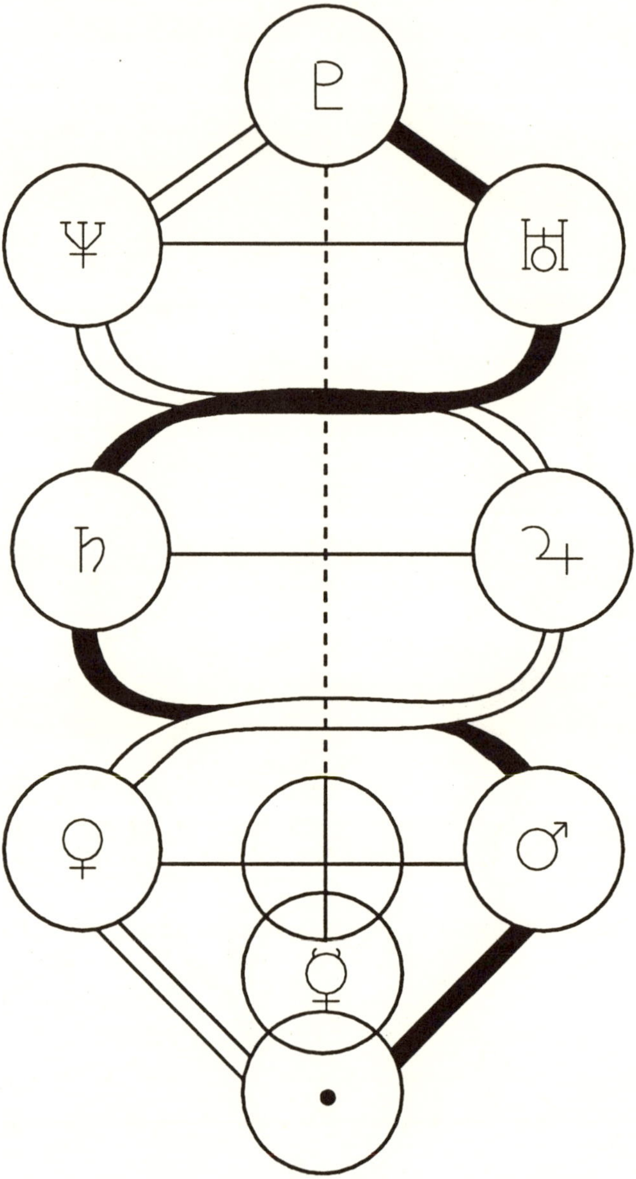

Yin and Yang polarities. Interestingly enough, the same solution was required in order to solve the incongruous "noise" generated by the modern day electric guitar. This phenomenon seems to be a universal dilemma concerning the laws of physics governing polarity in general.

The first electric guitars to hit the U.S. market were equipped with single coil pick-ups. These were a long flat magnet, with a definite north and south pole, which were placed underneath the strings so as to "pick up" their vibrations. The most popular of these early electric guitars was the "Fender stratocaster." This model has three single coil pickups placed under the strings, all laid out parallel to one another. They quickly gained a reputation as noisy guitars which captured all sorts of electrical fields in addition to the string's frequencies.

The problem with the guitar was ultimately found to be the same one as with our two-dimensional Tree. All of the magnets had their south poles and north poles aligned with each other. This was the source of all its polar disturbances. All that needed to be done was a slight modification to the arrangement of pick-ups. By simply flipping the middle pick-up 180°, essentially reversing its two poles, the entire guitar became dynamically balanced in terms of its polarity. This completely canceled out all of the extraneous noise being picked up by the guitar. All that remained was the sweet sound of music!

In our own particular case, the end result of all this polar juggling is a Tree that is completely balanced on a dynamic level. This gives us perfect Yin-Yang harmony all the way around the perimeter of the structure (fig. 11e). We also wind up creating a form that looks remarkably like the DNA spiral.

There are four proteins, or nucleotides, that form the joining "rungs" of the DNA molecule. These are Adenine, Thymine, Guanine, and Cytosine. Adenine can only join with a Thymine molecule. Guanine can only pair off with a Cytosine molecule (fig. 11f).

In our spiral/Tree, we have four basic human archetypes. They also prefer to pair off quite selectively. Mars and Venus, Warrior and Lover, always pair off together. This is depicted by the universal symbol of the Martian sword or arrow piercing the Venusian heart! The Sun and Mercury, King and Magician, are always seen working together. Mercury must translate and interpret for the Sun.

Venus and Mercury are primarily Yin in nature, because they lack any satellites of their own. This is because they are strictly subservient to the power of a larger gravitational body, the Sun, and do not control the orbits of any moons of their own. The Sun and Mars are both predomi-

Figure 11e

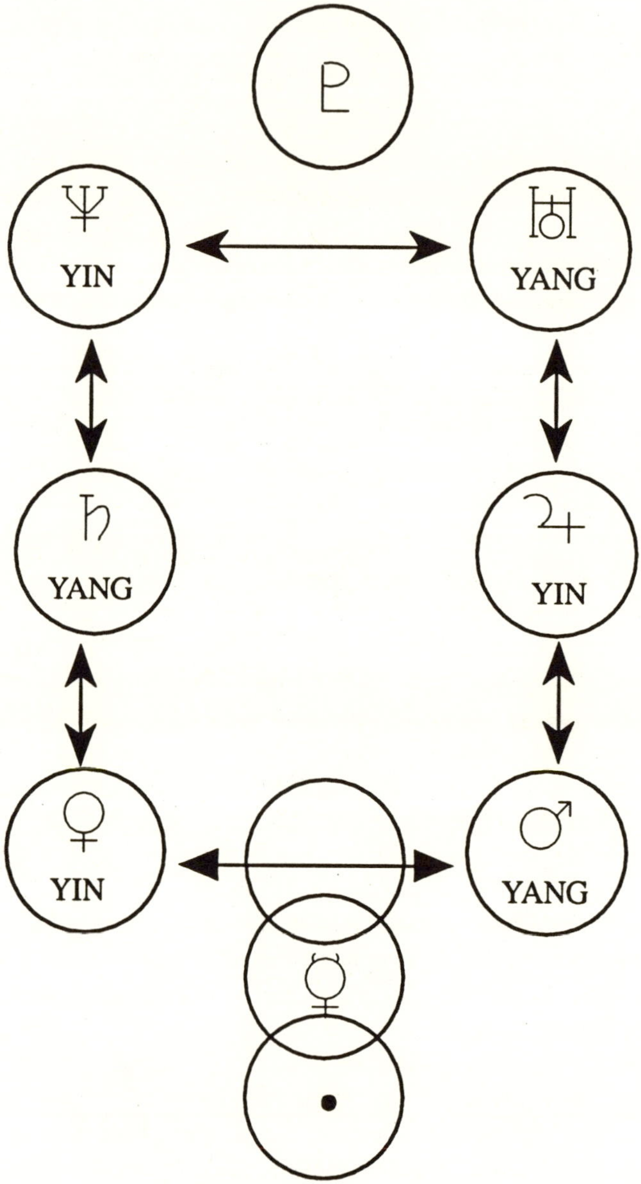

Figure 11f

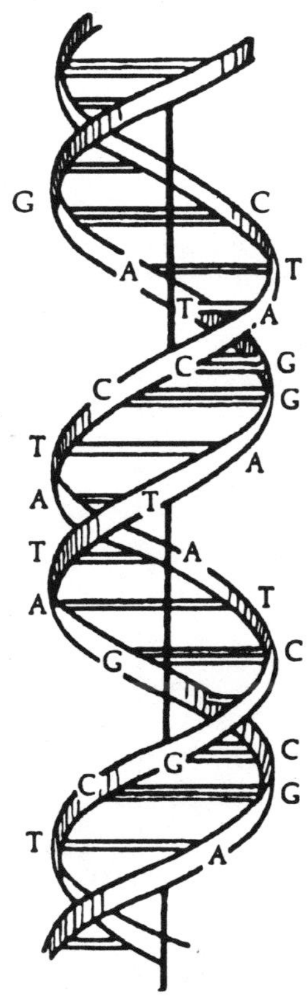

T = Thymine
A = Adenine
C = Cytosine
G = Guanine

Figure 11g

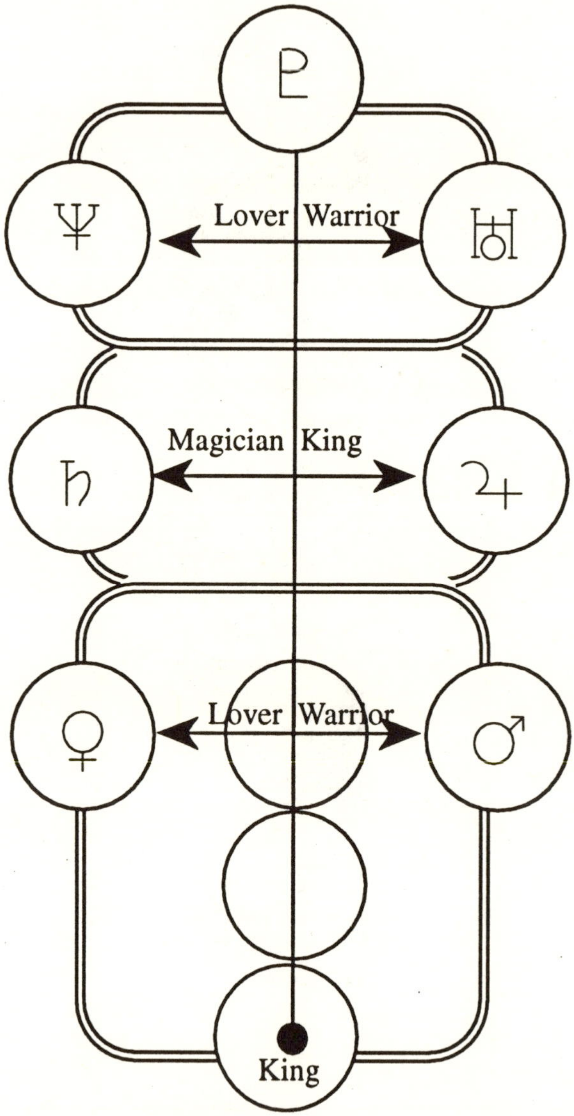

nantly Yang because they both are in control of lesser, smaller orbiting bodies. Keeping this in mind will help us understand how the archetypes selectively combine in much the same way as Adenine-Thymine and Cytosine-Guanine (fig. 11g).

We have Sun-Mercury at the bottom of our Tree, arranged in a vertical pairing. Then we have Mars-Venus pairing off at the first horizontal "rung." Next we find a repeat of the King-Magician polarity, represented by Jupiter-Saturn. Jupiter is the resurrected King or White Osiris in Egyptian mythology. Saturn is the dark alchemical magician, Set, who must kill his brother Osiris so that he may live again. They carry a different flavor than Sun-Mercury, but share the same archetypal principles.

Finally we have a repeat of the Warrior-Lover energy pairing off on the third horizontal rung. Uranus is the spiritual Warrior or rebel. Neptune, of course, represents the spiritual lover or mystic. The parallels are staggering if one can read between the lines. Life reflects itself holographically on many different levels. I believe we have simply begun to uncover another one.

The electro-magnetic spectrum is perceived as consisting of various wavelengths. It is my belief that these waves are actually spirals. They are really spiraling through space. In order to measure their length and height, we simply view them from the side where their depth cannot be seen. This has been a long standing fundamental error in our thinking concerning the movement of particles (fig. 11h).

Instead of calling it the Particle-Wave theory, we should really call it the Particle-Spiral theory. We need to grow out of our two-dimensional way of thinking. Is light a particle or a wave? Any physicist knows that it is both at the same time. It's not a black and white, all or nothing situation. Life is shades of gray. Both are valid and both are needed.

Male/Female Modes of Feeling

I believe we have discovered the root core difference between what Robert Bly calls the "male mode" of feeling, versus the "female mode."[1] The male mode of feeling, through which a man learns about the world, is to view life as particles. The female mode of feeling, through which she learns about the universe, is to see all of life as waves or spirals.

A woman's foundation or reality map is to consider all things as one, as all connected. Her mind seeks to unify everything, much like an analog computer. Being identified with the wave gives women an

Figure 11h

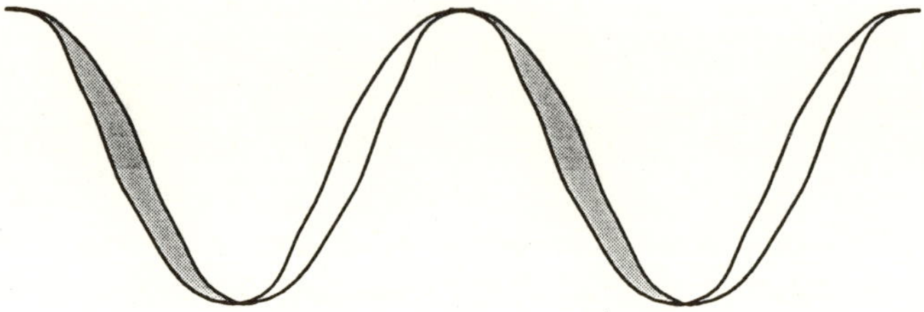

Spiral (3 Dimensional)

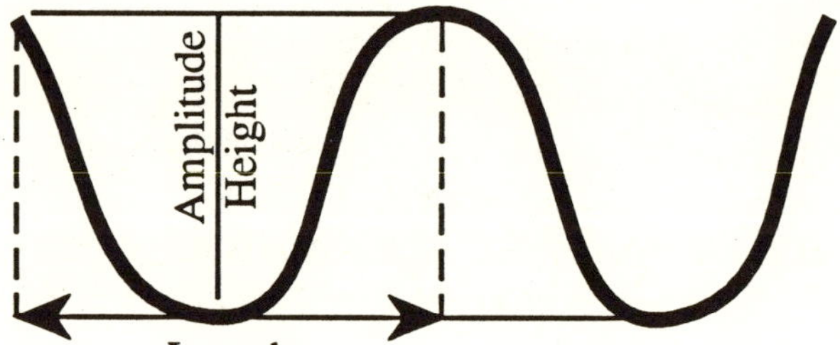

Wave (2 Dimensional)

intuitive pathway that is almost non-verbal. They simply "know" what other people are thinking and feeling with a greater degree of accuracy than most men are capable of.

Within a man's foundation, or reality map, there is a strong need to be guided and taught through particles or specifics. His mind seeks to break down information into its components, much like a digital computer. Men learn and communicate best through ritual and symbol. "Show me the way, initiate me. Give me a map that makes sense." The beauty of this is that both of these paths will lead us collectively into the light!

These two modes can also be seen clearly in the spiraling Yin-Yang pillars of our Tree. The Yin, female, mode of feeling is expressed by the soft, passive nature of Venus-Juno/ Jupiter-Neptune. This energy is moist and nurturing. It is empathetic, warm and social.

The Yang (male) mode of feeling is represented by the harsh, active nature of Mars-Saturn-Uranus. This force is dry and ruthless. It is stoic, cold and antisocial. He has a "code" or sense of duty.

We also can see the Amor-Roma polarity very clearly. The female-Yin mode is amorous by nature. The male-Yang mode is romantic by nature. These two extremes are meant to create a healthy balance.

John Gray, has also written about these two distinct modes in his book *Men Are from Mars Women Are from Venus.*[2] I find it interesting that this psychologist chose to accurately confirm what we already know from the astrological perspective. The male mode of feeling emanates from the Yang pillar, at the root of which lies the Warrior archetype, Mars. The female mode of feeling emanates from the Yin pillar, at the root of which lies the Lover archetype, Venus. The symbols for Mars and Venus have always been known to represent the two sexes.

The danger of splitting these modes apart has already been alluded to in Chapter 9. Robert Bly offers further proof through his analysis of the work of Wilhelm Reich. According to Reich, there are three levels of feelings within the human psyche. We shall find that they correspond perfectly with the three pillars of our Tree.

First level emotions relate to the mode of the Yin pillar. They are the pleasant, soft, cozy and sweet emotions of life. A person can become stuck here in the new age consciousness of cultivated kindness. They become imbalanced and phony, by denying their second level emotions.

These second level emotions correspond to the mode of the Yang pillar. Here we find anger, rebellion, grief, melancholy, envy and fear. Many of us shame and repress this side of our nature. We don't acknowledge its existence within others, or ourselves. As a result we never reach the third level emotions imparted by the central pillar of enlightened clarity.

Bly states that for every person who denies their second level emotions, there is someone else on the planet who must carry this burden for them. Nature abhors a vacuum. This is how she seeks to balance our imbalance. For every fluffy new age person ascending into the clouds, there is a homeless person carrying their pain.

I think that the lesson here is pretty clear. We must all take full responsibility for our own pain and grief. Through embracing the entire archetypal structure of the Tree, we leave others free to do the same. This is the only way that we, as humans, might someday heal our collective wounds.

The lower group of planets represent the personal (human) archetypes which help fuel the Ego. This is the hard drive of our human computer. It must contain solid, mature programming within it, in order for us to make use of Jupiter-Saturn.

These two master teachers help us to interface with the "software" of the upper triad, Uranus-Neptune-Pluto. After passing through the veil or gate of the asteroid belt, we encounter these two great guardians. Like the two huge lions on either side of a doorway, we cannot pass until we appease their appetites.

It is important to know what to feed these lions. We need to speak their language in order for interface and access to take place. Michael Meade tells the story of a boy who tries to get past these two lions. His goal is to retrieve the waters of life (Neptune) contained within the inner castle.

The boy feeds them loaves of bread which symbolize the physical body. While they are busy eating the bread, he passes through the portal with his spirit still intact. The boy goes on to re-discover his gold and awakens to find the water as well.

This initiatory rite of passage is what life is really all about. Most of us never get past these portals, because our hard-drive never makes a complete interface. Our personal programming is so botched up, so wounded, that we have trouble even getting the system to boot-up.

The tragedy of all this is that we have this incredibly advanced computer called the human psyche. When we finally go to use it, we discover that the programming is all fouled up. The system fails to boot and crashes instead. In searching through the box it came in, we discover that no instruction manual was included.

The Archetypal Tree is, in my eyes, the schematic diagram of our soul. We can use this schema as a guiding structure for the process of self exploration. A working knowledge of our selves, developed through personal and spiritual exploration will allow our inner worlds to blossom and unfold once again.

There are many people whose work provides us with invaluable tools for this exploration, especially when combined with the knowledge of astrological archetypes. Robert Moore, Douglas Gillette and James Hillman are three brilliant therapists who have uncovered and synthesized some very powerful information. Robert Bly's work on grieving is indispensable. John Bradshaw and Lucia Capacchione are wonderful sources of information on the inner child. We must access childhood to heal the wounds.

The inner child is a very nebulous term which can lead to much confusion, or delusion. Its energy is very tangible and is easy to access through guided imagery. The inner child's presence can feel much like the way a restless infant in the womb feels when we put our hand on the mother's womb. We can feel it squirming and hear it calling, but we can't pierce through the membrane and connect with it, we cannot touch it until it is fully developed and ready to be born. A wounded inner child will not come out, it is too damaged and resists birth. This frustrating feeling of woundedness can keep us stuck, unable to move forward and incapable of birthing our whole self.

Much of our problem may center on a belief that there is only one inner child. We hear a voice that we think is "his" and categorically reject any other inner voices that we may hear.

The truth is we've got a whole bunch of inner kids in there, all kicking and screaming for attention, all longing for re-birth. There is the wounded King-child, Magician- child, Lover-child, and Warrior-child. We must find them, contact each one, and guide them forward into healing. But how do we recognize them individually?

The left hand-right hand dialoguing of Lucia Capacchione is very effective.[3] Working with the same approach as Bradshaw and others, Capacchione goes a step further by recognizing the multiple inner children that are present. She has different names for them: the "angry child," "vulnerable child" and the "brat," etc. John Bradshaw's work is primarily focused on contacting the Divine Child archetype. His book, *Homecoming,* is an excellent place for the beginner to start.[4]

It is the ground breaking work of Moore and Gillette, however, that allows us to advance further along in our abilities to heal our inner kingdom by realizing that we have a whole constellation of archetypes and archangels within us.

This inner initiation process was externally represented by King Arthur and the Knights of the round table. Through learning in this setting, these students were being consciously reminded of the structure of their own inner round table. All the Archetypes have child sub-personalities and each has his own chair at the round table. This sacred space is where the true healing and integration can occur. Our inner King plays his flute and calls the meeting to order. Differences are discussed and worked out. The end result is a powerful alliance of energies that collectively offer themselves up for sacrifice to the King of the other world.

It is here that we discover our true purpose and commit to it devoutly. We have here, in the center, the perfect opportunity for complete balance. The two crossing axes of the King-Magician, act to counterbalance the "square" created by the two Lover-Warrior polarities (see 11i).

The intersection of all four archetypes marks the eleventh sphere, or Kings chamber of our inner Great Pyramid. The Archetypal Tree represents this central meeting room within. It is here that we achieve a proper balance between our inner archetypal structure and the Earth's magnetic field. Through the initiation of this process, we can invoke true healing within ourselves.

This happens when we enter into the fourth dimension. Up till now, our Tree has been an interesting three-dimensional "form." The fourth dimension is when our spiral becomes animated with the dynamic life-energy of Eros. This can only take place on the fourth planet, Earth.

The Egyptians represented this process with their word for eternity (fig. 11j). Here we see the Sun, in the middle of the glyph, representing the central pillar. It is flanked on either side by two twisted pieces of flax. These represent the left and right pillars. They even have the same number of twists as our Tree does.

The Hindus developed the whole science of Kundalini Yoga based on this same principle. Through balancing the energies of the ida and pingala, the kundalini could then rise up the central sushumna. This led to a complete energizing and balancing of the soul. Wisdom, serenity, health and ecstasy were experienced.

This is the true meaning behind the very symbol for the medical profession. We have the cadusus or magic wand of Mercury, the central pillar. This is surrounded by two serpents spiraling three times around its length (fig. 11k). The use of serpents to represent the side pillars is very appropriate. Handled separately, these pillars can turn quite venomous.

Figure 11i

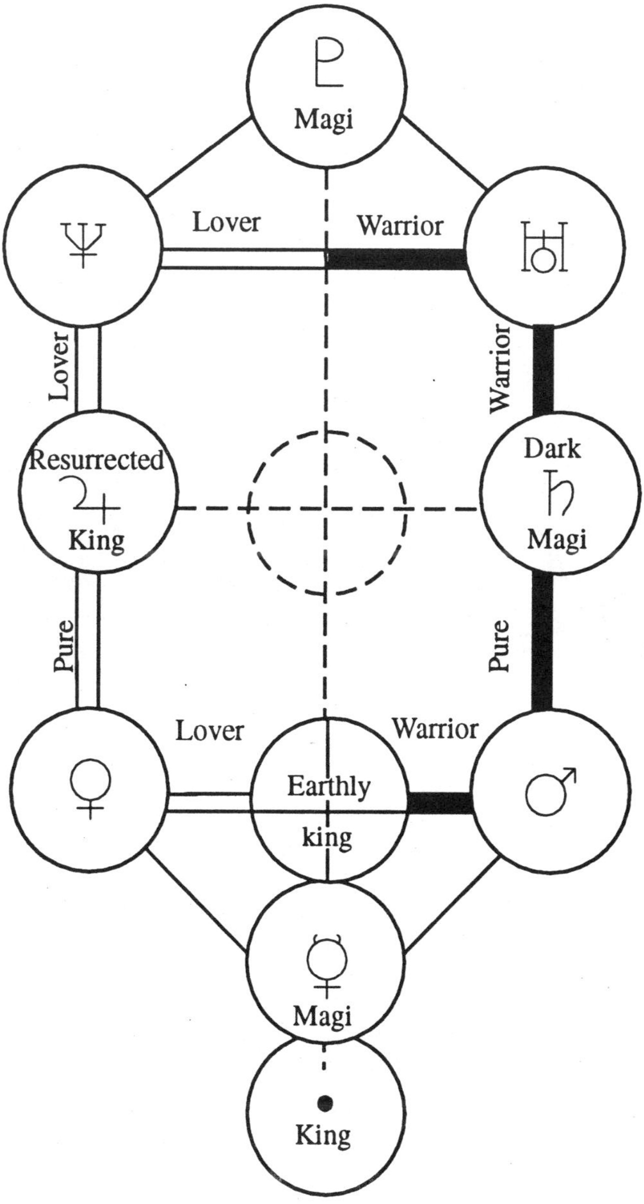

Magi
Lover
Warrior
Lover
Warrior
Resurrected
King
Dark
Magi
Pure
Pure
Lover
Warrior
Earthly
king
Magi
King

Figure 11j

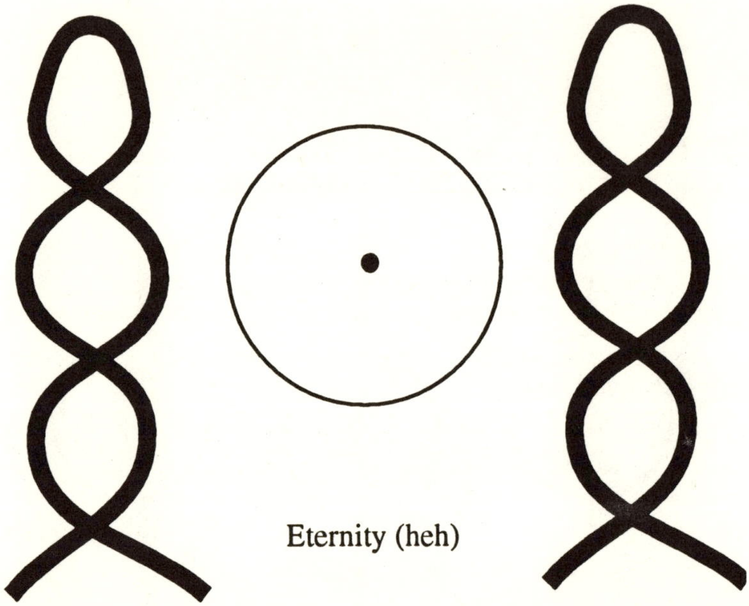

Eternity (heh)

Figure 11k

Caduceus

The pure Yin and Yang threads form these two curved paths that spiral around each other. These are the pathways of the male and female modes of feeling. They also represent the two counterbalancing functions of the sympathetic and parasympathetic nerve branches.

These two branches comprise the autonomic nervous system which, as a whole, is ruled by the Moon/Earth. The sympathetic branch is pure Yang and is ruled by the male mode (Mars-Saturn-Uranus). The parasympathetic branch is pure Yin, and is ruled by the female mode (Venus-Juno/Jupiter-Neptune). They have the ability to accelerate and decelerate the body's functions.

The autonomic system's nerves run along either side of the spine. They can be effectively accessed through shiatsu and various other forms of bodywork. We can actually tap directly into the archetypes of the two outer pillars via their connections to the two branches of this nervous system.

It is for this very powerful reason, that bodywork often accesses and releases "body memories" from deep with the archetypal unconscious. They are, in reality, archetypal memories. Here we find all the trauma of our wounds which have been stored up in the body's nervous system.

The body actually has an innate intelligence all its own. The sum total of all our evolutionary experience, instincts, memories and traumas are stored within the archetypes of our internal Tree. The future lies wide open now to all these new branches of healing. Many of them, such as network chiropractic, are leading the way towards an exciting new horizon.

Comparison of Key Words

Female "Yin" Mode	Balanced Mode	Male "Yang" Mode
Venus-Jupiter-Neptune	Pluto-Sun	Mars-Saturn-Uranus
Peace		War
Hotep	Amen-Ra	Ptah
"Amorous" Lover	Magician-Priest	"Romantic" Warrior
Wet	Moist	Dry
Tefnut		Shu
Wave-Spiral		Particle
Hot	Comfortable	Cold
Earth & Water	Ether	Fire ¶ Air
Flesh	Nerves	Bone-Marrow
Liver		Spleen
Thymus		Adrenals
Yoni		Phallus
Passionate		Ruthless
Preserver-Nurturer		Destroyer - Conqueror
Absorber		
Stomach		Emitter
Expansion		Bowel
Accretion		Contraction
Receiver		Excretion
Lymph		Transmitter
CO-2		Blood
Carbon		Oxygen
Carbohydrate	Lipid	Nitrogen
Sweet	Salty	Protein
Alkaline	Saline	Sour-Acrid-bitter
Electron	Neutron	Acidic
"Halogens"	"Noble Gases"	Proton
Vegetable	Mineral	"Active" Metals
Para-Sympathetic	Central	Animal
Ida	Sushumna	Sympathetic
Mother & Child	Holy Spirit	Pingala
Isis & Horus	Osiris	Father
Vishnu	Brahma	Set
Social		Shiva
Dependent		Anti-Social

Merging		Independent
Joy		Separating
Soft		Grief
Passive		Hard
Leisure		Aggressive
Art	Mythology	Laborer
Generous		Science
Proud		Economical
Liberal		Humble
Bountiful		Conservative
Naive		Rational
Trusting		Calculating
Relaxed		Guarded
Emotional		Tense
Open		Stoic
Public		Closed
Yes		Private
Socialite		No
Extravert		Loner
Light		Introvert
		Dark

CHAPTER TWELVE

Integrating Archetypes and Medical Astrology

We have discussed the need for personal and spiritual exploration and examined the use the Archetypal Tree as a structure for this inner search. I'd like to present a few ideas that will help integrate this information on an even deeper level.

In Chapter 11 we made mention of the relationship between the three pillars of the Tree and the Hindu system of Kundalini. To explore this correlation further we must introduce the significance of Chiron and the Asteroids.

The Yogic system of Kundalini is an ancient method of understanding the human body and soul. There is believed to be a coiled serpent at the base of the spine. This serpent energy will rise up the central sushumna when the Yin-Yang energies of the Ida and Pingala are balanced. As the serpent rises, it will illuminate the seven chakras (energy centers) along the way (fig. 12a).

I believe that our Archetypal spiral can be seen in much the same way. When superimposed over the human form, we shall find that there are many exciting discoveries to be made. We are not attempting to invalidate the Hindu system. The objective is to introduce a new perspective that, in many ways, corresponds to the chakras.

In the diagram (fig. 12b), we can see that the central pillar corresponds to the sushumna. This was known to the Egyptians as the pillar of Ra. The Pingala relates to the Yang pillar of the tree (Mars-Saturn-Uranus). The Egyptians called this the "dry" pillar of Shu. The "moist" Yin pillar (Venus-Jupiter-Neptune) was called Tefnut in Egypt, and is related to the Ida.

The two side pillars cross over each other twice, at both the throat and the solar plexus. This is very significant, and allows for the double inversion principle upon which life is based. We also wind up with three distinct sections to the spiral and the body. Interestingly enough, they

Figure 12a

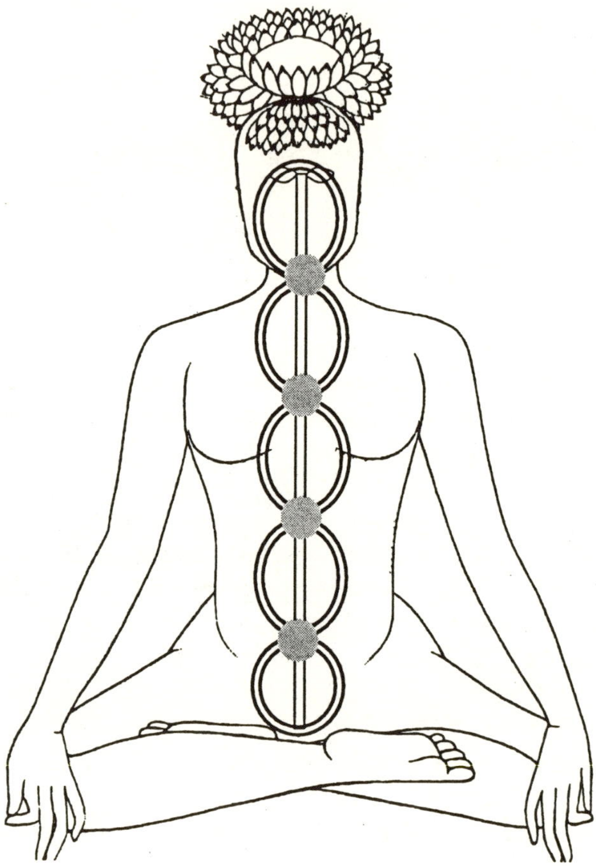

Figure 12b

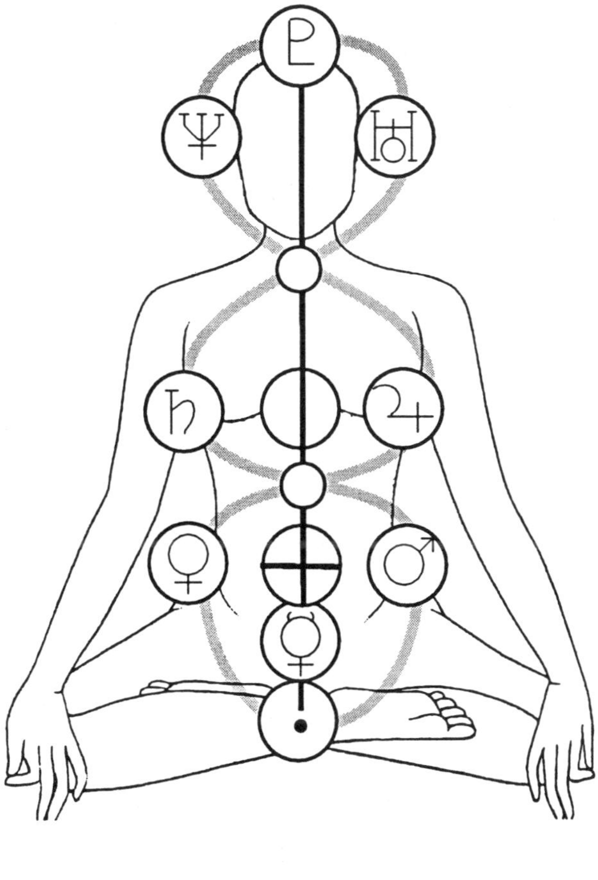

correspond to the head, thorax and abdomen. These three divisions are present in virtually all living creatures.

They are a direct reflection of the principles embodied by the three horizontal axes of the Tree. I shall start at the base of this structure, and work my way upwards. Each significant aspect will be expanded on as we come to it.

At the base of the spine we find the Sun, which represents the source of all creativity. It is most appropriate that the King archetype should be located at the root of the sacral area. Sacral has always signified that which pertains to the King.

The first horizontal axis is very crucial to understand. Venus and Mars fall perfectly in place over the Adrenal glands, which they rule. The cross-hairs of the Earth-Moon lie perfectly over the navel. This is the center of the gut, where the bulk of our assimilation takes place within the small intestines.

This axis contains the third, fourth and fifth planets respectively, and is representative of what the Pythagoreans call the 3-4-5 triangle! Here we have the foundational power axis of the human ego, which generates our *chi* force. These three planets share many other parallels besides the same axis.

Venus is virtually identical to Earth in size. It is often called the twin of the Earth. Mars, as mentioned in chapter 5, has virtually the same axial tilt as the Earth roughly 23.5 degrees. It also spins on its axis in the same 24 hour time frame.

Midway between the Sun and Moon is Mercury. Here we experience the awareness of the abdominal brain. This is situated three inches below the navel, and is known to the Buddhists as the ha-ra. I believe that these are the two primal sounds, chanted to invoke the combined Lunar-Solar energy of the gut. "Ha" is Lunar, Ha-thor, and "Ra" is obviously Solar, the name of the Egyptian Sun god.

The power of this chant invokes the awareness of the conception and fertility inherent within the new moon phase. This occurs when both luminaries are fused together in the act of copulation. The Ha-Ra is our sexual energy chakra, which is magically aroused by the ritual invocation of Mercury. It is interesting that the navel is the most evident proof of our birth into Earthly flesh. This is only possible through the reproductive urges of the Moon. Here we experience the "fire in the belly," that primal passion that drives us to crave both sex and food. This is the home of the Wildman archetype.

The Lunar cycle is responsible for creating peristalsis within our body. This is the rhythmic wave of contractions that move our food from the esophagus to the rectum. The circular motion of the Moon around the Earth (navel) can be seen by the circular path of the large intestine itself, which encircles the abdomen.

Mars and Venus also represent the physical expression of the pillars of Shu and Tefnut (dryness and moisture). For this reason they rule the kidneys which control water balance within the body.

The ovaries are located in this very same region, and owe much of their functions to the Yin-Yang energies of this Mars-Moon-Venus axis. I believe this is why each ovary tends to ovulate during alternate months.

As a whole, this lower region controls digestion, assimilation, elimination and regeneration. The abdominal cavity is largely instinctual by nature. It is concerned with our primary survival needs.

As we move out of the viscera we pass through a veil or barrier. This is known as the diaphragm, which physically separates the gut from the chest cavity. It is indicated, on the Tree, by the first point of crossing, the solar plexus.

In the solar system, this is represented by the asteroid belt, which is located between the orbits of Mars and Jupiter. It denotes a region of transition or interface, where we leave the physical and enter the emotional. The asteroid belt is populated by thousands of asteroids or minor planets, circling around the Sun as a scattered trail of rubble.

Their orbits are usually highly elliptical or oval shaped. It is interesting to note that all the central pillar components are both the smallest, and most erratically orbiting bodies in the solar system. Pluto, Chiron, the asteroids, the Moon and Mercury all have very many of the same magical qualities in common. They all comprise various aspects of the central magic wand of the Tree.

This zone of the asteroids can best be understood by looking at the entire realm of inner planets. The central "ego" structure of the solar system, which incorporates the Sun through Mars, can be seen as a living organism. The nucleus of this cell would be the Sun. We find that these asteroids act collectively in the same basic capacity as that of a cell membrane.

Here we find the castle wall of the King's domain. Mars patrols watchfully along its borders, always on guard against outside threats. The asteroids are predominantly Yin, and act as the protective feminine matrix of the ego. They decide who gets in and out of the castle, in much the same manner as a cell membrane regulates the passage of materials into and out of the cell.

In reality, there are thousands of asteroids spread out across the 360° arc of the sky. You can take your own birth chart and find numerous asteroids within every single degree of its zodiac. How do we know which ones are pertinent to our own personal reality?

The asteroids that become the activated receptor cells of our personal cell membrane are the ones that make contact with the angles of the chart, and the ten planets. Since there are so many asteroids, we read only those which are located within one degree of a planet or angle, thus keeping our focus strictly limited to those asteroids that are truly active. Whether asteroids are active or not is a purely hit or miss situation, which will keep their influence highly personal.[1]

The asteroid belt acts to create a kind of protective, magical static. This serves to initiate (interface) us with the emotional world of the thorasic area.

Entering the chest cavity, we find the principles of Jupiter-Saturn powerfully at work. Nowhere else in the body are the forces of expansion and contraction so evident as they are here! The heart and lungs are both ceaselessly working to keep us alive, through the assistance of these powerful principles. Without them, the heart would stop and the lungs would collapse.

The heart is the seat of the emotions and the understanding which they impart. The two most powerful emotions that teach us wisdom, are joy, Jupiter, and grief, Saturn. The Greeks understood the value of the theater as a classroom for these emotions of Jupiter-Saturn. It is from this, that the two faces of comedy and tragedy were created.

It is absolutely essential for us to experience both joy and grief in our life. In the process, our emotional spectrum is matured and expands into true wisdom. These are the only two emotions that lead to our developing of morals, values and character. From this balanced perspective, we can proceed further in our evolution towards the upper Mental-Spiritual realm.

The breath is inextricably connected to the emotions. With each breath, we experience both inflation (Jupiter) and deflation (Saturn). The breath is our secret teacher of the mystery of life and death. In meditating upon its rhythm, we can calm and balance our emotional world.

This sense of harmony we experience is realized within the eleventh (inferred) sphere, which lies directly over the heart. In chapter eleven we described this point as the place where the entire Tree is balanced. The heart truly is the King's chamber of the body.

The second point of crossing on the Tree marks the passage from the heart to the head. This is represented by the throat chakra, which is ruled by Chiron. This powerful little sphere is a recently discovered minor planet, found circling between the orbits of Saturn and Uranus.

It is interesting to note that Uranus rules the Thyroid, and Saturn governs the Parathyroids. These are both located in the throat, directly in front of the windpipe. Chiron represents an energy that "mediates" between the orbits of Uranus and Saturn. Its elliptical orbit carries it as far out as Uranus, and also brings it as close to us as Saturn.

It is for this very reason that I believe Chiron is the perfect mediator, or regulator, of the thyroid-parathyroid functions. These are very difficult energies to balance, and Chiron is perfectly suited for the task.[2]

Chiron was a teacher, healer and sage in Greek mythology. He taught horsemanship, hunting, archery and medicine, all survival skills, as well as music, philosophy and astrology. This planet combines the energies of the alchemical magician (Saturn) with the fierceness of the spiritual warrior (Uranus). In Mythology, Saturn was Chiron's father and Uranus his grandfather.

Chiron was a centaur, half man and half horse. Most centaurs were savage creatures, more beast than man. Chiron, however, was gentle and compassionate in his ways and, as a result, became the leader of the centaur race. He can thus be linked with the Wildman archetype, but a healed integrated Wildman known for his skill and wisdom. He represents the mastery of the human soul over the more primal animal roots from which we have evolved.

I believe that Chiron represents the purest essence of what Robert Bly describes as a male mentor or male mother. Many of the gods completely entrusted their young sons into his care. Chiron would raise them and love them as his own. He taught them all the skills they would need to become young men. In this capacity, he was the most esteemed initiator of the gods.

Chiron was referred to as an oracle. His wisdom was taught orally, hence his connection to the throat! Music, chanting and all forms of invocation come under his powerful magical influence. He is a high shaman, who fully knows the healing power of spells and incantations. Persistent infections of the throat are a sign that we posses a "wounded healer" archetype within us.

I have two close friends who both suffer from Grave's disease, a thyroid condition, usually caused by stress. They both have stressful aspects to all three planetary rulers of the thyroid region (Saturn-Uranus-Chiron). One of them has Uranus opposed Chiron, T-square to Saturn. The other has Mars opposed Chiron, Mercury opposed Saturn, and Moon opposed Uranus.

Many of the healing arts are named after Chiron. chiropractic being the most obvious of these. Interestingly enough, most chiropractors agree that the key to a good adjustment is a proper aligning of the cervical (neck) vertebrae. If this is achieved, then the rest of the spine can be easily adjusted.

Chiropractic also works predominantly with the spinal column. This is the central pillar of the Tree, expressed on a physical level. Chiron is an intricate part of the central pillar.

I believe that the Egyptian god who rules this planet was known as Anubis. He was represented as a jackal or wild dog. I base this parallel on the work of Robert K.G. Temple and his marvelous book "The Sirius Mystery."[3] He explains that Sirius, (also known as the Dog star) is part of a double star. It is orbited by Sirius-B which has a cycle of fifty years.

Temple reveals that the Egyptians named these two stars Isis and Nephthys. Their orbit of fifty years was represented by Anubis. Schwaller de Lubicz claims that the jackal fed on carrion. He therefore represents the principle of extracting life (Uranus) from dead flesh (Saturn). The orbit of Chiron is also 50 years in length, which directly connects him to the principles of Anubis.

This parallel also ties Chiron together with the myth of Jason and the 50 argonauts. Jason was Chiron's pupil. The centaur gave Jason his name, which means healer. Another one of Chiron's pupils, Actaeon, was eventually killed by his own pack of fifty hunting dogs! The connection to both fifty and to dogs are central to the meaning of this planet ruling the second critical crossing.

It is also worth noting that King Arthur has very many connections to the Chiron myth. He was a hunter and a warrior knight who was trained in the arts of war and horsemanship. He initiated young men into knighthood by teaching them all the aspects of chivalry. There were also fifty seats at his round table. This initiating energy of Chiron is incorporated into the myths of many different cultures.

Anubis, the Egyptian parallel to Chiron, was also known by a second name. The translation of this name *Ap-uat* means "opener of the ways." Here we see yet another obvious reference connecting Chiron-Anubis with the role of an initiator, one who opens pathways and leads us through.

As we interface into the upper realm, via Chiron, we enter the world of the mental and spiritual planes. The axis of Uranus-Neptune runs right through the third eye or sixth chakra! These two planets actually represent the two petals of the ajna chakra in the Hindu system.

This chakra corresponds with the pituitary gland. On a physical level, Jupiter and Saturn rule the functioning of this gland. Neptune is the higher vibration of Jupiter, and Uranus of Saturn. These two, therefore, correspond to the higher spiritual aspects of that gland (chakra).

Uranus is the highest form of left-brain thinking. It is fiercely individualistic and quick witted, bordering on pure genius. Neptune is the purest essence of right-brain reality, and represents our highest aspects of creativity and mystical inspiration. Neptune's genius is realized through surrendering to the collective.

When all the archetypes are balanced and evoked properly, then the pineal gland ignites. This corresponds to the highest chakra of the Hindu system known as the "thousand petaled lotus". The sacred power of Ra or Kundalini shoots up the central pillar and illuminates the mind. The enlightened consciousness of Pluto, the underworld, actually becomes one with the overworld of King Ra. The Egyptians spiritually understood this state, calling it the "Eye of Horus."

This was the path of the magician-priest of Amen-Ra. (Amen is an Egyptian word meaning "that which is hidden.") The young priest would take this hidden power of Pluto and merge it with the conscious power of the Sun-Ra. This, in effect, literally turned his world upside-down.

Here we understand the meaning of the Alpha and the Omega. Christ said, "The first shall become the last, and the last shall become the first." The actual tri-partite nature of our body and soul can bee seen in the symbolic Christian blessing. As you form the sign of the cross in the act of blessing oneself, you actually touch all three parts of your body and soul. We touch the third eye first, which is the seat of the father (Uranus-Yang pillar energy). The hand then comes to the navel, which is the son. This is really the nurturing energy of the Yin pillar.

The Yin pillar is always Mother and son. It is that nurturing pregnant energy symbolized by the virgin myths of Mary and Jesus, and Isis and Horus. Isis was the goddess of the Moon which rules the navel center. This is the location of the womb itself.

When Isis was referred to in her lunar form, she was called Hathor. The actual Egyptian name was Het-Hor (temple of Horus). The hieroglyph itself, was that of a hawk perched inside of a square temple (fig. 12c). Hathor represented the quadrated temple of the Earth-Moon. She symbolizes the womb from which the archetype of Horus arises to avenge his father, as Jesus arose to serve his father.

The final part of the Christian benediction is to cross the chest. In doing so, we divide the heart into its four chambers. These are the four directions of the Earth, within which the holy spirit may safely reside. The energy of the holy spirit emanates from the central pillar of the Tree. The heart is the place where we balance the head and gut, in order to gain true understanding. The Egyptians saw the heart as the location of a man's soul.

The tri-partite nature of the body and soul can also be seen in the mechanics of the brain. In his book *Homecoming,* John Bradshaw summarizes the brain research of Ronald Melzak. Melzak believes that the brain reflects the entire evolutionary history of consciousness within its design.[4]

These three parts are most commonly known as the cerebrum, cerebellum and medulla oblongata. The medulla is also called the brain stem and is located at the top of the spinal cord, as it enters the skull. It is referred to by Melzak as the visceral brain, and corresponds to the reptilian phase of our evolutionary experience (fig. 12d).

The most common creature that comes to mind is the serpent. All reptiles are strictly concerned with their own survival and reproduction. The instincts of this primary consciousness can be powerfully seen in our very own visceral serpent. This wisdom is physically stored within the thirty foot long coiled snake, which is better known as the intestinal tract. The medulla regulates the functions of these visceral memory banks.

The cerebellum evolved out of the medulla (reptile) phase of our evolution. Melzak calls this the paleo-mammalian brain. It sits on top of the brain stem and, as a result, contains access to all the evolutionary experience of the medulla in addition to its own functions.

During this early mammalian stage of our development, we learned to care for, and raise our offspring. This allowed for the developing of the first signs of compassion, nurturing and bonding. Melzak referred to this as the emotional brain, or the limbic system. The correspondence to the lunar autonomic nervous system is quite obvious.

The most recent phase of our evolution is called the neo-mammalian period. Here we find the development of an advanced thinking brain the

Figure 12c

Figure 12d

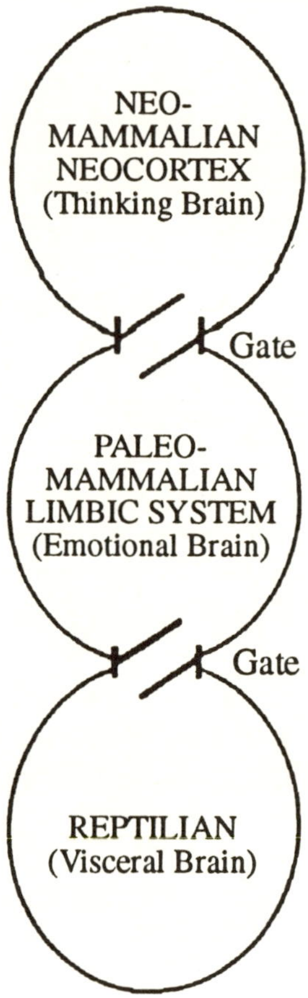

From *Homecoming: Reclaiming and Championing Your Inner Child* by John Bradshaw.

cerebrum. Humans and other higher mammals have the unique ability to reason and relate to their environment intelligently. They form more advanced social colonies, each with their own particular hierarchy, or government.

A human being is a complete walking, genetic library of his own historical roots. When healthy, he should have access to all his experiences. According to Melzak, this is possible via neuron gates that allow the three separate brains to inter-relate and talk to each other.

These gates are represented in our archetypal spiral by the two interfacing junctions, ruled by Chiron and the asteroid belt. Bradshaw explains that these neuron gates will shut down when the person is exposed to trauma or abuse. Through the course of time, if the abuse is persistent enough, they may become stuck in the closed position.

Melzak's diagram is amazingly similar to our Tree in all respects. His work only serves to emphasize the extreme importance of keeping the gates open. Astrologically speaking, this puts an entirely new emphasis on Chiron and the asteroids. Including and synthesizing them within the client's natal chart are paramount to the progressive astrologer's work.

In the future, I believe we will see many new shamanistic practices developing. The astrologer and psychologist of the 90s will best be able to help their clients by assisting them in their own personal magical journey towards self actualization.

The re-introduction of ritual and creative visualization will be an integral part of the methods used by the truly effective healers of the future. A close astrological colleague of mine, John Van Zandt, has already developed his own personal method of counseling clients in this way. Needless to say, he has Chiron very powerfully placed in his own birth chart.

John's life has taken a very shamanistic turn, both personally and professionally. His work is very transformative, centering closely around the synodic cycle. This is very poignant, because he was born during a full moon. His chart has Chiron conjunct with the Moon, opposed to the Sun, and squared to Saturn.

The synthesizing of Chiron into the understanding of my own natal chart has led to a most powerful awakening in my life as well. It sits exactly on the lower meridian of my chart, and colors the whole of my inner being. Chiron also conjuncts Venus/The Lover, is sextile to Mercury/The Magician, and quintile to the Moon.

The major interests in my own life have always been astrology, music and the healing arts. I have been a singer-songwriter and guitarist for more than half my life. My other passions—Egyptology, herbology, iridology and psychology—have occupied my attention for over fifteen years. I still remember building a scale model of the Great Pyramid in fourth grade!

Our spiral contains some amazing correlations with the Enneagram as well. This esoteric diagram was developed by Gurdjieff from Sufi mysticism. The Enneagram verifies our Tree numerically. It also reveals the three pillars in the process (fig. 12e).

The first feature that becomes readily apparent, is the equilateral triangle (trinity) composed of the numbers 3-6-9. These are the numerical values of the planets of the Yin pillar. This is the nurturing pillar of love, expressed on all three axes or planes of consciousness. It truly confirms to us that all you need is love.

The three remaining numbers, 5-7-8, on the left side of the Enneagram, are the 3 numerical values of the Yang pillar. Mars is the root of the Yang pillar, and connects by lines of force to both Saturn (7) and Uranus (8).

The final three numbers on the right hand side of the Enneagram represent the base of the Central pillar: Sun (1), Mercury (2) and Earth-Moon (4). At the top of our middle pillar is the number 10, Pluto. This confirms the fact that the central pillar represents the tetractys of Pythagorean thought. The Tetractys was a mystical equation which stated that:

$$1 + 2 + 3 + 4 = 10$$

Sun + Mercury + Yin pillar trinity + Earth/Moon = Pluto

Within this number sequence are all the central pillar planets.

Returning again to the Enneagram, we find an interesting hint of the significance of Chiron and Pluto. There are only two lines that cross-connect the left triad (5-7-8) with the right triad(1-2-4). The first line links 1 (Sun) with 7 (Saturn). The second one connects 2 (Mercury) with 8 (Uranus).

The key to this mystery is remembering that Chiron oscillates between the orbits of Saturn (7) and Uranus (8). It therefore can represent both of these numbers simultaneously. Here we have the perfect mediator or rainbow bridge. The Enneagram's line which connects 7 to 1, shows this vacillation between 7 and 8 (8 = 7 + 1).

Chiron allows the lower central pillar archetype of the Sun (1) to cross-over from right to left on the Enneagram. This, in effect, acts to transport the Solar consciousness up the middle pillar and mingle its power with

Figure 12e

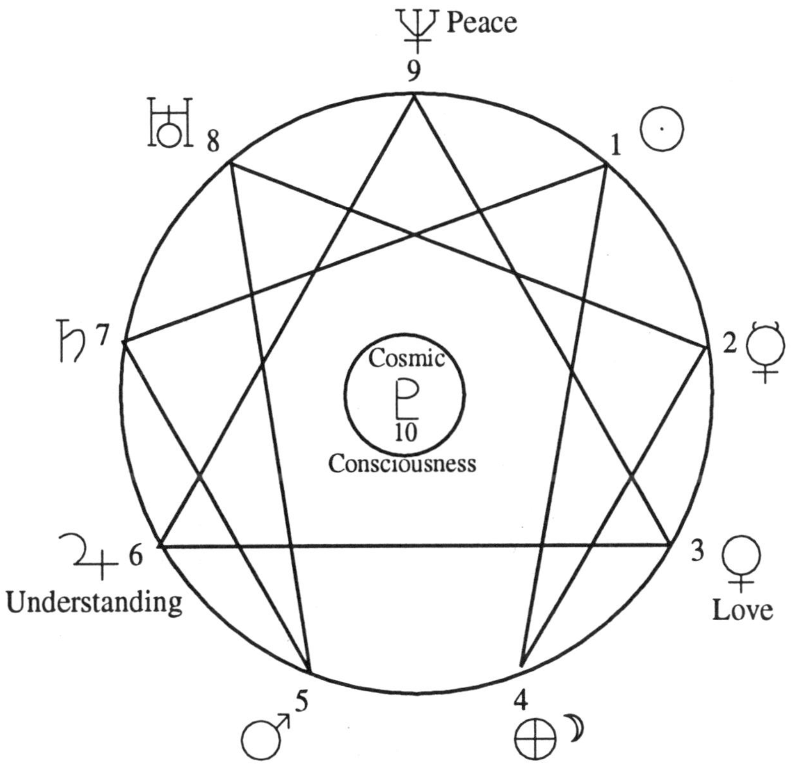

Peace
9
8
1
7
2
Cosmic
10
Consciousness
6
Understanding
3
Love
5
4

the principle of 7 (which in turn becomes 8). These are the highest aspects of the Yang pillar (Saturn-Uranus).

Many authors have referred to Chiron as a rainbow bridge, and the Enneagram helps illustrate this point. We see him acting in the capacity of an archetype that raises our awareness by octaves. He takes us from the 7th note (of dynamic tension) to the 8th note. He initiates us full circle. We have returned again to the beginning but are now an octave higher.

Chiron is one of only two places on the Tree where the energies of the Central and Yang pillars can experience a true relationship. The lower energy of Mars is bypassed. In so doing, Chiron represents a very high expression of the spiritual Warrior-Magician.

Pluto is the other place where Central and Yang pillar energies can be effectively blended. He is represented by the second crossing line of the Enneagram, which connects the numbers 2 and 8. These add up to Pluto (10). Here we find, contained within the crown of the Tree, the highest synthesis of the Spiritual-Warrior (Uranus) and the Magician (Mercury).

There is yet another interesting and significant application of our spiral. The Archetypal Tree can also be superimposed over the body in its inverted form (fig. 12f). We find that this symbolism also correlates nicely with the information laid down in the previous chapters.

The Sun represents the cerebrum and our conscious faculties. Mercury ties in with the voicebox or larynx. The dualistic nature of Mercury resonates through our 2 vocal chords! Hermes/Thoth has always been the spokesperson for Ra. His magical attributes combine well with Chiron, who oversees the functioning of the endocrines that lie directly on top of the voicebox.

The Earth-Moon rule the heart on a physical level. As alluded to earlier, the four quadrants of the Earth correlate nicely with the four chambers of the heart. Venus and Mars rule the blue and red blood which flows through opposite sides of the heart. These two halves are divided by the septum.

It is worth noting that the left side of the heart is larger than the right, and contains more muscle mass. It is not a truly symmetrical organ. I believe there is a definite reason for this.

If the quantity of muscle mass contained in the left side of the heart was compared to that of the right side, I would venture to say that the proportion of one to the other might possibly reflect the Pythagorean golden section or Phi. This mystical number is crucial in the proportioning of all living organisms.

Figure 12f

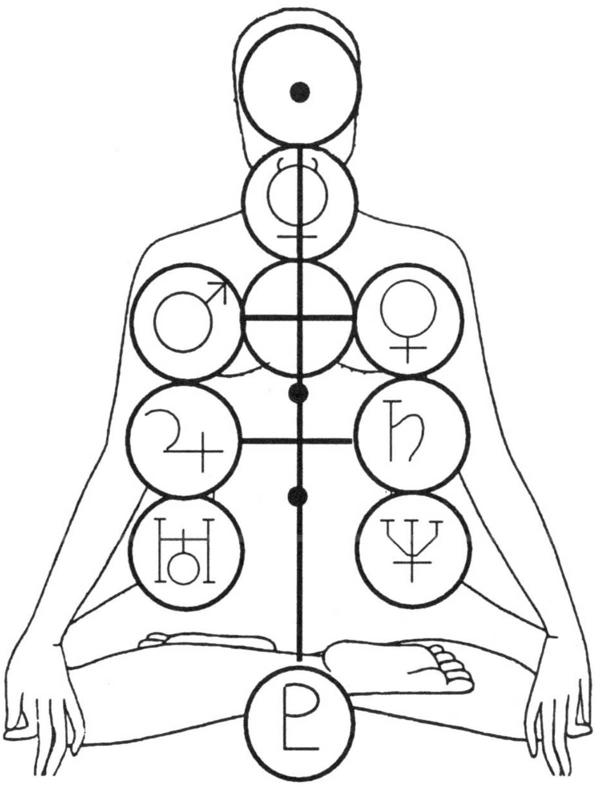

Phi is a mathematical proportion that can best be represented by means of a straight line (A-B). This line is then divided in such a way that the proportion of the smaller segment to the larger one is the same as the larger piece is to the whole. I believe that it represents the true relationship between Yin and Yang.

If the middle pillar was exactly in the mathematical center of the Tree, there would be no dynamic tension or Eros to bring about life. The universe would have remained neutral, or static, and evolution would simply not exist as a force. Phi actually represents a principle or process and not a number. Roughly speaking, on a mathematical level, it represents a proportion of 2 to 1 (2/3-1/3).

This proportion is amazingly revealed in the crown of our Tree. In Chapter 10 we pointed out that Charon was roughly half the size of Pluto. This puts them in a Phi(2:1) relationship. Here we truly see the forces of Yin-Yang(life) represented in their proper dynamic balance. Phi is that principle which allows for conception, re-evolution, and creativity, the very essence of Pluto and Charon.[5]

The Venus-Mars axis can be seen working within the thymus gland, which is positioned in front of the heart. Venus rules the overall functioning of this gland, as covered in Chapter 3. Mars answers her beckoning call by producing the army of immune factors that are issued forth to do battle on the cellular level.

The asteroid belt corresponds to the solar plexus. This is truly representative of that mystic place of divine static, which is composed of thousands of minor planets. They collectively mediate and translate a magical transformative power all their own. Among these is the power of the asteroid named Eros.

Jupiter correlates to the liver on a physical level. It aligns perfectly with this organ in the diagram. Saturn falls on top of the spleen which is ruled by the ringed planet. It also has some jurisdiction over the stomach as well. Here we see the corrosive acidic effect of Saturn upon proteins, acting to break them down. The bowel and the stomach are the two most acidic regions in the body, and Saturn's influence is attributable to both.

Chiron sits right on top of the navel center. In Greek mythology his grandmother was Gaia, the Earth, which rules this center as well. Even though both of these diagrams are starting from opposite ends of the body, they overlap with a wonderful common sense wisdom.

Neptune correlates nicely with the function of the mesenteric (lymphatic) system of the gut. The twenty-two foot coiled snake, which we call the small intestine, is where Neptune's principles of absorption and osmosis take place. Through the influence of some five million villi (fingerlike protrusions), the overall surface area of the small intestine covers more than five times the surface area of the skin.

Within each of these millions of villi, we will find a lacteal or lymph duct. These microscopic lymphatic sponges absorb fatty acids directly into the lymphatic system, which is the domain of Neptune.

Venus rules the mesenteric and portal veins, which return the nutrient rich blood from the gut to the liver. Neptune rules the finely dispersed venous capillaries that eventually merge into these larger veins. Neptune also corresponds to a wealth of lymph nodes in the groin and gut area.

Mars rules the larger mesenteric arteries which deliver fresh oxygenated blood from the heart to the intestines. As these arteries break up into finer and finer capillaries, Uranus takes over the task of delivering the fresh red Warrior's blood to each cell. He is the higher spiritual force behind the "fire in the belly."

Pluto co-rules the root chakra with the Sun. He is the generator of Tantric Kundalini as it rises within the sex glands. Pluto-Charon are the transformative powers of the collective unconscious manifesting through the primal urges of elimination and procreation-conception. This is why transits of Pluto offer us a chance to clean house and start over.

Pluto spiritually rules the dark secret depths of the uterus where conception miraculously occurs. The Moon physically rules over the functions of the uterus. This organ is centrally located in the abdomen, which correlates nicely with the fact that both of its ruling influences are central pillar archetypes.

Many of the lower abdomen's organ systems also reflect the 3-4-5 axis of the Tree. Venus (3) and Mars (5) rule the left and right extremes, and are joined in the middle by the Moon (4). As previously mentioned, the kidneys are also split left and right in the body. The physical axis which connects them are the two ureters that lead to the bladder.

The urinary bladder is centrally located and acts as a reservoir for the renal fluids. This connects its functions, quite obviously, with the Moon. The same 3-4-5 parallels can be made with the female reproductive organs. The ovaries are ruled by Mars-Venus. The physical axis connecting them would be the fallopian tubes, which lead to the uterus, ruled by the Moon.

The human body is an absolute poetic miracle on all levels. The exquisite beauty of its design can be appreciated by all. This information need not be limited just to those interested in medical astrology or metaphysics.

There are definite reasons why these two tri-partite spirals manage to overlap so well, even though they do start from opposite ends of the body. It is my belief that they represent the anima and animus of our soul. These are the two halves of the octahedron or the two overlapping triangles of the Star of David. We are dualistic beings on many different levels.

This chapter has been the longest and most involved so far. I truly hope that I have been able to avoid losing anyone along the way. The material may require re-reading, in order to let this onslaught of new ideas have a chance to sink deeper into your psyche. The more you learn of these associations, the better you can forge connections within your own physical being as influenced by your natal chart.

CHAPTER THIRTEEN

Astrological Aerobics

The whole purpose of aerobic exercise is to gradually warm up the muscles in preparation for a full-scale work out. That is what we shall attempt to do, in an astrological sense, within this chapter. Through the charts we examine, I will try to convey my methods of prioritizing and interpreting the information contained within each of them.

Although there are some definite guidelines to be followed, I personally shy away from any heavily systematized approach to astrology. There are many "cookbook" style approaches to astrological interpretation which ultimately serve only to restrict the astrologer's creative clarity. This creative clarity emanates from the right brain functions and must never become boxed in by excessive left brain dominance.

In my first draft of this book, I deliberately avoided using the charts of well-known people like Marilyn Monroe, Adolph Hitler and John F. Kennedy, precisely because their charts appear, ad nauseam, in so many astrology cookbooks. On working through the material, I decided to include several familiar charts after all, because although the charts have been done before, they've never been analyzed in this manner before. You may want to compare the charts of these familiar personalities to their interpretation in the cookbook of your choice to see just how different and more accessible my approach is.

In the following series of charts, I will teach you how to immediately pick out the most dominant factors contained within each of them. By knowing just what to look for, you can obtain a wealth of information before you even begin analyzing the chart in depth. You will soon discover that there is no definite order assigned to my interpretive guidelines. Each chart will dictate its own order of priorities.

The seasoned astrologer will notice that all of my charts are calculated in the Sidereal zodiac instead of the more popular Tropical one. As will be reiterated at the close of the chapter, the zodiac is essentially irrelevant to the purpose of my system. Either one will suffice for the simple process

Reference Key for All Charts

PLANET	SYMBOL	LONGITUDE	ASPECT	HARMONIC	KEY
Sun	☉		Conjunction	First	
Moon	☽		Opposition	Second	— — —
Mercury	☿		Trine	Third	———
Venus	♀		Square	Fourth	▬▬▬
Mars	♂		Quintile	Fifth	▪ ▪ ▪ ▪ ▪
Jupiter	♃		Sextile	Sixth	— — — -
Saturn	♄		Septile	Seventh	- - - - - -
Chiron	⚷		Octile	Eighth	
Uranus	♅		Novile	Ninth	
Neptune	♆				
Pluto	♇				
Ascendant	ASC.				
Midheaven	M.C.				

of positioning the planets within the chart. My use of the Sidereal zodiac is simply a leftover preference from my days of membership within the Fagan/Allen school of thought. It offers me the luxury of not having to correct for precession when doing forecasting work for my clients.

At the end of this chapter, I will give instructions on how to convert a "standard" astrological chart into my type of chart system. This will allow you to interpret your own birthchart, or any other birthchart, according to my methods. We shall find that this conversion is a relatively simple and straightforward process.

Robin Williams

We shall start with the chart of a celebrity whose personality was already alluded to back in Chapter 8. I described Robin Williams as a Uranian type. It was only later, when I cast his chart, that I realized just how right I was!

As we begin to examine his chart, there is one important feature that should be looked at first. I call it the "quadrant distribution" of planets. These numbers, located at the lower left of the chart, indicate the total number of planets contained within each quadrant of that chart. Any variations from a normal random distribution should be duly noted.

The first factor that can be immediately determined from the quadrant distribution is whether the person has any marked predisposition towards either extroversion or introversion. Robin has a total of three planets below the horizon and a whopping eight above! This reveals a very marked predisposition to be extroverted in nature.

The extrovert thrives in the outer, public world. The bulk of his planetary archetypes receive their stimulation from outside sources. The extrovert is most at home when in the public eye. He receives his most powerful validation through the approving accolades of others.

William's personal planets (Sun, Mercury, Venus and Mars) are all located in the most elevated region of the chart: near the mid-heaven. This indicates an extreme need for the approval of others. Much of his sense of self esteem and Ego comes directly from this public acknowledgement. When an extrovert is cut off from this external source of validation, they will usually wind up feeling uncomfortably empty and insecure inside.

The next thing to look for is any quadrant that contains a heavy concentration of planets (five or more). Here the Warrior quadrant is quite busy with five planets located there. This is an indication of a

Name: Robin Williams Birthdate: 7/21/51 Time: 1:34 pm Place: Chicago, IL

C.D.T.

Zodiac: Sidereal

Longitude: 87 W 38

Chart Type: Natal

Latitude: 41 N 53

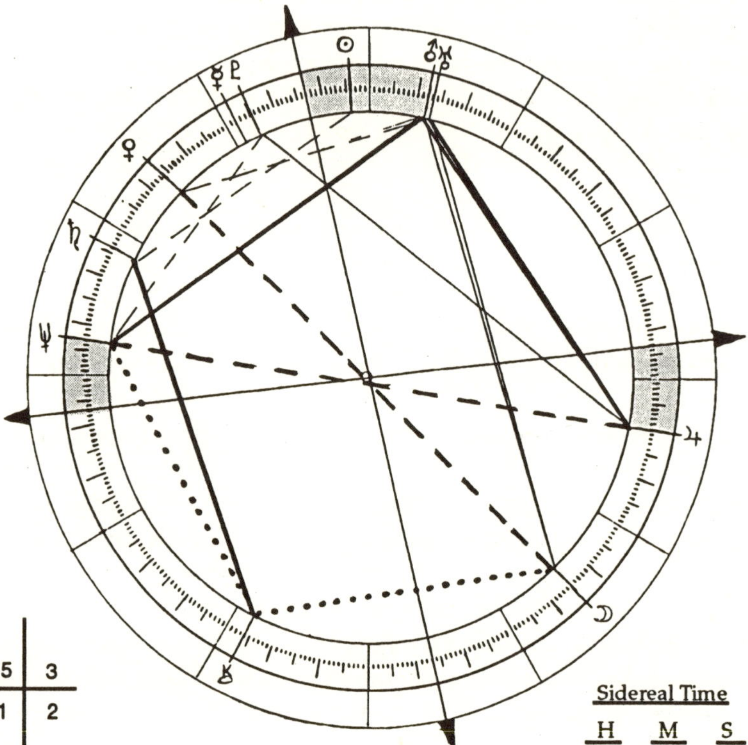

5	3
1	2

Quadrant Distribution

Sidereal Time

H	M	S
8	38	20

person who is very self motivated and dynamic. They don't wait for things to happen, they make them happen. They contain tremendous drive and are constantly in motion trying to achieve some personal goal. They can sometimes be headstrong and bulldoze others with their intense willpower.

After noting the variations in quadrant distribution, we should now concern ourselves with any planets located within the Gauquelin power zones. These zones house the planets most proximal to the four angles of the chart. This cross is indicative if the quadrated nature of the Ego structure. Any planetary archetype that is closely aligned with these four angles becomes a leading actor in the play of our live's drama. We will identify strongly with these angular archetypes in terms of how we define ourselves.

Williams's most angular planets are the Sun as well as the Mars/ Uranus conjunction. They are located in the power zone associated with the King quadrant. To have the actual planet which embodies the King archetype (the Sun) located within the power zone of the King quadrant is a very significant arrangement. It places a double emphasis on the King archetype.

The Sun could not possibly be located in a more powerful spot. He is completely exalted on his throne of the mid heaven, where he can bestow his brilliance and blessing upon all who behold him. This is reminiscent of the Biblical saying: when one has a lamp, he does not hide it under a bushel. He places it high upon a hill for all to behold. As a performer, Williams must feel a tremendous need for others to behold this brilliance which he undoubtedly senses very powerfully within himself.

The planets located in this upper power zone of the King often have much to say about one's career. They help to significantly define the type of blessing or gift that we feel it is our destiny to give to the world. If we are living our life's true purpose, our career will powerfully embody our particular "calling" in life.

Adjacent to the Sun, Williams also has a Mars/Uranus conjunction. Mars represents the immediate personal sense of the Warrior archetype. Uranus represents the immense spiritual aspects to the Warrior that lie more within the unconscious level of our psyche. When the two combine forces, the effect is extremely powerful. The result is a person who fights energetically (Mars) to break down and rebelliously destroy all repressions of freedom (Uranus).

The Mars/Uranus type refuses to be hemmed in and often has difficulty dealing with authority. They are staunch individualists and are constantly challenging the status quo through shocking people's sense of complacency. "Freedom above all else" is the credo by which they live.

There is a down side to this planetary pair as well. When in conjunction, their energies combine in a very subjective way. The native is very rarely fully conscious of how these rebellious urges can run him around by the nose. They are often daredevils at heart and pure suckers for living life on the edge. The Mars/Uranus type craves instant gratification and intensity in all that he does. This can lead to fixations with gambling and the quick buzz drugs like crack and cocaine.

The blessing, and the curse, of the angular Mars/Uranus configuration is that these people want to live life as a "pedal to the metal" experience *all the time.* They have no time for useless activities like sleeping. There is simply too much life to be lived! The major lesson that Robin Williams has had to learn in his life is temperance, all things in moderation. His admitted bout with cocaine addiction is ample testimony to this.

Williams's comedy style is so blatantly Uranian in nature that he makes an excellent case study. He loves changing gears by engaging in sudden, shocking segues from one topic to another. He is unpredictable and uncompromisingly blunt at times. This Mars/Uranus conjunction does not act completely alone in this case. It is moderated by the influences of many other planets (archetypes).

After taking note of the angular planets in a chart, the next order of business is to see if these archetypes are further influenced through their connection, via aspects, to any other planets. It is also necessary to start looking for any larger amalgams of planets. The bulk of these multiple archetypal alignments usually happen in various groups of three. I like to refer to them as "triangulated power structures."

These larger lattice grids are equivalent to corporate monopolies and are immensely powerful and richly diverse. Williams has one of these common patterns present within his chart. It is called a T-Square. It is a triangle formed by the Mars/Uranus conjunction being exactly perpendicular (90°) to both ends of the Jupiter/Neptune opposition.

Any opposition brings with it the tremendous opportunity for complete awareness of the two planets in question. Williams possesses the potential to be completely aware of a blending between the archetypes of Jupiter (expansiveness, optimism, faith, joviality and gregariousness) and that of Neptune (spiritual, intuitive, vulnerable, impressionable and impressionistic).

This opposition lends itself powerfully to his talents as a very respectable actor. One can observe that the planets which make up the three corners of this T-square are all in angular power spots! This simple fact allows the whole of this structure to access the outside world. This incredible arrangement allows Williams's Warrior archetype (Mars) to be powerfully supercharged through dynamic contact with three of the four outer gaseous planets (Uranus-Neptune-Jupiter).

Neptune is situated nicely within the power zone of the Warrior quadrant. This rising planetary archetype strongly colors the way in which Williams appears to act and interface with his environment. The Neptune rising person can fool anyone. They are like an amoeba or a chameleon. They adapt through a process of osmosis and flow with their immediate environment. This is where Williams's tremendous ability to ad-lib and improvise comes from.

Additional factors to consider are the Moon/Venus opposition and the Mercury/Pluto conjunction. Although neither is angular, their influences are integrated through aspects to his angular planets. Moon/Venus indicates a powerful awareness of love (Venus) for his mother (Moon) and nature in general. Frequently, this opposition can signify an awareness of separation or distancing from the mother, emotional and/or physical. (See Krishnamurti — Chapter 14)

The Magician archetype (Mercury) is conjunct with Pluto the god of the underworld. This planetary combination can often lead to mental aberrations as tremendous upwellings of material from the collective unconscious (Pluto) blend with the conscious mind (Mercury). This subjective fusion of the two worlds can cause the native to feel crazy and remote from others. They feel that nobody could possibly fathom the darkness of their secret thoughts. The potential for paranoia is obvious.

Williams channeled this energy beautifully into the role he played in *The Fisher King*. The Mercury/Pluto conjunction provided the rich source of his ability to so convincingly portray his character. We even got to see his Wildman archetype (Moon) express itself boldly (trine to Mars/Uranus) when his character danced around naked in central park under the full Moon!

There are still other background influences that can be interpreted (Saturn and Chiron). As I don't want to spend too much time on any one chart at this point, I will leave it to the reader to complete the delineation. This should challenge you to develop your own skills at reading charts. I can also suggest that the reader complete the remainder of the book and then come back to these charts in order to test their familiarity with this new method.

Bobby Fischer

Our next subject was also briefly mentioned in Chapter 8. Bobby Fischer is one of America's most enigmatic celebrities. During the early 70s he captured the imagination of the country as he rocketed toward the World Chess Championship. I was 14 at the time and can still remember watching the analysis of the games on television. Everyone seemed to be caught up in the excitement as chess became the rage.

At first glance, we can see that Fischer's chart has eight planets above the horizon. This would classify him as an extrovert. Some might be inclined to argue this point vehemently because of his reclusive lifestyle since retiring from competition in 1972. His choice of this hermit-like existence is due more to his innate rebelliousness and Egoic arrogance than to any sense of real introversion. This will become apparent as we proceed.

Fischer's chart contains five planets within the Warrior quadrant. This automatically gives him an inner attunement to the aggressive, self-assertive nature of the planet Mars. Mars is, itself, quite prominent through its angular placement within the Lover power zone. Already, we have a strongly reinforced theme of a very competitive personality due to the powerful presence of these Martian influences.

His chart also contains four other angular planet archetypes (Venus, Neptune, Jupiter and Pluto). This will rather complicate and enrich the diversity of his Ego. With Venus located in the King power zone, it is no wonder that America fell in love with the young prodigy from Brooklyn. Our endearment was soon to decay into a love/hate relationship due to the simultaneous angularity of both Venus and Mars. His brilliance enthralled us, yet his arrogance insulted us!

Unfortunately, Mars is much more powerfully aspected than Venus. As a result, it took over the leading role within his personality as time went along. As much as the extroverted Fischer needed the approval of the public for his self esteem, the growing rebel within him sabotaged a promising career, causing him to thumb his nose at the world and disappear in a huff.

This rebelliousness is powerfully generated by a complicated inner structure, of which Mars is an integral part. The structure alluded to is a four planet pattern composed of Mars, Uranus, Neptune and Pluto. In

Name: Bobby Fischer Birthdate: 3/19/43 Time: 2:39 pm C.W.T. Place: Chicago, IL

Zodiac: Sidereal Longitude: 87 W 39

Chart Type: Natal Latitude: 41 N 52

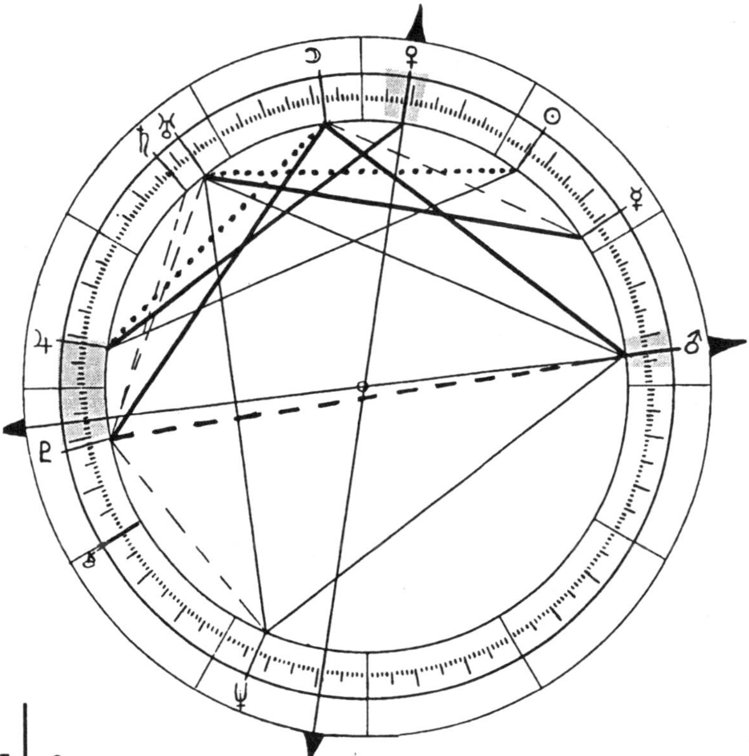

5	3
3	0

Quadrant Distribution

Sidereal Time

H	M	S
0	54	53

its totality, this pattern looks very much like a kite. The "spinal cord" of this kite is the Opposition aspect between Mars and Pluto. This is a highly volatile combination of archetypes and presents immediate potential for difficulties.

Mars (the Warrior) is quite aggressive in his own right. When combined with Pluto, it tends to sway the native towards the dominant tendencies inherent within Pluto's desire to control and manipulate others. Fischer would grow increasingly aware, through this Opposition, of his Warrior's ability to intimidate and subversively control others. When Pluto does not get what he wants, he will go underground in an attempt to secretly obtain it.

This Opposition is further modulated by the incredible Grand Trine between Mars, Uranus and Neptune. This adds fuel to the fire by connecting the highly sensitive and reactionary natures of Uranus and Neptune to the Warrior archetype. This puts the entire outer trinity of Unranus/Neptune/Pluto in direct contact with Mars. This is an awful burden for anybody's Warrior archetype to deal with.

We must break the Grand Trine down in order to analyze it completely. The Trine between Mars and Uranus connects the physical and spiritual Warriors together. Recall that Robin Williams has this pair in conjunction. The Trine, by comparison, offers a harmonious, flowing connection where the rebellious energy of Uranus effortlessly empowers Mars with an even more uncompromising nature. This was from where Fischer got his stubborn competitive spirit that refused to allow him to lose. It also had much to contribute to his downfall as well.

The Trine between Mars and Neptune further inflamed his Warrior through its attunement to this emotionally sensitive planet. The Neptunian fear of betrayal found its way into the Warrior's bag of fears. This paranoia plagued Fischer as he frequently would accuse other players of cheating through various means. Even recent interviews have him throwing bitter accusations at the Russians.[1]

As if this wasn't enough, Fischer has the Moon in a T-Square arrangement with his Mars/Pluto Opposition. The highly emotional and reactionary nature of the Moon becomes the "odd man in" adding additional energy to the equation. It also reflects Fischer's often abrasive relationship with his mother. His mother (the Moon) was at odds because of her square aspect to the two key focal points of his "kite" formation (Mars and Pluto).

Fischer's mother frequently embarrassed and enraged him by constantly seeking donations for his budding chess career from wherever she could. She often went behind his back, which a Mars/Pluto person like Fischer would find outrageous. Pluto hates to be outmaneuvered and controlled by others. He is much more comfortable doing the controlling himself.

Having the Mars/Pluto Opposition laying right across the horizon of the chart is why this whole setup is so unavoidably volatile. The horizon of any chart depicts our methods of "action" (through the ascendant's Warrior power zone) and "reaction" (through the descendant's Lover power zone). The central axis of symmetry, in Fischer's kite formation, is inextricably connected with his immediate environment (the Earth).

The end result is that Fischer reacts to others through his highly inflamed angular Warrior archetype (Mars). On the other hand, we might expect his actions to be somewhat dictated by Jupiter since it is located within the Warrior power zone. In this case, however, Pluto will overpower Jupiter because of its involvement with this crucial kite pattern. Fischer's manner of "acting" towards others is therefore likely include the secretive, subversive planning tactics of an all out revolutionary. He must win at all costs even if that means self-banishment in order to prove his point!

Leo Buscaglia

Leo Buscaglia is famous for his books and teachings on the subject of love. Over the years he has clung firmly to his belief in his simple message. Here we have an excellent opportunity to test our theories.

Since Buscaglia's message is so streamlined and specific, we should expect to find some evidence of a highly developed "Lover" archetype within his personality. Well, we don't have to look far to notice that Venus (the Lover) is angular and therefore quite active. She resides within the angular power zone of the Lover's very quadrant! This is where Venus is exalted and can express her nature most optimally.

Looking further still, we should immediately notice the Grand Trine connecting Neptune, Jupiter and the Mercury/Chiron conjunction. Any time there is a Grand trine you have a powerful triangulated harmony between the archetypes. To understand the specifics of this, we must examine the planets that compose the Grand Trine. In Buscaglia's case, he is considerably more fortunate than Bobby Fischer. The planets composing Buscaglia's Grand Trine are a lot more compatible by nature than Fischer's combination.

Gazing at Buscaglia's arrangement, we can see that Mercury is an integral component of the Grand Trine. This is poignant because one of

Name: Leo Buscaglia Birthdate: 3/31/24 Time: 11:00 pm Place: Los Angeles, CA

P.S.T.

Zodiac: Sidereal Longitude: 118 W 15

Chart Type: Natal Latitude: 34 N 04

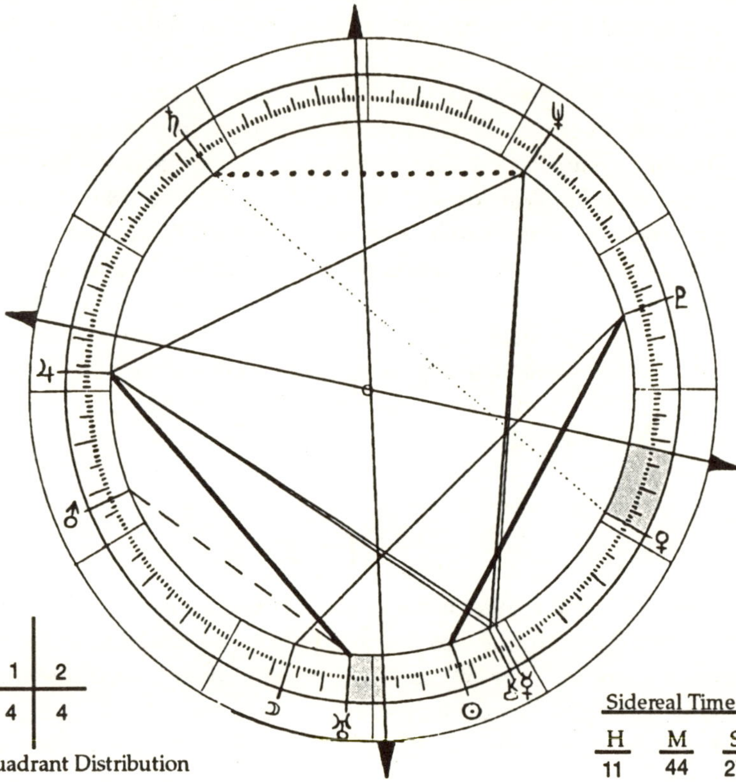

1	2
4	4

Quadrant Distribution

Sidereal Time

H	M	S
11	44	27

Buscaglia's most emphatic beliefs is that love is a "learned behavior."[2] In his own personal reality map, this is certainly the case! He cannot help but expound this viewpoint. His Magician archetype (Mercury) is wired directly into the wisdom of both Jupiter and Neptune.

These two planets, together with Venus, compose all three aspects of the 3-6-9 Lover trinity which makes up the left pillar of the Archetypal Tree. Buscaglia is tapped into an awareness of love which spans the entire spectrum from the most physically tangible (Venus), on past the expansively inspirational (Jupiter) and ultimately arriving at the most sublimely spiritual (Neptune).

The presence of Chiron in this Grand Trine will serve to modify the agenda of the Magician archetype (Mercury). Because Chiron is fused with this planet, this indicates the burning purpose behind Mercury's choosing to "learn" about love. The whole reason for this is to heal others and oneself with this knowledge. Buscaglia's chart is short and sweet and to the point, just like his teachings!

Joseph Campbell

Joseph Campbell is responsible for single handedly inspiring millions of people, worldwide, to reexamine the myths of our antiquity. He spent his life educating himself in all aspects of ancient cultures, mythologies and spiritual practices. Many have benefited from his teachings, praising him as a pioneer in documenting the many parallels which connect these seemingly different cultures.

Robert Moore is one who refers to Campbell's work quite often. In fact, it was due to a lecture of Moore's that I was inspired to look into Joseph Campbell's chart. Moore was speaking on the various archetypes and stated that he believed that Joseph Campbell was well developed within the Lover and Magician and not very fond of Warrior and King energy. I decided, based on his viewpoint, to look into it myself using the astrological chart to either confirm or dispute Moore's assertions.

As we can well see, Moore was right on the money. If we look at the quadrant distribution of planets, we will note that the Lover quadrant is by far the most busy (with six planets residing there). Venus herself is found comfortably within her own quadrant. If we look to the Lover power zone, we find Mars on the fringe and the triple conjunction of Sun/Mercury/Jupiter right in the heart of it! This tempers the extroverted tendencies of both the Warrior and King archetypes because of their more passive (Yin) locations within the chart. The two envoys of

Name: Joseph Campbell Birthdate: 3/26/04 Time: 7:25 pm E.S.T. Place: New York, NY

Zodiac: Sidereal

Chart Type: Natal

Longitude: 74 W 00

Latitude: 40 N 43

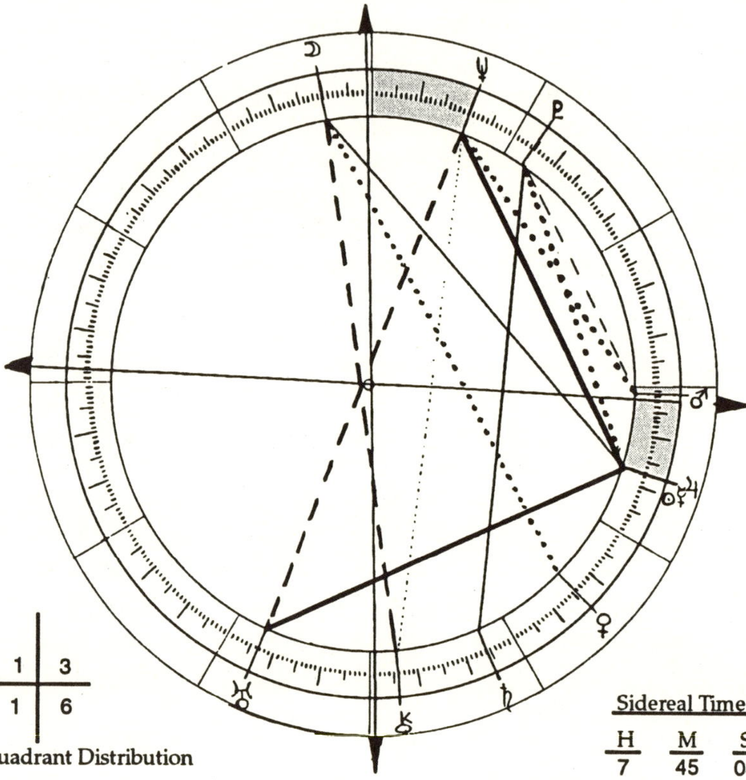

1	3
1	6

Quadrant Distribution

Sidereal Time

H	M	S
7	45	03

King energy (Sun/Jupiter) are mellowed by their placement within the Lover power zone, as is Mars. These normally assertive, expansive archetypes are pacified as a result. The same can be said of the rebellious Warrior nature of Uranus which is introverted through its sublimated placement within the Magician power zone.

The Magician archetype is wonderfully empowered through its conjunction with both Sun and Jupiter as well as its angular placement right within the heart of the Lover power zone. In addition to this, Mercury is in dynamic Square aspect to Neptune. This gives Campbell a direct understanding of the mystically sublime world of the spiritual Lover (Neptune). Neptune is also regally placed right in the center of the King power zone.

Campbell's gift to the world, his purpose for being here, was ultimately spiritual, thus his credo to "follow your bliss"! Through his magnificent placement of Neptune, he enchanted us with his wonderful versions of classic stories and myths. His excitement in telling them was generated by the square of Mercury/Sun/Jupiter to Neptune. It is further enhanced throughout the Opposition of Uranus to Neptune as well. This Opposition gave him an awareness of an unconventional (Uranus) view of spirituality (Neptune) that he was able to communicate directly through the T-Squaring influence of Mercury.

The fusion of Jupiter with Mercury always brings with it the potential to strive for the highest quality expressions of wisdom in one's pursuit of such. Joseph Campbell certainly achieved this. He succeeded in causing many a person to fall in love with the wonders of mythology as a medium for transmitting timeless spiritual wisdom.

Robert Moore

The reader should, by now, be well acquainted with the work of this man. Robert Moore's chart gives wonderful testimony to the undeniable influence of quadrant distribution and angularity. The first thing that should be immediately noticeable to us is that all of his planets are located on the left side of the meridian. This has tremendous significance in determining basic dispositions crucial to the native's outlook on life.

Just as a concentration of planets above, or below the horizon determines the degree of extroversion or introversion respectively, a concentration of planets to the left or right of the meridian has an impact on the personality as well. The right half of the chart represents a passive Yin

Name: Robert Moore Birthdate: 8/13/42 Time: 6:28 am C.W.T. Place: Little Rock, AR

Zodiac: Sidereal

Chart Type: Natal

Longitude: 92 W 17

Latitude: 34 N 45

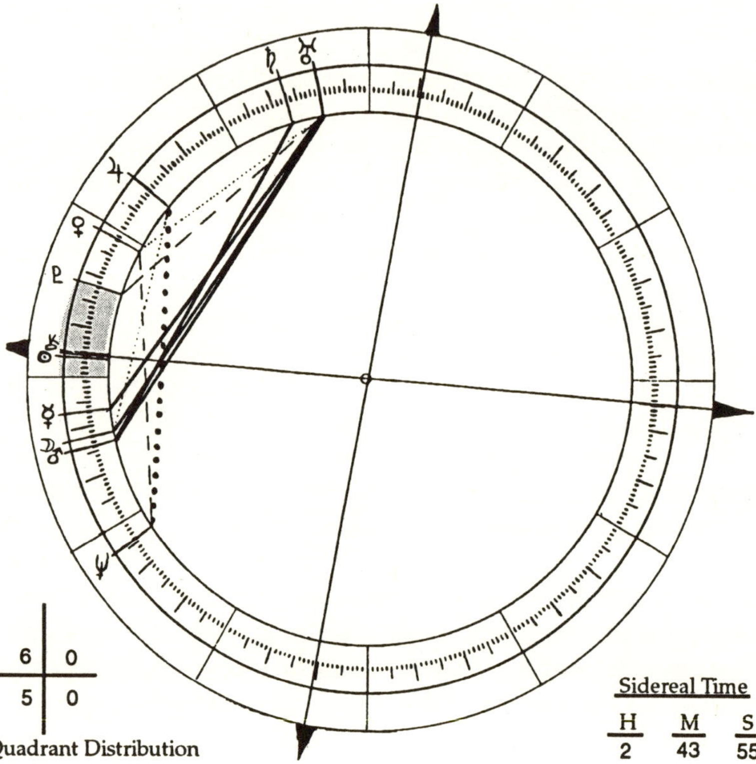

6	0
5	0

Quadrant Distribution

Sidereal Time

H	M	S
2	43	55

energy, because a planet will be setting or waning in energy when located there.

In Moore's case, all of his archetypes are on the left side of the meridian. This half of the chart represents an energy which is quite active and assertive by nature. This "Yang" energy is decidedly masculine in tone and concerned with coming into being or "becoming."

The whole thrust of Moore's work centers around his development of a psychology based distinctly around masculine issues and the men's movement. The basic orientation of his chart precludes him from seeing life any other way. This means that the wisdom of his "feminine" planetary energies (Moon/Venus/Neptune) will be imparted to him through various masculine forms of experience and initiation.

This is the chart of a man with a pioneering spirit and a keenly developed intelligence due to the high numbers of planets occupying the Warrior and Magician quadrants. Most therapists must have a strongly developed Magician archetype in order to be accomplished at their craft. Moore's Mercury is comfortably located within the Magician quadrant and squared off to Uranus. This gives his intelligence the ability to regenerate itself through venturing into exciting and unexplored terrain (Uranus).

Moore's angular planet/archetypes really tell the whole tale. Here we find a Sun/Chiron conjunction and the enigmatic Pluto all residing within the Warrior power zone. This zone will succinctly determine the way(s) in which we "act" in terms of the first impression that we seek to impose onto others.

This could be interpreted in the following straightforward manner: I act in the capacity of a healer, mentor and initiator (Chiron) of men. I strive to embody a Kingly manifestation of blessing towards others (Sun) that will empower them in the pursuit of inner wisdom (Pluto). Moore would only be capable of such a task through having accomplished some degree of this ongoing process within his own life. I, for one, approve of and applaud his responsible methods for helping men to reclaim a healthy and mature form of masculinity within their own lives.

Jimi Hendrix

Jimi Hendrix was one of the most gifted rock musicians ever to sling a guitar around his neck. He pioneered an entirely new sound that caught the ears of other famous rockers who attended his concerts, leaving them in complete awe. His music was innovative, passionate and hypnotic.

Name:	Jimi Hendrix	Birthdate: 11/27/42	Time: 10:15 am	Place: Seattle, WA

Zodiac: Sidereal

Chart Type: Natal

P.W.T

Longitude: 122 W 20

Latitude: 47 N 36

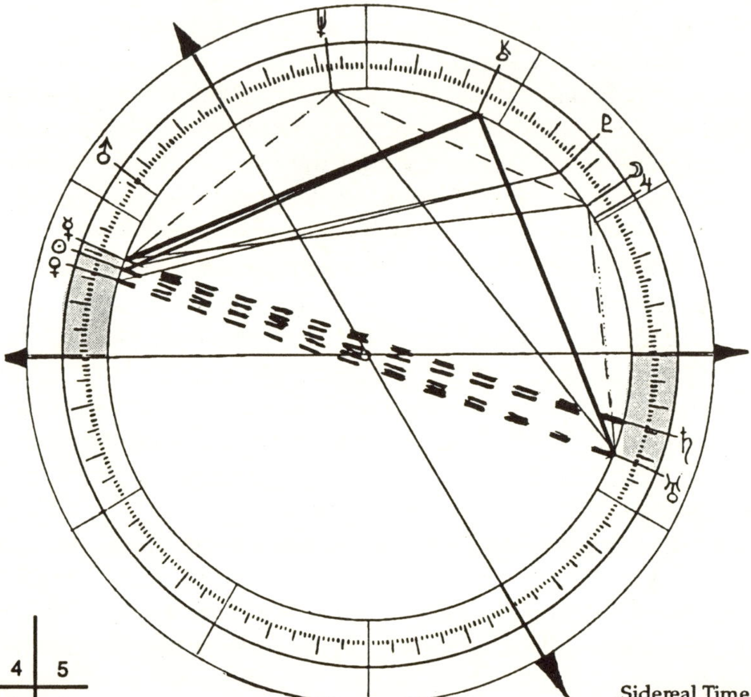

4	5
0	2

Quadrant Distribution

Sidereal Time

H	M	S
13	29	36

The most striking feature of his chart is that five of his eleven planets are involved in a massive complex of interlocking Opposition aspects. This central hub, or axis, of his personality generated a tremendous amount of Magician energy. Both planets which resonate Magician energy (Mercury/Saturn) are part of this huge Oppositional structure. This gave him a powerful predisposition towards the pursuit of awareness and wisdom. He saw himself as a powerful alchemist.

In many of his songs, Hendrix often referred to himself as a magical boy or child. The mind-expanding drugs which he took only served to fuel this awareness of inner Magical abilities. He viewed himself as *experienced* in this inner realm. His lyrics often fantasized of buying entire towns, making love to women and of leveling mountains with his bare hands and fashioning islands from the debris (*Voo Doo Chile* and *Hear My Train a Comin*).

All these fantasies are primarily radiating out of his triple conjunction of Venus (making love), Mercury (the magic boy) and the Sun (the creator of all, re-shaping matter). This triple conjunction generates plenty of energy all on its own. The fact that it is Opposed to the Uranus/Saturn conjunction makes his awareness of its presence even that much more pronounced.

This whole arrangement is further fueled by the fact that both ends of this huge five planet Opposition are located within power zones! The Venus/Mercury/Sun conjunction finds a very active mode of expression through the Warrior power zone. We can thus infer that Hendrix acted in the capacity of a Lover, King and Magician who was completely aware of this uniqueness (Opposition to Uranus).

Hendrix was a legend among the throngs of "groupie" women who traveled and slept with famous musicians. He was rumored to have been blessedly endowed and passionately prolonged between the sheets! Aside from having an active Lover archetype, Hendrix was seen as a shining star whose light was too brilliant and burned out too quickly (Sun Opposed Uranus). Many also felt that he was a lyrical prophet of freedom and unrestricted awareness (Mercury Opposed Uranus). Unfortunately the negative repercussions of drugs brought an end to his grandiose fantasies of self.

Jimi Hendrix was human after all. Unfortunately he failed to integrate the urgent message of Chiron to heal the inherent grandiosity of this overpowered Opposition. Chiron is T-Squared to this entire 5 planet Opposition. Chiron is energetically challenging Hendrix to heal the wounds to his King, Magician and Lover archetypes. Many of a man's King wounds center around issues with his own father.

Had Hendrix tended to this inner source of pain, he might have regenerated his life instead of self-destructing through his overinflated self concept. The defense mechanism of his grandiosity never allowed him to come down out of the high chair. In living up to his public image, he abandoned his true self and all hopes of inner healing. The sadness of this abandoned hope can still be heard echoing amidst the bittersweet notes of his blues, forever captured in time.

Marilyn Monroe

Marilyn Monroe is one of the most famous sex symbols in American history. She was beautiful, desirable and oh so sensual. One would naturally expect her to have a very pronounced Lover archetype (Venus). Upon first glance, it can be quickly determined that Venus is the most angular planet in her chart. It sits quite exalted within the power zone of the King quadrant.

Persons who have Venus placed here have a strong need to be publicly appreciated and valued for their beauty in some way, be it looks and/or inner beauty. Because of this extroverted placement of Venus, Marilyn was able to publicly display and embody the full spectrum of the Lover's sensuality. It was her calling and ultimately her career.

Venus connects, via Quintiles, to both the Moon and Pluto/Persephone. This means that, as an actress, she was able to willfully call upon her Wildwoman archetype (the Moon) to help empower the Lover within her. This vivacious spontaneity was readily perceivable in many of the roles she played. At other times she could just as willfully create the innocent pouting Persephone with the simple batting of an eyelash!

Her inner awareness of the Lover was also powerfully fueled by the Opposition of Neptune and the Moon. Neptune is the idealistic, ethereal, dreamy Lover that always has her head in the clouds. Having the Moon so close to the descendant gave Marilyn a strong emotional need for relationship. This placement of the Moon, and its opposition to the idealistic Neptune, drove her to marry many men. She was searching for that elusive Mr. Right, driven by her inner Neptunian fantasies.

Unfortunately the T-squaring position of Saturn would not allow any happy endings to this pursuit. It threw a monkey wrench in her dreams by constantly challenging them, challenging her to see beyond them. Her

Name: Marilyn Monroe Birthdate: 6/1/26 Time: 9:30 am P.S.T Place: Los Angeles, CA

Zodiac: Sidereal

Chart Type: Natal

Longitude: 118 W 15

Latitude: 34 N 03

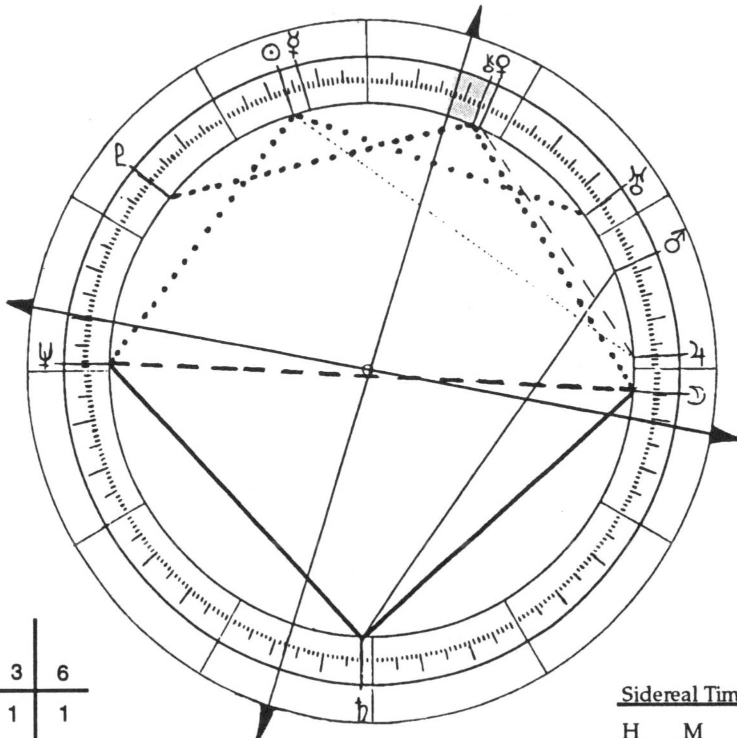

Quadrant Distribution

3	6
1	1

Sidereal Time

H	M	S
2	14	45

world of personal relationships was poignantly epitomized by the bittersweet struggle between Saturn's square to Neptune.

Another significant factor is Chiron conjunct with Venus. Whenever Chiron contacts another planet, it usually signifies the archetype within us that is most in need of healing. In Monroe's case, it is the Lover within her that is crying out for healing. In Greek mythology, Chiron was a healer to everyone else but himself. For all his wonderful skills in this area, he was unable to heal a wound which he suffered from an arrow. Monroe, a victim of childhood sexual abuse, was similarly able to grace us all with her eternal beauty and love, yet was unable to soothe and heal her own inner Lover. This paradoxical twist is often present when Chiron contacts an archetype.

John F. Kennedy

J.F.K.'s chart is another excellent example of the importance of noting the quadrant distribution of planets. There are two facts that are immediately apparent. The first is that, with nine planets above and two below the horizon, Kennedy was unquestionably an extrovert. He thrived in the public eye and was quite at home with handling the media.

The second fact is that he has a whopping six planets in the King quadrant. This automatically gives him a strong attunement with the King archetype. Both of the planets which embody the energy of the King most strongly, Sun and Jupiter, are both comfortably situated within the King quadrant as well. As if all this wasn't enough, Kennedy has a powerful triple conjunction radiating from within the King quadrant. Remember that all conjunctions generate King energy.

Kennedy was a born leader. The Zeus energy radiating powerfully from the conjunction of Jupiter with Mercury and Mars was apparent to all. We were caught up in the immense charisma of this man's leadership qualities, so much so, that the Kennedy administration was referred to as Camelot! Kennedy had the natural ability to forcefully (Mars) speak out and verbalize (Mercury) the highest quality ideals for all (Jupiter).

All of Kennedy's inner personal archetypes are located in the upper third of the heavens. This means that all of his personal charm was quite visible to all. His elevated position of Venus, square to the Moon and loosely conjunct the Sun, made him seem quite endearing to the public. A person's innate ability to lead can be determined by the planets occupying the King's quadrant. In Kennedy's case we have Pluto (shear

Name: John F. Kennedy Birthdate: 5/29/17 Time: 3:00 pm E.S.T Place: Brookline, MA

Zodiac: Sidereal

Chart Type: Natal

Longitude: 71 W 07

Latitude: 42 N 20

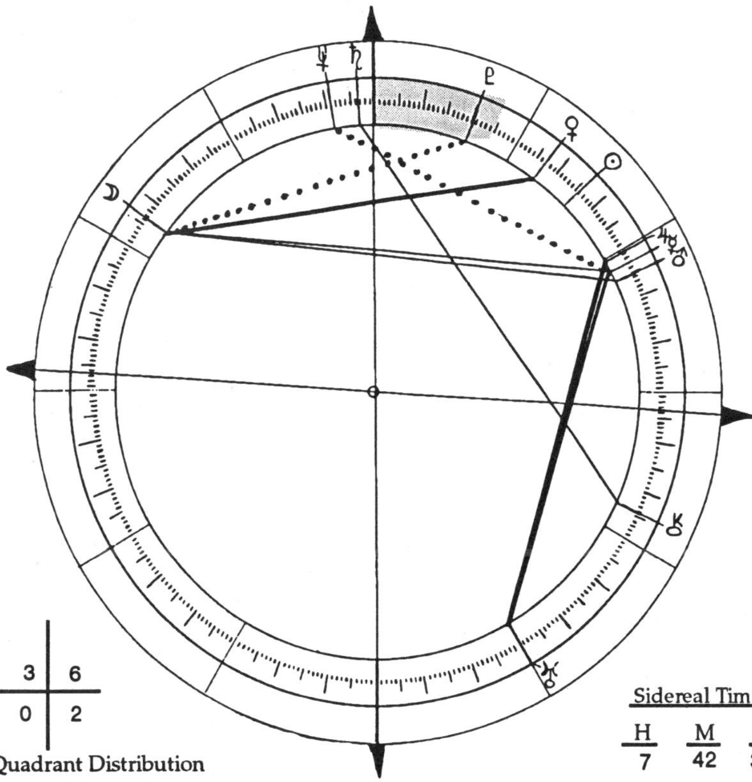

Quadrant Distribution

3	6
0	2

Sidereal Time

H	M	S
7	42	37

power), Venus (charm), the Sun (charisma and integrity), Jupiter (optimism), Mercury (oratory skills), and Mars (forcefulness).

Kennedy had a lot of archetypal energy available to him when it came to leadership ability. His ability to powerfully envision the future and verbalize optimistic goals, which radiates from the triple conjunction, was further enforced by the Quintile aspect between Mercury and Neptune. This gave him additional willpower to forcefully express productive ideas (Mercury) that seemed almost dreamy and too fantastic to believe (Neptune).

We need only remember his confident claim that America would be the first nation to put a man on the Moon, and would do so within a decade! Only in retrospect can we fully appreciate the far reaching vision of Kennedy's ability to dream of a futuristic event that would indeed come true.

Many of the leftover conservative elements from the paranoid McCarthy era saw Kennedy as a threat. His expansive far reaching vision, generated by Jupiter/Mercury, was also energetically squared by the planet Uranus. Many of his ideas, as a result, were seen as too radical by the right wing ultra-conservatives. Many saw him as a loose cannon who nearly precipitated World War III with his disastrous Cuban policies.

The square aspect, as we know, offers the dual possibility of both death and regeneration. It is a double edged sword. Kennedy's ability to take chances and break with convention (Uranus) would both excite (regenerate) some folks, and terrorize (kill) others. The conservative crowd saw him as the evil Set, one who would hack the political system to death and cause massive chaos.

John Kennedy had possibly a little too much King energy for one man. His grandiosity led to him taking a few too many liberties with Cuba. When a King gets dangerously out of control with his power, exercising liberties belonging only to God, someone has to forcefully remove him from power. Kennedy was literally be-headed just like many Kings throughout history when their power becomes a fearsome force.

Adolf Hitler

Here is a man in whose chart we would expect to find ample evidence of internal difficulties. His brutal quest for world domination and annihilation of the Jewish people would be more than enough cause for suspecting a highly developed shadow expression of Warrior energy. A

Name:	Adolf Hitler	Birthdate: 4/20/1889	Time: 6:30 pm L.M.T.	Place: Braunau, Austria

Zodiac: Sidereal

Chart Type: Natal

Longitude: 13 E 02

Latitude: 48 N 15

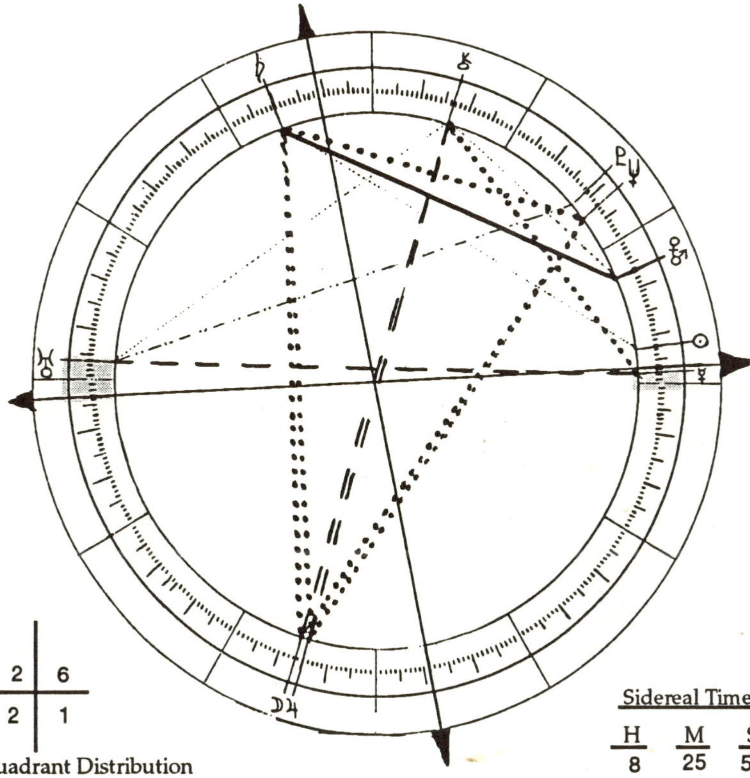

2	6
2	1

Quadrant Distribution

Sidereal Time

H	M	S
8	25	58

person's shadows are a direct result of childhood wounds. We must then also examine Hitler's past in order to uncover the whole picture.

The first thing we can note is that Hitler was an extrovert. He has eight planets above and three below the horizon. He craved the public's worship and approval. The quadrant with the single highest concentration of planets is the King's quadrant which contains six. Again, like Kennedy, we see evidence of a born leader. We are not concerned with methods here, merely the propensity and desire to lead and control others for better or for worse.

There are two facts about Hitler's chart that, when combined, add up to a potentially volatile situation. First, notice the complete absence of the softer harmonious aspects (Trines, Sextiles and Noviles). Next, notice the massive proliferation of Quintile aspects in his chart (a total of six). Five of the six Quintiles are arranged in an extremely powerful triangulated structure which I call the "spike." It is composed of a Quintile aspect between Neptune and Saturn, and 4 Bi-Quintiles from the Moon/Jupiter conjunction to both Neptune and Saturn. This gave Hitler a caustically intense development of Warrior energy.

This does not condemn the Spike arrangement as an astrological curse. Many people have this structure present within their chart. Yet why did it cause such toxic devastation in Hitler's case? The answer lies in his horrible childhood. Because of his spike, Hitler was a child who simply contained a propensity for Warrior development. Had his parents honored and blessed his internal strength, and channeled it in a healthy direction, he might have grown up with a moral desire to valiantly protect the rights of the weaker and less fortunate.

Instead Hitler suffered relentlessly under the totalitarian regime of his father's iron fist.[3] His mother and he were helpless victims of this dictator-like father. Hitler's home was like a concentration camp in many respects. At the age of 11 he was nearly beaten to death for merely thinking about running away!

Hitler gradually learned to repress and deny the pain of his beatings to the point where he would simply count the number of blows as he was being beaten. All of his more vulnerable archetypes (Moon, Venus and Neptune) are all crushed and repressed by harsh arrangements of aspects. Poor Venus is smothered by the conjunction of Mars and the oppressive square to Saturn. Hitler refused to allow himself to love, being too afraid of the risk involved.

Neptune and Moon are both repressed and controlled by their interlocking relationship with Saturn via the willful, duty-like code of the

Quintile's energy. Not only did Hitler's chart lack the soft aspects, but the softer Yin planets were all imprisoned as well! The result is that Hitler's proliferation of Quintile energy is left unregulated within his psyche. With no inner freedom of Yin to balance it, his Warrior development simply ran amuck!

The fact that Hitler's Moon is involved in the spike means that he carried all of his mother's repressed rage towards his father. He also carried his own rage towards his mother for never protecting him from being beaten. His experience of the feminine was that of it being useless and weak, incapable of offering safety. As a result, he made the decision, based on his internal design, to repress his feminine side under the restrictive disciplinary code of both Mars and its Quintiles.

The following quote reveals just how completely Hitler resolved to live this way. "I want the young to be violent, domineering, undismayed, cruel. They must be able to bear pain. There must be nothing weak or gentle about them."[4] This shows us just how completely his own inner child archetype (Moon) was under the rigid willful code of the spike configuration which connected it to the repressive Saturn.

The way Hitler perceived his father can be seen by the aspects to his Sun. Hitler has a Septile aspect connecting the Sun to Saturn. This means that he perceived his father as one who caused him much grief and suffering through his oppressive child rearing methods (Saturn). In mythology, Saturn/Cronos was the titanic god who ate his own children for fear that one of them would live to dethrone him. Saturn represents the ultimate paranoid regime of fear, which Hitler experienced within his own human father.

There are also two other Septile aspects involving Chiron. Chiron is Septile to Mars/Venus and Bi-Septile to Uranus. This means that Hitler had issues of sadness and loss which involved both of his Warrior archetypes (Mars/Uranus) and his Lover as well (Venus). Unfortunately, the opportunity for healing (Chiron) never manifested itself within his life. He never had a mentor to offset his father's devastation.

The ultimate outlet for all of Hitler's rage and inner turmoil was vented through his angular archetypes. As we can see, Hitler has Uranus rising in the Warrior power zone and Mercury setting within the Lover power zone. Uranus, the rebellious inner Warrior, is explosively placed within his chart. Remember that planets within the Warrior power zone define the way(s) in which we "act." This means that Hitler would act in the capacity of a total rebel, refusing to acknowledge any authority except his own.

The fact that Mercury is opposed to Uranus adds more deviousness and cunning to Hitler's modus operandi through the input of the Trickster shadow of Mercury. The shadow content of his Magician and rebel archetypes gave him an inner awareness of his talents as a detached manipulator of thoughts and information (Mercury). Hitler's toxic Nazi propaganda was second to none in its scapegoating of Jews and exaltation of the Aryan race. He burned and confiscated books and distributed his own in their place.

Because of its alignment with the horizon of the chart, this powerfully angular opposition of Uranus and Mercury strongly affected the way in which he interfaced with his immediate environment. Within Hitler's mind (Mercury) he saw himself as having the right to defiantly break all the rules (Uranus) and shock others with his complete disregard for any social morality. In this respect he unfolded into the ultimate sociopath, a cold and calculating Trickster whose anarchistic methods devastated Europe and the entire world.

Hitler's life was poignantly reminiscent of Uranus, his most angular planetary archetype. The god Uranus, in mythology, was awesome and powerful in his ability to create massive weapons with the potentiality for devastating destruction. He created the Cyclops, a titanic creature whose explosive ability to destroy came from the lightening bolts which flashed from its one immense eye. Uranus created countless monsters, some with a hundred hands with which they could wreak havoc. Ultimately, the other gods knew that Uranus had gotten out of hand. Saturn, his son, had to disempower him through castration.

Hitler's creation of massive armies for destruction are strangely reminiscent of Uranian monsters. Uranus ultimately became paranoid of some of his creations. He chose to imprison them within the bowels of the Earth. Hitler did the same with the Jews, whom he saw as a threat. He rounded them up and imprisoned them in concentration camps. Ultimately, the entire world rallied to stop Hitler's campaign for global conquest. Like the gods' fear of Uranus, we collectively feared Hitler's potential for runaway destruction.

It is no coincidence that this man embodied the worst shadow expressions of his angular archetype (Uranus). The outward impact of his horrific childhood, coupled with his internal wiring produced the most demonic expression of Warrior energy ever known to man. Hitler simply had to be castrated and brought down. It is interestingly rumored that Hitler had only one testicle, a poignant parallel to the Uranian myth.

Converting a Standard Chart

It is now time to provide you with a description of how to convert a standard astrological chart into the type that you see displayed in this book. This will allow you to take your own charts and apply this new method to them. We must first come to appreciate how these two chart methods differ from each other. Only then will the conversion process make sense to us.

A standard chart is usually drawn onto a blank twelve house template. The longitudes of each house "cusp" are inserted on the periphery of the wheel. The planets are then placed within the house which encapsulates its zodiacal longitude. The problem with this method is that it severely limits the astrologer to merely using the sign and house placement of each planet. This method will visually preclude the astrologer from being able to see any of the aspects which may exist between planetary bodies. He remains essentially trapped within the framework of houses and signs.

The first objective of my method is to strip away this potential roadblock to an effective delineation of the chart. It accomplishes this by eliminating the twelve houses and the zodiac from the framework of the chart. The zodiac is used *only* as the system of coordinates by which each planet is assigned its position relative to the others. Beyond this task, the zodiac plays no further role in my system.

The first order of business is to obtain or create a blank chart template similar to the one used in this book. The essential ingredients are as follows. It should have a grid of 360° marked around its periphery. This should be divided into twelve segments of 30° each. Inside of this grid, the chart should be completely blank. This type of chart template is obtainable at many astrology book stores. If you are handy with a protractor, you can easily design your own version.

The first chart element to be converted is the line of the horizon. This is the same as the 1st/7th house cusp line in a standard chart. Find the zodiac degree of the 1st house (ascendant) and draw in a small line, which marks this position, within the 30° sector which is farthest to the left of your grid. Now, directly across from this point, you should draw another line to mark off the same degree within the opposite 30 degree sector. Finally, we need to take a ruler and draw a line across the middle of the chart which connects these two points. This is the horizon of the chart.

Figure 13a

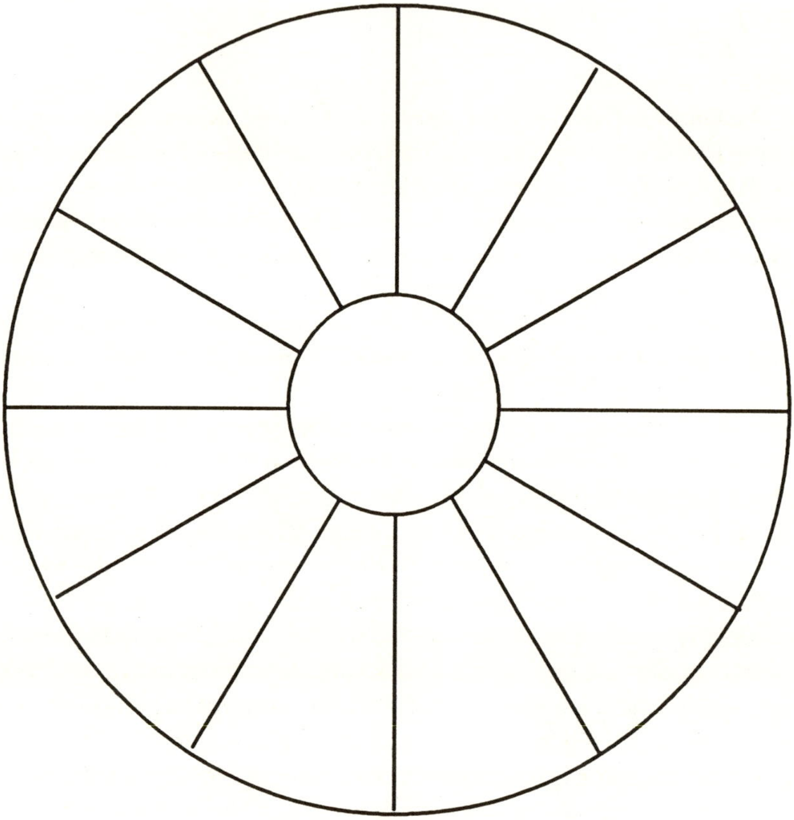

Standard Conventional Blank Chart

Now we need to temporarily draw in the symbols for the corresponding 12 zodiac signs. I recommend using pencil so they may later be erased. Start by drawing in the sign of the ascendant and listing the rest in counterclockwise order. It is best to list them around the outside edge of the chart. It will now be much easier for us to draw in the remaining axis of the meridian and insert the planetary positions.

Follow the same procedure, when drawing in the meridian axis, as we used to insert the horizon. Draw two opposing marks to denote the positions of the 10th and 4th house cusps. These are also known as the upper and lower meridians. Use the ruler and connect these two points as well. You now have the primary quadrated grid within which to place the planets. Take each planet and insert it into its appropriate degree of the relevant sign. Make a mark on the grid at this point and then draw the planet's symbol to the outside of this mark.

Once this is complete, you can now safely erase the penciled in symbols for the signs. They are no longer necessary for our purposes. You can leave them, if you prefer, but they will most likely serve only to distract you from an impartial interpretation of the aspects between the planets. I suggest you try it first without them so that you can focus completely on the planetary aspects.

To effectively be able to tell the difference between a Trine and a Square, for example, you should assign a color code to each aspect that will remain constant. Buy yourself a box of colored pens, pencils or markers and set up a color for each aspect (harmonic). I am assuming that your standard chart is computer generated and contains an "aspectarian." This will provide you with a list of all the aspects between the planets of that chart.

Simply take your colored pencils and draw connecting lines between the planets which have mutual aspects between them. An example will suffice. Lets say that you assign the color purple to represent all Opposition aspects. You should then look through the aspectarian and note any and all Oppositions between planets. Simply draw a purple line between these planets on the chart grid. After you have drawn in all the colored lines, your chart is ready to be interpreted!

This color coded system allows you to begin recognizing the distinct shapes of the larger triangulated power structures to which I constantly refer. These larger conglomerates of archetypal energy are the crux of the biscuit in terms of understanding the core of the native's personality. Their presence should therefore be made readily apparent, in this manner, instead of being hopelessly obscured by signs and houses.

One final suggestion is that you should use a yellow highlighter to mark the four power zones of the chart. Remember, the central "peak" of these zones lies 12-15° to the clockwise side of each angle. The zone itself begins at the angle and then climbs to this peak, and will ultimately fade off after another 10° or so. Any planets which are present within these zones will be immediately apparent to you by using this method of highlighting them.

CHAPTER FOURTEEN

Complete Chart Delineation and Synthesis

In this chapter I would like to fully delineate some charts, in order to show how all this information might be applied towards a better understanding of human nature. As seen in the partial interpretations in the last chapter, the theories that we've laid down do show some very valuable applications. Now that you have warmed up your delineating skills, it should be relatively easy to follow the three in depth delineations that will follow.

I've chosen to interpret charts of people who have been significant in my own life. We've covered the charts of some fairly popular celebrities in the previous chapter. Now I would like to delineate the charts of some well known teachers, whom I see as positively affecting the planet.

I must again re-emphasize to traditional astrologers, that I will not be using any houses or signs. Instead, I wish to demonstrate the ability to achieve a deeper understanding of the person, by avoiding these distractions. I will confine myself, exclusively, to the use of planets, aspects and angularity.

This should prove interesting to anyone who has experience in the standard method of delineation. I ask only that you keep an open mind. To do so requires you to leave all your previous experience behind. You should hopefully, then, be able to add to your abilities as an astrologer. Of course, no prior astrological skill is needed to use this method in order to come to a deeper understanding of yourself.

This is a new way of interpreting, and I will therefore reiterate a lot of basics so as to reinforce them in your mind. It is extremely important to always remember the inseparable connection between number, aspect and archetype/planet. For example:

3 = Trine = Venus.

In this new way of understanding, we completely eliminate the need for referring to the signs and houses. As a result, we wind up finding more true meaning within the chart itself.

Carl Jung: Plutonian Teacher of Transformation

Carl Jung is perhaps the most charismatic and enigmatic mind ever to grace the field of psychology. We are still sorting through the legacy of his life's work. Many believe that Jung's greatest contribution to psychology was the concept of the "collective unconscious."

Throughout this book, we have referred to Pluto as the ruler of the collective unconscious. If astrology is based on any kind of certainty, we would expect to find Pluto centrally and intricately involved in Jung's chart. Observing Jung's chart, one might even call that an understatement.

Pluto is right at the root of Jung's chart, being conjunct with the lower meridian! The overall concept of the meridian is "I AM." The lower meridian is our private, or hidden sense of I AM-ness. Having Pluto in this location would translate as: I AM (inwardly) transformative and reflective.

The lower meridian, and the Gauquelin power zone, just to its left are both associated with the Magician archetype. Jung has Pluto, Moon, Neptune, and Chiron all strung together in this magical zone. This was the fountain of his psyche, out of which flowed the wealth of creative ideas that are his legacy.

Jung considered himself an introvert. This is confirmed by the the fact that eight of his eleven planets are in the lower, private half of the chart. Four of them are buried in the deepest and most personal, sacred, region of the map. Jung was truly a Magi in every sense of the word.

Starting at a very young age, three or four, Jung began experiencing powerfully symbolic and cryptic dreams. Having the Moon wedged in between Pluto and Neptune, gave him a tremendous sensitivity (Moon) to both the collective unconscious (Pluto), and the great feminine absolute (Neptune). He was literally swept away in these powerful primordial influences.

Jung himself stated it best, "All other memories of travels, people and my surroundings have paled beside these interior happenings. My encounters with the 'other' reality, my bouts with the unconscious, are indelibly engraved upon my memory. In that realm there has always been wealth in abundance, and everything else has lost importance by comparison."[1]

As a youth, Jung was constantly struggling with depression caused by his own sensitivities. This is revealed by the Square aspect (90°)

Name: Carl G. Jung Birthdate: 7/26/1875 Time: 7:40 pm L.M.T. Place: Kesswil, Switzerland

Zodiac: Sidereal

Chart Type: Natal

Longitude: 9 E 19

Latitude: 47 N 34

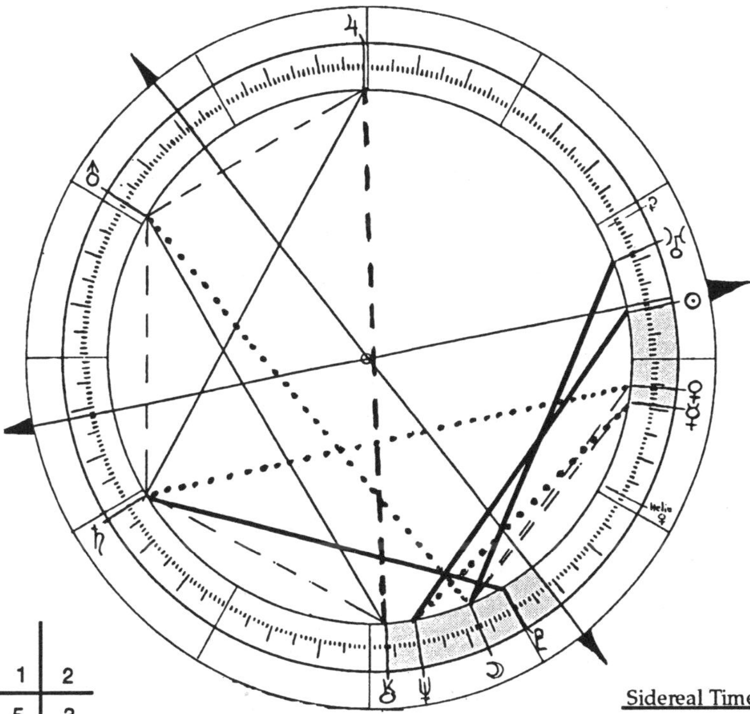

1	2
5	3

Quadrant Distribution

Sidereal Time

H	M	S
15	56	15

between Saturn (grief) and Pluto. Through this dynamic struggle, he matured and grew past it by age 18-19. This is often a time of critical growth for people. It is at this time that the 19 year cycle of the Moon's nodes comes to fruition.

Jung had difficult and challenging relationships with both of his parents. This is revealed by the square aspects to both of his luminaries. The Sun represents the Father archetype and the Moon denotes the Mother archetype within each of us. The aspects we have to the Sun and Moon will color our perception of our earthly parents, as we project these archetypes out into the world.

The Moon in his chart is square to Uranus, changeability. Jung said of his mother, "My mother was very good to me... and then her unconscious personality would *suddenly* put in an appearance. That personality was *unexpectedly* powerful. I was sure that she consisted of two personalities, one innocuous and human, the other *uncanny*."

Her kind and human side which Jung alluded to, is revealed by the Sextile between the Moon and the Venus-Mercury conjunction. The "crazy" half is shown by the Square of Moon and Uranus. This was, in reality, his own personal blueprint of the Mother archetype, which colored the way he saw his earthly mother. The outer responds unconsciously to the inner.

Jung's Sun was square to Neptune (denial) in his chart. In *Portrait of Jung*, Gerhard Wehr writes of Jung's father, "Not only did the father not understand those things which moved the boy most deeply; he was not even aware of them." This is in agreement with Jung's own description of his father within his autobiography.

This internal struggle between his Father-Mother archetypes and the principles of both intelligence and spirituality (Uranus-Neptune), led to his awareness of two personalities within himself. Being so deeply rooted within the realm of Pluto, led to the realization of that middle ground between left brain (Uranus) and right brain (Neptune) consciousness.

Having Pluto conjunct with the meridian places him within the central throne of the pineal gland, the whole of Jung's consciousness was positioned in such a way that allowed him to observe from between two realities. His own notes are full of references to this phenomenon.

Jung described the two distinct personalities within himself. The first was an image of a schoolboy who felt obliged to work hard at his studies. Of the second, Jung said "...there existed another realm, like a temple in which anyone who entered was *transformed* and suddenly overpowered by a vision of *the whole cosmos*." He explains further: "Here lived the 'other,' who knew God as a *hidden*, personal, and at the same time *suprapersonal secret*." Embedded in Jung's description are many key-words of Pluto. It is from this personal experience that his ideas on the relationship between the Ego and the Self arose.

Jung took many years to decide on becoming a psychologist. He studied initially to become a medical doctor, like his grandfather for whom he was named. As we can see, Chiron (the healer) is powerfully placed in his chart. It is opposed to Jupiter, which created the awareness of separation that he wrestled with for so many years before choosing his profession.

Jung himself said: "I continued to waver between science and the humanities. Both powerfully attracted me." When a chart contains only one opposition, it then becomes the central unresolved polarity within the person's life. He was torn between the empirical science of medicine (Chiron), and the social humanities of Jupiter.

These also represent the paths of his father, who was a Lutheran minister (Jupiter) and his grandfather, who was a medical doctor (Chiron). Jung chose to resolve the opposition in the only way in which one truly can. This is achieved by owning both halves and consciously integrating them.

In the process of becoming a psychologist, he wove together the highest aspects (Jupiter) of healing (Chiron). He became a male mentor in the truest sense. The powers of the Warrior (Mars) and the dark alchemical Magician (Saturn) are both tied into this opposition via trines and sextiles. These archetypes all harmoniously interrelate to form a huge power structure.

This larger "pattern" represents four of the six points needed to form a Grand Sextile. If the advanced astrologer considers the addition of the asteroid Ceres and the heliocentric position of Venus, the pattern is then perfectly complete. The Grand Sextile is an awesome power structure that represents the highest attainable essence of six-ness or Jupiter.

Jung reveals his own passion and interests in numerology, alchemy and philosophy. "Above all I was attracted to the thought of Pythagoras, Heraclitus, Empedocles and Plato, despite the long-windedness of Socratic argumentation." Jupiter is the most elevated planet in his chart which drove him to aspire to the highest quality synthesis of all these interests.

The Grand Sextile forms the occult symbol of the Star of David. This signifies the two overlapping triads of the Ego and the Self. It also represents the Anima and Animus! It was inevitable that Jung would discover all these powerful terms. His own personal "archetypal structure" embodies them so undeniably.

Astrologers owe a tremendous debt of gratitude to Carl Jung. With the publication of *The Interpretation of Nature and the Psyche,*[2] Jung made it quite apparent as to his profound interest in astrology. He relied on it to help him statistically prove his theory of synchronicity. Jung admits as evidence the astrological charts of married couples. They consisted of three groups of 180, 220 and 83 couples respectively. He monitored the frequency in which certain planetary combinations occurred. Through his study, the entire field of synastry (chart comparison) was born. Synastry illustrates the astrological forces at work within relationships.

Jung spent the whole of his life studying the subjects of mysticism, alchemy, spirituality, mythology and comparative religion. Like a true magician, he saw his life as an ongoing experiment. Through his own personal inner experience, he formed his understanding of Grandiosity (Jupiter) and the mystical Numinosity (Neptune) of something immensely spiritual.

Carl Jung was a man consumed by the collective unconscious. He developed the concept of the shadow based upon his own experiences within the dark murky depths of his Plutonian netherworld. It is virtually impossible to convey to the reader the full scope of this man's life in any amount of words. Jung was truly a living enigma in the fullest Plutonian sense. In reflecting back over his life, at age 83, Jung wrote, "Today as then, I am solitary, because I know things and must hint at things which other people do not know, and usually do not even want to know." He suffered the Plutonian isolation of only meeting a few souls in his life who could both challenge and comprehend him.

Jung found one such soul in Sigmund Freud. The sychronicity of their meeting was impeccable. They had both just completed major astrological cycles within their own personal masculine development. Jung was 32, and had just experienced his Saturn return. Freud, at 51, was just emerging from the Chiron return. They were separated in age by 19 years, which is the perfect age difference for the typical mentor-student relationship. This represents the complete cycle of the Lunar Nodes. Freud even formally adopted Jung as his eldest "son." Here we see the energy of Chiron accepting a pupil. Jung would eventually go on to outshine his master, just as Asclepius did of Chiron.

Jung's chart also contains another rarity. There is a powerful presence of five-ness represented by a whole array of Quintiles. These aspects are indicative of forging new links via the powerful will of the Warrior. They represent the union of 2 + 3, (objective reasoning and form), which is further reinforced by the conjunction of Mercury (2) and Venus (3).

Neptune is quintile (72°) to Mercury. This indicates the ability to forge a productive working relationship between the mind (Mercury), and the great feminine absolute (Neptune). From the depths of this link, Jung willfully entered the ocean of Nut and retrieved his most profound spiritual insights.

Venus is biquintile (144°) to Saturn. This allowed Jung to willfully forge a productive relationship between the Alchemical Magician (Saturn) and his Lover archetype. It is no secret, at this point, of Jung's love for alchemy. The fact that Mercury is conjunct with Venus allows these two separate quintiles to mingle their combined forces.

The conjunction of the Magician and Lover (Mercury-Venus) is situated right in the power spot of the Lover quadrant. This double reinforcement, of his Lover nature, gave him tremendous sensitivity. Upon Jung's first encounter with Emma Rauschenbach, he simply knew that he had met the female embodiment of his anima. They were married seven years later.

The final biquintile (144°) is between Mars and the Moon. Jung was able to forge a conscious working relationship between the Warrior and the Mother archetype. This link allowed his spiritualized and integrated Warrior to be able to descend down into the dream world of the feminine (Moon). He was able to return with many victorious and productive interpretations.

Jung's chart shows a most advanced state of evolution. The astrological map is simply the blueprint to the soul of the person. Jung's birth chart reveals serious development of his internal awareness of the Pythagorean principles of 1, 2, 3, 4, 5 and 6. This all culminates in the Grand Sextile.

His powerful attunement to six-ness is what attracted him so strongly to the I-Ching. This ancient Chinese system of divination uses a hexagram composed of six lines. Jung spent many years of his life consulting this oracle and studying its innate structure. He even collaborated with Richard Wilhelm, who produced one of the best translations of the I-Ching.[3]

Very few birth charts ever reflect this level of integration of so many different dimensions. It is the sign of a very diversified soul, one

Name: J. Krishnamurti Birthdate: 5/12/1895 Time:12.25 am Place: Madanapalle, India

Zodiac: Sidereal

Chart Type: Natal

Longitude: 78 E 30

Latitude: 13 N 33

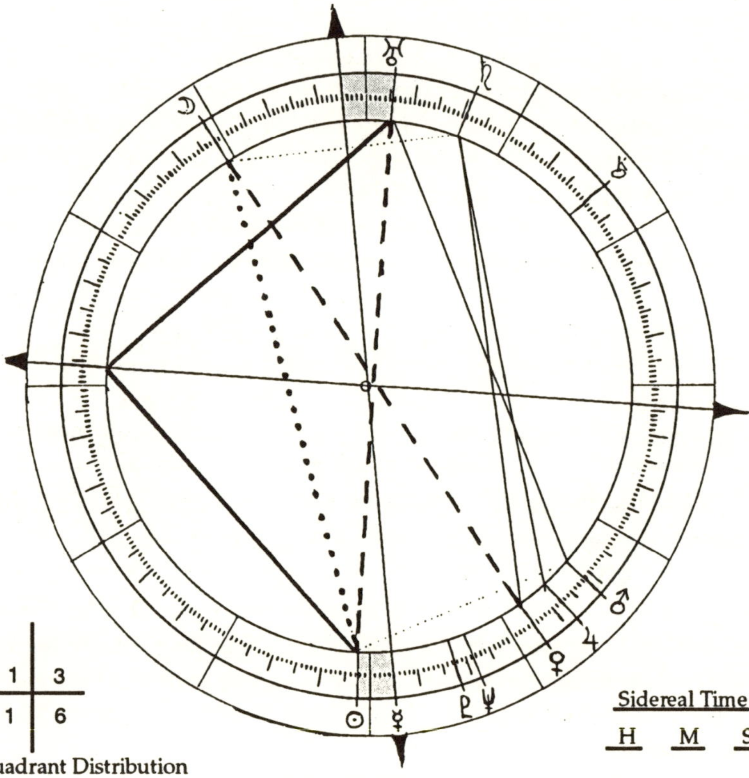

1	3
1	6

Quadrant Distribution

Sidereal Time

H M S

fascinated by the conscious interplay of various aspects of pure number. The next chart shows a completely different way of achieving self actualization. Each man blazes his own glorious path, on the way to his Great Self.

Krishnamurti: Uranian Teacher of Freedom

Krishnamurti is one of the most powerful spiritual teachers to have lived in this century. As a child he was groomed by the Theosophical Society to be the next messiah. He was led through their process of initiations, so as to eventually become a channel or vehicle for the Lord Maitreya to manifest through. All during his later twenties, he experienced a mysterious process in his body that caused him much suffering as these initiations continued.

Just around this time, at the beginning of Saturn's second cycle (about age 30), he started becoming aware of his separation. The world of the messiah started to appear ridiculous to him. He saw his own human limitations and those of others, wanting to cling to him.

Krishnamurti started to consciously and deliberately let go of and grieve for the ending of this role. He saw this as standing in his way towards real enlightenment. The power of Saturn's eliminating urges began to rise to a conscious (Mercurial) level. This is typical of Saturn's second cycle. The quality of two-ness, remember, relates to Mercury and objective awareness.

Krishnamurti proceeded to disband the order in a purely Uranian way. It was a sudden decision, shocking everyone. Nobody saw it coming. In his final speech to them, he said, "I refuse to be your crutch. As I am free,..I have found this truth, which is limitless,...without beginning or end. *I will not be conditioned by you!*"[4] Here we have the archetypal Uranian teacher.

The rest of his life was spent lecturing and teaching, on the straightforward path to freedom. He was the quintessential mouthpiece of Uranus. Through him, this principle spoke to us in its pure, unadulterated form.

Uranus is the most elevated planet in his chart. It is situated just past the meridian, in the Gauquelin power zone. (I shall refer to these four power zones from now on, as the "G" spots for the sake of brevity.)

Uranus, being on the upper G spot, is therefore identified with the upper meridian, which has a Solar-Kingly quality. Adding to this energy, he also has the Sun opposed to Uranus. This aspect joins the archetype of the King (Sun), with the principle of freedom (Uranus).

The Opposition carries a flavor of two-ness, or Mercury. He was very aware of his magical power as a King of freedom, or a teacher of the inner kingdom of freedom. His books had titles such as: *Freedom from the Known, The Ending of Time, The Awakening of Intelligence,* and *The Impossible Question.*

Mercury itself is exactly on the lower meridian, and very close to the Sun. This further reinforces the link of teacher (or Magician), with the King archetype, and the concept of freedom. Both the Sun and Mercury are located within the lower "G" spot, which is the power zone of the Magician.

How could Krishnamurti help but speak out for the inner spiritual liberation? Uranus-Sun is also Squared, perpendicular to the horizon. This connects the power of Uranus, to his body (the Earth).

The square aspect (90°) represents the concept of four-ness, and relates to the Earth-Moon. In this case, the square is between Uranus-Sun and the horizon which is the Earth itself. Again we have double reinforcement. His body was constantly affected by this energy which explains the mysterious "process" which plagued his physical body. The voltage of the Uranian-King was intense within him. He was, literally, a human lightening rod.

The other major aspect in his chart is an opposition between Venus and the Moon. Krishnamurti had tremendous love (Venus) for his mother (Moon). His mother died a few months before his tenth birthday. The opposition aspect reflects the painful awareness of separation he experienced by this. He grieved deeply for his mother, as he clearly expressed in many of his letters. Those close to him say it was a loss from which he never fully recovered. I believe this is the wound that propelled him into the life he was to live. His wounded Lover was offered up as a sacrifice towards his chosen lifestyle of a spiritual renunciate.

Krishnamurti was never married and lived his entire life in celibacy, an intense sacrifice. His Lover, instead, expressed itself in his gentleness and love of nature. He loved the simplest objects of beauty.

I consider myself blessed to have heard him speak once, in Ojai California, a few years before his death. The night before, I camped out in a nearby State forest. That very evening, there was a beautiful conjunction of Venus and the crescent Moon in the sky, just after sunset. These planets were central to his awareness, because of their opposition in his chart.

The next morning, as he spoke, people were asking him all kinds of heavy duty existential questions. He sort of blew them off, in a typically Uranian fashion. Instead of responding to them, he simply asked, excitedly, "Did anyone see the Moon and Venus last night?"

My heart leapt with joy. I felt very connected to this man at that moment. A part of me knew that my ability to appreciate beauty and simplicity, was being acknowledged by this King. I am, only now, fully realizing the blessing I received back then.

Krishnamurti was described as a stunningly beautiful man in his youth. The reflection of Moon-Venus caused many to say he was more beautiful than most women. He was a painfully shy and private man. This is reflected by the fact that all of his personal-private planets (except the Moon) are below the horizon. The lower hemisphere is the private (subconscious) half of the native's awareness and life.

In his public life, people saw him as a nurturing (Moon) manifestation of freedom (Uranus). Saturn is also elevated close to the upper G spot. It has a trine aspect to both Venus and Jupiter. This combines high quality (Jupiter) love (Venus) with Saturn, who teaches through adversity and loss. Saturn also has a septile to the Moon.

This forms a triangulated structure between Moon-Venus-Saturn. It is composed of an opposition (2), septile (7), and a trine (3). These three aspects, as we know, are those of Mercury (2), Saturn (7), and Venus (3) respectively. They give this larger power triangle, an overall meaning of an awareness of separation involving grief and loss, with which he would eventually reach reconciliation.

The grief principle of Saturn is, therefore, intimately tied into the loss of his mother (Moon). This wound to his Lover archetype, was his personal cross that he carried throughout his whole life. He intuitively knew and accepted his grief, with an inner resolve that led to a true awareness of healing in his life.

We also find the same exact triangulated power structure involving the Sun. There is a septile connecting Mars to the Sun. Mars is also applying into a trine aspect with Uranus. This means that his Warrior archetype must learn to grieve the loss of the father (Sun), through becoming a nurturing expression of liberation (Uranus).

The oppositions to both Sun and Moon show the complete "awareness of separation" which he experienced from his father and mother. He was taken away from them at a very early age, and raised by the Theosophical Society. His surrogate parents became Annie Besant and C.W. Leadbeater who oversaw his initiations.

We see further evidence of how this would be internally experienced by him. This is revealed by the bi-quintile (144°) aspect between the Sun and Moon. He would therefore come to experience the relationship between his surrogate father and mother to be one involving duty, work and service. These keywords express the nature of the Quintile aspect which harmonizes with the nature of the fifth planet (Mars).

This is indicative of a productive working relationship with his surrogate parents, Besant and Leadbeater. His sole purpose of involvement with them was to study and pass his initiations, so he could eventually become the next messiah and deliver the new gospel of salvation to the world. The septiles to Sun and Moon reveal that he would also let go of and grieve his connections to this second pair of parents as well!

It was through the deep sorrow and restriction of these early experiences of being consciously manipulated that he developed his own way of teaching. His own mood of conveying his spiritual philosophy was very somber and Saturnian. He did not paint a pretty picture, and offered no shortcuts. The road to spiritual liberation, in his view, was a solitary and individual one. It was a pathless path, and he therefore offered no directions or roadmaps.

Krishnamurti lived to be almost 91 years old. It is rare that any of us lives long enough to experience a complete cycle of Uranus. This takes 84 earth years to achieve. It seems fitting that this great teacher of Uranus should live long enough to enjoy the awareness of its second cycle!

In this final chart I will work with delineating some of the asteroid archetypes. Their meanings are very specific, much like a laser beam. They lack the rich diversity of the larger planets, but they add very pertinent information despite this limitation. I work with a narrow orb of 1° when dealing with the asteroids. Their significance will become apparent in the following delineation.

Robert Bly: Saturnian Teacher of Grief

Robert Bly has in recent years come into the public eye through the publication of his best selling book *Iron John: A Book about Men*. A poet for most of his life, it has been through his work as a teacher and initiator of men into the world of mythology that Bly has truly come into public awareness.

Name: Robert Bly Birthdate: 12/23/26 Time: 7:20 am C.S.T. Place: Madison, MN

Zodiac: Sidereal

Chart Type: Natal

Longitude: 96 W 12

Latitude: 45 N 01

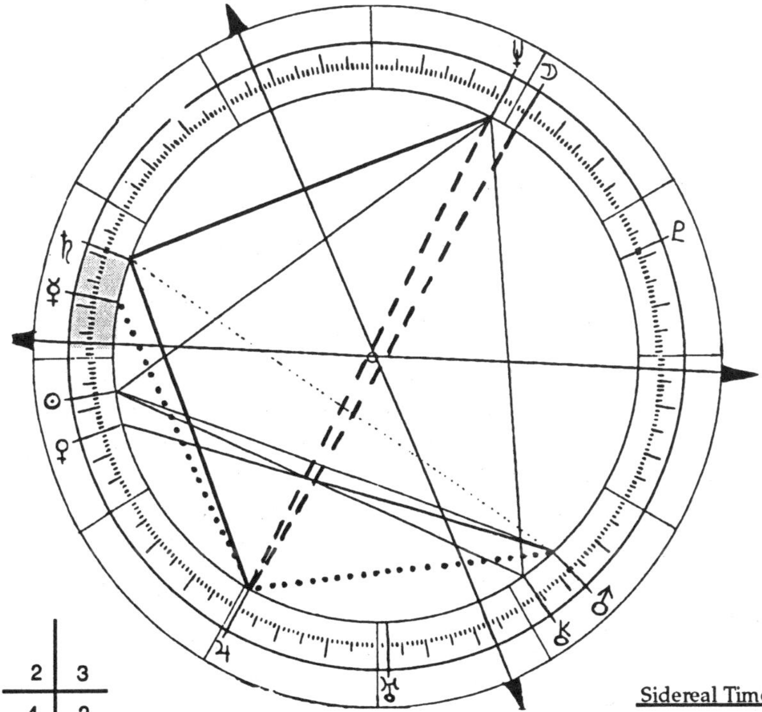

2	3
4	2

Quadrant Distribution

Sidereal Time

H	M	S
13	00	30

The mythology which Robert teaches places a strong emphasis on the importance of recognizing and honoring grief as an essential part of male spiritual growth. In my opinion, there is no one who speaks more convincingly of the positive aspects of grieving than Bly. His conviction comes from his own hard fought victories within the realm of Saturn.

If we look at Bly's chart, we find Saturn and Mercury in the angular G spot on the ascendant. These are the only angular planets within his chart. They fall specifically within the power zone of the Warrior quadrant. Any planets within this rising hot spot take on the active, assertive qualities of the Warrior.

This can be interpreted as follows: I act assertively in the capacity of a teacher and writer (Mercury) of the principles of grief (Saturn)! This connection between the active nature of the Warrior archetype, and the planet Saturn is further emphasized by the tri-septile aspect (154.29°) between Saturn and Mars. Remember, the Septile is 1/7th of the circle (51.4°) and corresponds to the energies of the seventh planet, Saturn.

We therefore have an exact mathematical link between the archetype of the Warrior (Mars) and the process of grieving (Saturn). This signifies that Bly would come to realize the full potential of his Warrior through the process of utilizing the energy of Mars for his own grief work. This can best be illustrated by his own teachings on this subject.

In explaining the difference between depression and grief, Bly has the following thoughts:

> Depression means you have refused to go down into your own grief, and a hand pulls you down. There is no purpose in it, no passion. But grief is a different process. Grief has *activity* in it, where one chooses to go down. You use your *energy* that men have used as *hunters* for thousands of years. Instead of going out and hunting out there, you go down and *hunt* inside your childhood in various places.[5]

Bly is the only teacher I know who places such a strong emphasis on the active nourishing qualities of grieving. He calls it the gateway to male feelings.

Men have responded passionately to this vital new approach. Bly has found a much needed place within our society as a teacher and initiator of men. This was not achieved until much later in his life, after he had passed through the Chiron return (age 50) and done his own personal healing. He has become a role model and spokesman for many American men.

In his acclaimed PBS video *A Gathering of Men*, Bly reveals that his own father was an alcoholic. Through sharing of his lack of connection to his father, he hit a raw nerve in many men, myself included. His early life was a struggle to gain a sense of masculinity in the face of an overwhelming predominance of the feminine within his life.

Many men, without a strong male role model, get swallowed up by the powerful presence of their mothers. Bly has been able to verbalize this swallowing from his own personal experience. The most predominant aspect in his chart is the opposition of Jupiter to the Moon-Neptune conjunction. This is a powerful alliance of feminine (Yin) archetypes. I know, because I have Moon opposed to a Jupiter-Neptune conjunction.

Having Moon-Neptune as the most elevated planets in his chart gave Bly a powerful awareness of his immersion within the realm of the Mother. This is the source of his early poetry. The feminine energy of this opposition dominated his early life, before he had a clear sense of his King and Warrior archetypes. Bly has lectured on the plight of the man overly adapted to the feminine, which he calls the "naive male."[6]

He, once again, hit a chord in many young men, myself included. In his lecture on naivete, he has cited his early poetry as a poignant example of the male who is submersed in the world of the great feminine absolute (Neptune). Bly's writings reveal the presence of the archetypes of the Moon and Neptune, as they speak through his psyche. Bly described himself in his thirties:

> What I saw when I looked at the world was innocence. I was sort of poignant and sensitive, self-enclosed, dreamy, floating, spiritual, impractical, hoping for the best.[7]

One couldn't ask for a more perfect description of Neptune! The following poem, from Bly's book Silence in the Snowy Fields, will reveal more of Bly's poetic attunement to the energies of Neptune. Remember Neptune's links to water.

> These pines, these fall oaks, these rocks,
> This *water* dark and touched by wind—
> I am like you, you dark *boat*,
> *Drifting* over *water* fed by cool *springs*.
>
> Beneath the *waters*, since I was a boy,
> I have *dreamt* of strange and dark treasures,

Not of gold, or strange stones, but the true
Gift, beneath the pale *lakes* of Minnesota.

This morning also, *drifting* in the dawn wind,
I sense my hands, and my shoes, and this ink—
Drifting, as all of this body *drifts*,
Above the clouds of the flesh and the stone.

A few friendships, a few dawns, a few glimpses of grass,
A few *oars* weathered by the *snow* and the heat
So we *drift* toward shore, over cold *waters*,
No longer caring if we *drift* or go straight.[8]

Within this poem, there is also evidence of Saturn's influence. Saturn is in square aspect to both Neptune and Jupiter. This forms a larger power structure called a T-square. The references to "dark, rocks, and stone" are all Saturnian. The struggle of Saturn to express itself in his poetry (indicated by the square aspects to Saturn) would not gain any real prominence until his later works.

Excerpts from another of his early poems entitled "Laziness and Silence" also show the dominance of the Moon-Neptune energy at this point of his life.

On a Saturday afternoon in the football season,
I lie in my *bed* near the lake,
And *dream* of moles with golden wings.

While the depth of the *water* trembles on the ceiling,
Like the tail of an enraged bird,
I watch the dust *floating* above the bed, *content*.

I think of *ships* leaving lonely *harbors*,
Dolphins playing far at *sea*,
Fish with the faces of old men come in from a blizzard.

A *dream* of moles with golden wings
Is not so bad; It's like *imagining*
Waterfalls of stone deep in mountains,
Or a wing *flying* alone beneath the earth.

I know that far out in the Minnesota *lake*
Fish are nosing the mouths of cold *springs*,
Whose *water* causes *ripples* in the *sleeping* sand,
Like a *spirit* moving in a body....[9]

I find the reference to the "wing flying alone beneath the earth" to be very revealing. The cadusus of Mercury has two wings, as does our archetypal Tree. Each "wing" represents half of the balanced psyche. We need two wings to fly straight. We require both our Yin and Yang nature to proceed through life. Bly was expressing here, that he was unconsciously aware (the wing is flying under the earth) that he was not yet whole or complete.

He was flying on his feminine side only, the Yin pillar, Neptune-Jupiter-Moon. The masculine archetypes of the Warrior (Mars) and the King (Sun) were still dormant in his unconscious. This is shown by the fact that they are in the lower half of the chart, underneath the earth! These energies were to unfold later on in his life, as he turned his focus onto his unresolved wounds surrounding his own father.

At the age of 46, Robert started writing poetry that specifically dealt with his own father and his feelings of grief. As he actively delved into his own unconscious, he started to salvage and resurrect his Warrior and King archetypes. These two planets (Mars-Sun) are in trine aspect (120°) to each other. This shows an affinity for the Warrior to work in harmony with the King and serve him well.

The only problem with trines is that, despite their beneficial influence, they are essentially lazy aspects. By this I mean that they sort of float, like a boat at sea with no sail. In order to make use of their benefits, we need to consciously and actively invoke their energy, raise the sail. Many people only become aware of these subtle gifts (trines) at the later stages of their lives.

Bly also has the tremendous gift of a Grand Trine between the planets Neptune-Chiron-Sun. After passing through his Chiron return, at age 50, Bly began to experience the full power of this gifted Grand Trine. He has become a compassionate (Neptune) mentor-initiator (Chiron) and even father figure (Sun) to many younger men who respond to his ability to teach and heal the male spirit.

In this later period of his life, he also began to reap the benefits of the Quintile energy in his chart. Mars-Jupiter-Mercury form three-fifths of a Grand Quintile. This creates a powerful working relationship between the Warrior and the Magician as they seek to manifest the highest quality expression of their combined energies, via their link with Jupiter.

I would now like to show two examples of Bly's later poetry. The first one is an absolutely brilliant illustration of the energies of Saturn and Neptune struggling for position within his psyche. These planetary (archetypal) energies speak to us under the guise of the poem's two main characters. I will simply replace their names with those of Saturn and Neptune to make my point.

Aban Kavost and Ivar Oakeson

Saturn (A.K.)- What you love is gone; the worst have got it. The Stalinist shoves the papers to the floor; The priest cannot go on with the Mass; the singer tries to climb out through the porthole.

Neptune(I.O.)- You are a judge; a kind of demon judge- the hole in stones through which the wind blows.

Saturn (A.K.)- Who wants to remain in the world as it is? There are broken pieces of wood around the Jesuit; the log raft breaks up as it nears the falls; the spider runs quickly up the blinding path.

Neptune (I.O.)- You want to die, and leap off the earth!

Saturn (A.K.)- You are a coward to stay and be cheated—by landlord and Lord—again and again. *I suffered for years and you remained in ease! I am the strong one; I have endured pain. I suffer and do while you go into ecstasy.* Women love you, not me; and I raged at the start from my carrying you. No more. I will blind you.
Neptune (I.O.)- Have you put bonds on me? Are you that strong?[10]

This poem is an exquisite example of an archetypal debate. The struggle of the square aspect between Saturn and Neptune is being verbalized here. The three lines (which I highlighted) grabbed me as a powerful statement, one which contains obvious feelings of resentment toward Neptune. Saturn is demanding integration into Bly's psyche. He threatens to "blind" Neptune in order to achieve this.

This final poem shows the resolution of the preceding struggle. It clearly reveals the presence of Saturn within its structure. Instead of only hinting at things Saturnian, the entire mood of the poem is under the sway of this planet's influence, just as the first two were of Neptune.

Snowbanks North of the House

Those great sweeps of snow that *stop suddenly* six feet
    from the house...
Thoughts that go so far.
The boy gets out of high school and *reads no more* books;
the son *stops* calling home.
The mother *puts down* her rolling pin and makes *no more* bread.

And the wife looks at her husband one night at a party
and *loves him no more.*
The *energy leaves* the wine, and the minister *falls leaving*
the church.
It *will not* come closer —
the one inside *moves back,* and the hands *touch nothing,*
and are safe.

And the father *grieves* for his son, and *will not leave*
the room where the *coffin* stands.
he *turns away* from his wife, and she sleeps *alone.*

And the sea lifts and *falls* all night; the moon goes on
through the Sun attached heavens *alone.*
And the toe of the shoe pivots
in the *dust....*
The man in the *black* coat turns, and *goes back down*
the hill.
No one knows why he came, or why he turned away, and
did not climb the hill.[11]

The amount of Saturnian references in this poem are staggering. The mood is one of negation, heaviness, sorrow, grief, caution and fear. Bly's rising planets are now in full bloom, as Mercury eloquently and powerfully conveys the teachings of Saturn. His poetry has a way of helping us to embrace the inescapable presence of grief and to learn from it.

All of Bly's talents and abilities as a poet (Neptune) are now synchronized with the energies of the mentor (Chiron) and the King. Bly describes a poet as someone who filters the available mythology. Bly has a tremendous talent for knowing exactly the right types of poetry and mythology that will speak to men's souls. He often plays a bouzouki (Greek stringed instrument) while rendering his poetry readings. Chiron taught music to his students via the kithara, which was the precursor to the modern day guitar. Bly is the foremost example of Chiron in his role of a male initiator. He represents a spiritual (Neptune) foster father (Chiron) and King to many men seeking answers to the dilemma of understanding themselves.

There are quite a few significant asteroid archetypes that will serve to round out the delineation of Bly's chart. The asteroid Euterpe is exactly sextile (60°) to his Venus. Euterpe was the Greek muse of lyric, song and music. This further enhances his talent at rendering poetry to music. We also find the asteroid Chant in conjunction with Chiron to boot.

Another asteroid, named after the Greek muse of history Klio, is exactly conjunct with his Sun. Central to Bly's core theme of teaching, is a deep interest in the history of all tribal cultures. This is especially true as regards their use of mythology and ritual storytelling. He is concerned with keeping the wisdom of such cultures (Greek, Celtic, Native American, and Egyptian, etc.) alive and pertinent to modern man's needs.

Bly has the asteroid Eros in exact opposition to his Moon. The Moon, besides representing the mother, also represents the Wildman. This shows Bly's passionate belief and understanding of the Wildman archetype, as the gateway to spontaneity in men. One cannot attend a Robert Bly lecture or workshop without hearing him talk repeatedly about the energy of Eros.

The planet Saturn is conjunct with the asteroids Amor and Arthur. This gives Bly a deep understanding of the connection between grief (Saturn) and the Arthurian quest, coupled with a deep appreciation for this process.

The asteroid Paracelsus is conjunct with Jupiter. Sophia is also exactly square to Jupiter. This combination would manifest as an ability to bring out the highest expression (Jupiter) of alchemy (Paracelsus) and self knowledge (Sophia).

This is where Bly's Zeus energy comes from. Bill Moyers paid him this well earned compliment during their interview. (Zeus was the Greek equivalent of the Roman god Jupiter). The asteroid Sappho is Quincunx (150°) to Mars. Sappho was one of the most renown poets in Greek history. She also had a Women's initiation school on the island of Lesbos!

There are four asteroids that specifically indicate the probability of alcoholism being an issue in one's own life, or that of the family. All four show up connected to different archetypes in Bly's chart. Bacchus is square to Neptune, and Dionysius is Quincunx to the Sun. Vinifera is square to Pluto, and Beer is Quincunx (150°) to Pluto as well.

Quite a few proper first names have asteroids named after them. I have found that asteroids named after the members of one's immediate family will invariably show up in their birth chart.

The asteroid named after Bly's second wife, Ruth, is exactly square to the archetype of Pluto in his chart. Her relationship with him would most probably be as one who challenges him in his own personal inner transformation. She might also be one who inspires him within the realms of the collective unconscious by helping him with dream interpretation and deep primal forms of therapy and self-analysis.

The redundant, and therefore unavoidable, theme which runs through of all of the charts we have covered is that of angularity. We see irrefutable proof in favor of the Gauquelin's research. Jung's ruling influence, Pluto, is on the lower angle. Krishnamurti's dominant archetype, Uranus, is on the upper angle, and Bly's most powerful theme planet, Saturn, is on the rising angle. The charts from the preceding chapter confirm the undeniable influence of angularity as well.

Many astrologers are uneasy about abandoning the comforts offered by the houses and signs. I am hoping that the new method outlined in this book will help them to shed these dogmatic skins of outmoded and misleading methodologies. Astrology has always been, and should always remain, purely archetypal and numeric, or Pythagorean in nature. To lose sight of this central truth, is to abandon the science of astrology for mere speculation!

Conclusion

In the course of summarizing this book, I would like to include one last piece of supporting evidence. In the process of reading the latest work by Moore and Gillette, *The King Within,* I came upon the most stunning gem of validation for my research.[1] Contained within Appendix B, at the end of the book, was a diagram which absolutely amazed me.

This diagram was originally designed by George Everly based on brain research into the limbic system. Moore and Gillette have furthered his work by adding the names of the four human archetypes, plus that of the ego. What one sees is their representation of how they believe the archetypes to be situated "spatially" in relation to each other.

If one compares this diagram with the bottom (human) portion of my "Tree" design, they will see that the two match exactly. Line for line, position for position, the two are completely identical in every way! I think this only goes to prove the absolute existence of deep archetypal structures within the human psyche.

The fact that Moore and Gillette's findings parallel my own is overwhelmingly stunning to me, for we came upon our results via two seemingly different paths! It comforts me greatly to know that my approach is so closely aligned with such respectable and credible sources as these.

Moore and Gillette explain that the limbic system contains three primary subsystems:

1. The affiliative/attachment subsystem (equal to the Yin-female-pillar)
2. The autonomy/aggression subsystem (equal to the Yang-male-pillar)
3. The integrative/inhibitive subsystem (equal to the central pillar)

These correlations further affirm the physiological/psychological foundation upon which my research is based. Metaphysical information is useless unless it is grounded within a sound psychological foundation.

My own work continues to take astrology into even deeper realms of the psyche. In my next book, I plan to take the theories of Carl Jung, regarding the "double quaternio" and develop upon them by applying my astrological approach. I believe that we can thus achieve a greater understanding of the soul via its connection to the outer planet archetypes.

I feel that there are endless fields of rich soil still to be sifted through and explored regarding the connections between astrology and archetypal psychology. There is little, if any, value in the endless barrage of speculative approaches that have plagued astrology. I plan to continue on my journey of hopefully restoring some respectability to this field and turning it into a valid and useful tool for growth and self-exploration.

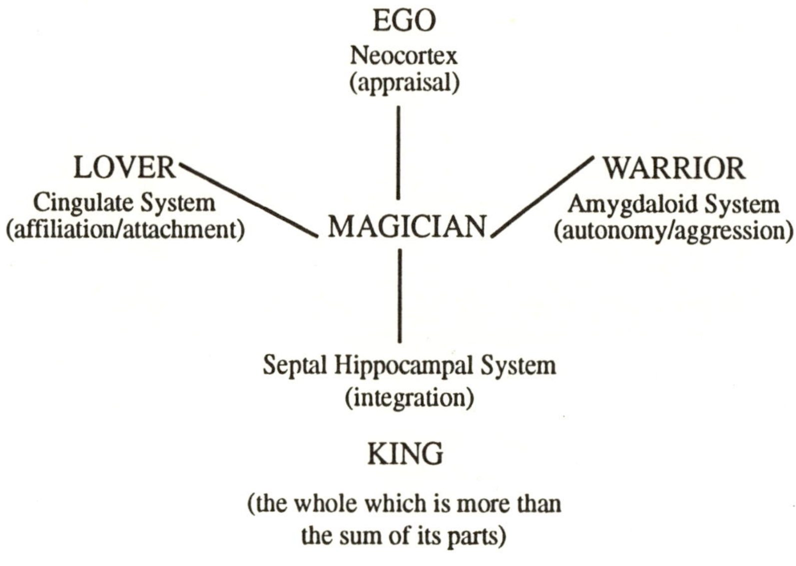

Limbic System Diagram, page 272 from *The King Within* by Robert Moore and Douglas Gillette. © 1992 by Robert L. Moore and Douglas Gillette. By permission of William Morrow and Company, Inc.

Glossary

Active imagination:

A term used by Jungian psychologists to indicate the process, initially developed by Carl Jung, in which one actively "dialogues" with the inner parts of oneself (shadow manifestations of the archetypes). The end goal is to align these parts of ourself so that they no longer act as subversive enemies within our unconscious, sabotaging our attempts at living a healthy life.

Alchemy:

An occult (secret) practice developed during medieval times of transmuting the base metal lead into the precious metal gold. Many mistakenly took the practice literally, believing that this could actually be accomplished on the physical level. Its adherents knew that it was an inner "spiritual" process, symbolized outwardly in this transmutive analogy of metals.

Angle:

An astrological term which refers to any of the four cardinal points of the astrological chart. These would be, the ascendant, descendant, midheaven and lower midheaven. They are also known as the cusps of the cardinal houses: first, fourth, seventh and tenth.

Angularity:

The astrological term for the method of determining the degree to which a planet (archetype) has the propensity towards outward concrete expression within one's life based on its mundane placement. This is all measured through the method developed by Michel Gauquelin. When one considers the "angularity" of the planets in a chart, they would look for those located within, or closest to, the Gauquelin "power zones." The angularity of these planets are strongest within that person's make up.

Archetype:
An essential component of the human psyche that contributes a distinct quality or trait which aids the soul in both its immediate survival and optimally in its prosperity. Archetypes support the survival and growth of the soul much the same as the organs do for the body.

Ascendant:
The eastern most point on the earth's horizon where the sun, moon and planets first make their appearance into to visible sky.

Aspect:
An astrological term which indicates the arc of separation between any two celestial bodies when viewed from the earth. When this arc approximates a definite mathematical fraction of the circle (1/2, 1/3, 1/4, etc.), it is said to constitute a specific aspect. For example: when two planets form a 90° angle, when viewed from earth, they are said to be in a square aspect. This square aspect has also come to be referred to as a fourth harmonic since it constitutes a quarter of the circle.

Aspectarian:
A special grid which is usually part of a standard astrological computer printout of a chart. It lists all the existing aspects between all the different planetary bodies and other sensitive points of the chart (the angles, etc.).

Black hole:
An astronomical term for a region of space that is apparently drawing all the surrounding stars and stellar material into its void, much like a whirlpool or a vacuum. All stellar material, entering into a black hole, is apparently being recycled by the universe through one of these many cosmic anal sphincters!

Cadusus:
The symbolic "magic wand" used by the Greek god Hermes (Mercury). This was seen as a shaft entwined by two serpents and crowned by two wings at the top. It is still alive and well and can

be seen, in its unchanged form, in our symbol for the medical profession.

Conjunction:

An astrological aspect whereby two celestial bodies are located in the same place in the sky (when viewed from the earth). This is also referred to as the first harmonic.

Descendant:

The western most point of the earth's horizon where the sun, moon and planets "set" in their daily course of travel through the visible sky.

Decile:

An astrological aspect equivalent to one tenth of the circle. This means that the two celestial bodies are separated by 36° of arc (when viewed from the earth). Also referred to as the tenth harmonic.

Ecliptic:

An astronomical term used to describe the apparent path that the Sun takes through the circle of the sky. This annual journey is confined to a definite band of constellations which has come to be known as the Zodiac. All the remaining planets (with the exception of Pluto) can be found to conform to the same general region of the ecliptic while traveling through their orbital journeys around the Sun.

Elliptical:

Any circular or orbital pattern that is more realistically "egg shaped" in appearance than circular.

Grand Trine:

A unique and harmonious arrangement of any three planets which occurs when each is found located 120 degrees from the other two. The result of this ensemble creates a perfect equilateral triangle.

Grand Square:

A unique and dynamic arrangement of any four planets whereby their positions collectively create a perfect cube. It can also be viewed as two opposition aspects that fall exactly perpendicular to each other.

Holograph:

A complex image or photograph generated with lasers instead of lenses. The result is a three dimensional image that can be seen within the whole, or any lesser part of the photograph. If one had a single 4" x 4" holographic photo of the earth, they could cut it into quarters and end up with four 2" x 2" photos. Each of these smaller photos would still contain the same exact image of the original picture, though obviously a smaller representation of such.

Horizon:

The visual boundary represented by that place where the edge of the earth and the sky meet each other.

Houses:

An astrological term used to refer to the 12 "compartments" that the sky is divided up into. The astrologer then assigns different meanings to a planet depending on which of these houses it falls into. This forms a major part of standard astrological delineation. There are numerous house systems that each offer a different mathematical formula for exactly how to divide up the circle into these houses. Some systems argue for an equal division of houses (30° each), while others vary considerably based on one's location in terms of geographical "latitude" (how far north or south of the equator one is).

I.C.:

An abbreviation for Imum Coeli. This Latin phrase means literally "lower heaven" or lower midheaven. It is the point in the sky where the Sun reaches its lowest point of daily travel. This is equivalent to where it would be found at "midnight" in local mean time. Every celestial body passes over this location in the sky, once a day, during the course of its travels. It is not a privilege restricted exclusively to the Sun alone.

I-Ching:

An ancient Chinese oracle or system of divination used to obtain guidance and wisdom. One poses a question to the oracle and then "casts" a hexagram. There are 64 hexagrams and each one has many meanings depending on the existence of any "changing lines" in its composition. Determining the nature of each of the hexagrams 6 lines is accomplished by either drawing sticks or tossing coins to arrive at the status of each line. Once the hexagram is constructed, its meaning is then consulted in the book of the I Ching.

Ida:

One of the three essential components of the Hindu theory and practice of Tantra. The Ida represents the left handed "Yin" path of energy that spirals around the central sushumna. It correlates, on a physical level, with the Para-sympathetic nervous system.

Kabala:

A Hebrew system of esoteric knowledge involving the deciphering of hidden, cryptic meanings believed to be contained within the old testament of the Bible. Most central to its teachings was a diagram referred to as the Tree of Life. This was a systematic arrangement of energy spheres (known as "sephiroths") into a cohesive whole. This larger energy grid or Tree bears a striking resemblance to the Archetypal Tree referred to in this book. Though structurally similar, they vary considerably when it comes to their specific placement of each sphere within their respective designs.

Kabalic:

Anything pertaining or relating to the Kabala.

Kundalini:

The spiritual or cosmic energy that was said to reside at the base of the spine in the form of a sleeping serpent. This is the central premise behind the Hindu practice of Tantra Yoga. The goal was to arouse this sleeping energy source and get it to rise up the Sushumna (spine) and illuminate one's entire being and consciousness.

Lunar Nodes:

These are astronomical terms that indicate the two points where the Moon's orbit crosses over (intersects) the ecliptic. In astrological literature they are referred to as the North node (Dragon's head) and the South node (Dragon's tail). When a new or full moon coincided with one of these points, an eclipse occurred. Their movement is cyclical, taking some 19 years, and was known to the ancient Babylonians and Mayans. This knowledge allowed them to forecast eclipses far into the future with great accuracy.

Mandala:

Any quadrated or fourfold image used by various cultures for the purpose of evoking a sense of order and calm in one's life. Examples of such are Navaho sand paintings, Tibetan and Hindu mandalas, etc.

M.C.:

An abbreviation for the Latin astrological term "Median Coeli," or "mid-heaven" in English. This is the point of local high noon where the Sun reaches the highest point of its celestial climb. All celestial bodies (including the Sun) transit this key point in the sky once every day. It is also referred to as the planet's "culmination."

Meridian:

The pivotal vertical line that divides the birth chart into two equal parts. The upper end of this line is called the M.C. and the lower end is referred to as the I.C. It is from this word that we also get the terms A.M. (ante-meridian) and P.M. (post meridian) which mark time.

Mesenteric:

Of or pertaining to the "mesentery." This is a supportive membrane that enfolds the intestines and organs of the gut, securing them primarily to the rear wall of the abdominal cavity. Contained within this membrane is a rich network of lymphatic ducts and blood vessels that transport nutrients throughout the abdominal region.

Natal:

An alternate term used in astrology to denote the birth chart. The natal chart is cast for the precise time of one's birth and reflects the exact position and arrangement of the planets at that point in time.

Native:

An astrological term used to represent the actual person for whom the birth chart has been cast.

Novile:

An astrological aspect equivalent to one ninth of the circle. This means that the two celestial bodies are separated by 40° of arc (when viewed from the earth). Also referred to as the ninth harmonic.

Octile:

An astrological aspect equivalent to one eighth of the circle. This means that the two celestial bodies are separated by 45° of arc (when viewed from the earth). Also referred to as the eighth harmonic. This 45° aspect is also referred to as the semi-square (constituting exactly half of the 90° square).

Opposition:

An astrological aspect equivalent to one half of the circle. This means that the two celestial bodies are separated by 180° of arc (when viewed from the earth). Also referred to as the second harmonic.

Orb:

An astrological term used in relation to aspects. It represents a kind of cut-off point, beyond which the effects of the aspect's strength are considered too weak to manifest. For example, let us work with a novile aspect (40°). An astrologer might allow an orb of plus or minus 1°. If two planets in a chart were separated by 39.5° of arc, they would be said to be well within the orb of a novile aspect. One would then seriously consider the influence of this novile on the person in question and weigh it in the balance of their complete delineation.

Partile:

An astrological term used in relation to aspects. It depicts a state of mathematical exactness or near perfection. Two planets separated by 119.9° would be said to be in partile trine aspect. Generally, a partile aspect is one in which the two planets are within one degree of mathematical exactness.

Pingala:

One of the three essential components of the Hindu Tantric system. The Pingala represents the right handed "Yang" path of energy that spirals around the central sushumna. It correlates, on a physical level, with the Sympathetic nervous system.

Power Spot:

An alternate astrological term used to represent the Gauquelin's power zones which act to energize or enhance the presence of any planet/archetypes found located there.

Quincunx:

An obtuse astrological aspect whereby the two planets are separated by 150° of arc. This aspect represents a state of transition (between other harmonic intervals) and does not relate directly to any particular harmonic.

Quintile:

An astrological aspect equivalent to one fifth of the circle. This means that the two celestial bodies are separated by 72° of arc (when viewed from the earth). Also referred to as the fifth harmonic.

Return:

An astrological term used to represent the exact time when any planetary body completes its orbital cycle and once again "returns" to the exact spot where it was located within a particular birth chart. It is said to have significance because it marks the initiation of a new cycle. That particular archetype's energy is renewed and rekindled within the native's psyche as a result of this. It is essentially a graduation of sorts which offers us the opportunity to mature and move onto greater things.

Septile:

An astrological aspect equivalent to one seventh of the circle. This means that the two celestial bodies are separated by 51.43° of arc (when viewed from the earth). Also referred to as the seventh harmonic.

Sextile:

An astrological aspect equivalent to one sixth of the circle. This means that the two celestial bodies are separated by 60° of arc (when viewed from the earth). Also referred to as the sixth harmonic.

Shadow:

A psychological term developed by Carl Jung to represent a largely unconscious presence within every human. The shadow contains dormant potential, both negative and positive, that has yet to be fully realized and integrated on a conscious level.

Square:

An astrological aspect equivalent to one fourth of the circle. This means that the two celestial bodies are separated by 90° of arc (when viewed from the earth). Also referred to as the fourth harmonic.

Synodic:

An astronomical term used primarily to refer to the monthly lunar cycle. The lunar synodic cycle is measured as the length of time between any two new moons.

Sushumna:

One of the three essential components of the Hindu Tantric system. The Sushumna represents the central column around which the Ida and Pingala entwine themselves. When these two outer spirals were activated, the Kundalini energy would then rise up the central Sushumna.

Tantra:

An ancient Hindu system of yoga (union) that seeks to invoke the tension of the opposites so as to facilitate an inner experience of their reconciliation. They sought to create as much awareness of this tension as possible. This was accomplished mostly through various meditative and sexual practices that culminated in the ecstatic inner experience of this all consuming union with all of creation.

Trine:

An astrological aspect equivalent to one third of the circle. This means that the two celestial bodies were separated by 120° of arc (when viewed from the earth). Also referred to as the third harmonic.

T-Square:

An astrological term used to refer to an aspect embodying a unique arrangement. It refers simply to any two planets that are in opposition to one another, while also having a third celestial body in square to each end of this opposition. This can also be viewed as three quarters of a grand square arrangement.

White Hole:

An astronomical term for a region in deep space where new stars and stellar material are being spewed out into the universe. It can be viewed as an entry point or the "mouth of God" breathing new life into the cosmos.

Notes

Preface

1. Garth Allen, *Taking the Kid Gloves Off Astrology* (Tucson, AZ: Clancy Publications Inc., 1955, 1956, 1975).

Chapter 1

1. Robert Moore and Douglas Gilette, *King, Warrior, Magician, Lover: Rediscovering the Archetypes of the Mature Masculine* (San Francisco: HarperSanFrancisco, 1990). Henceforth abbreviated as KWML.
2. KWML, Chapter 3.
3. Alice Miller, *For Your Own Good* (New York, Noonday Press, 1990).
4. John Bradshaw, *Homecoming: Reclaiming and Championing Your Inner Child* (New York: Bantam Books, 1990).
5. Robert Moore, *The Great Self Within: Men and the Quest for Significance.* (St. Paul, MN: Ally Press, 1991. Audiotape.)
6. KWML, 23-27.
7. Robert Bly, *Iron John: A Book About Men* (Reading, MA: Addison-Wesley Publishing Company, Inc., 1990).
8. KWML, 71.

Chapter 2

1. KWML, 27-28.
2. KWML, 28-33.
3. KWML, 100.

Chapter 3

1. KWML, 33.
2. Allen, *Taking the Kid Gloves Off Astrology*, 17.

3. KWML, 35-37.
4. KWML, 131-140.
5. Ibid.
6. Margaret H. Gammon, *Astrology and the Edgar Cayce Readings* (Virginia Beach, VA: A.R.E. Press, 1973.)
7. Allen, *Taking the Kid Gloves Off Astrology*, 20-21.
8. Robert Moore, *The Great Self Within*.
10. Allen, 20

Chapter 4

1. Robert Bly, *Iron John*.
2. See Jennifer Barker Wooljer and Roger J. Woolger, *The Goddess Within: A Guide to the Eternal Myths that Shape Women's Lives* (New York: Fawcett Columbine, 1989).

Chapter 5

1. David Hamblin, *Harmonic Charts*. (Wellingborough, UK: The Aquarian Press, 1983), 48.
2. KWML, 37.
3. Miller, *For Your Own Good*, 142-197.
4. KWML, 37-42.
5. Robert Bly, *The Naive Male*. (St. Paul, MN: Ally Press, 1988, Audiotape.)
6. The Pentagram is a symbol used by many religious and magical traditions, such as modern Wicca and Hermeticism. As a religious or magical symbol, it points upwards. So-called Satanists and some heavy metalists invert it, the same way they invert the crucifix.
7. KWML, 9.
8. Moore, *The Great Self Within*.
9. KWML, 84-85.

Chapter 7

1. Hamblin, *Harmonic Charts*, 64.
2. Robert Bly's best works in this area are *Iron John*, *Men and the Wild Child* (with James Hillman, Boulder, CO: Sounds True Recordings, 1990, audiotape) and *The Power of Shame*, San Francisco: New Dimensions Foundation, 1991, audiotape).
3. Allen, *Taking the Kid Gloves Off Astrology*, 3.
4. Bly, Iron John, 30-31.

Chapter 8

1. Moore, *The Great Self Within*.
2. Interview with Frank Zappa, published in Playboy, April 1993.
3. Allen, *Taking the Kid Gloves Off Astrology*, 32.

Chapter 10

1. Allen, *Taking the Kid Gloves Off Astrology*, 43.
2. Ibid., 44-45.
3. Moore, *The Great Self Within*.

Chapter 11

1. Discussion in Robert Bly's PBS television series, "A Gathering of Men."
2. John Gray, *Men Are from Mars Women Are from Venus*. (New York: Harper Collins, 1992).
3. Lucia Capacchione, *Recovery of Your Inner Child*. (New York: Simon & Schuster/Fireside, 1991).
4. John Bradshaw, *Homecoming*.

Chapter 12

1. For a deeper understanding of the asteroid belt and its significance, I recommend reading The 12th Planet by Zeccaria Sitchin (New York: Avon Books, 1976). This man's brilliant work is invaluable to any serious astrologer. He challenges the limits of conventional thought. For those readers who wish to understand the mythological background of the asteroids, I can recommend *Asteroid Goddesses* by Demetra George and Douglas Bloch (San Diego: ACS Publications, 1986) and also *The Ultimate Asteroid Book* by J. Lee Lehman (West Chester, PA: Schiffer Publishing, 1988) These are by far the best books for the astrologer who wishes to add the asteroids into his or her working knowledge of chart delineation.
2. I disagree with Barbara Hand Clow and her argument in *Chiron: Rainbow Bridge Between the Inner and Outer Planets*, (St. Paul, MN: Llewellyn Publications, 1987) of assigning Chiron to the pineal gland. The pineal corresponds to the highest chakra of the Hindu system, and is ruled by Pluto. *The Continuing Discovery of Chiron* by Erminie Lantero (York Beach, ME: Samuel Weiser, 1983) is the best source of information on this new planet.
3. Robert K.G. Temple, *The Sirius Mystery*." (CITY: Destiny Books, 1987).

4. Bradshaw, *Homecoming*, 73-75.
5. The work of Schwaller de Lubicz entitled *The Temple in Man* (Rochester, VT: Inner Traditions, 1981) explores this in great depth. One of his students, John Anthony West, has written an excellent work called *The Serpent in the Sky* (New York: Julian Press, 1987). I avidly refer the reader to both of these sources for further study on the significance of Phi and its connection to our inner divine temple.

Chapter 13

1. *Chess Life*, February 1993, page 39.
2. Leo Buscaglia, *Love*. (New York: Fawcett-Crest, 1972).
3. Miller, *For Your Own Good*, 147-80.
4. Ibid., 142.

Chapter 14

1. Gerhard Wehr, *Portrait of Jung*. (New York: Herder and Herder, 1971) All following quotes from Jung are taken from this biography.
2. Carl G. Jung and Wolfgang Pauli. (New York: Pantheon Books, 1955). Translated by R.F.C. Hull.
3. *I-Ching, or Book of Changes*. English translation by C.F. Baynes and R. Wilhelm. Foreword by C.J. Jung. Published by the Bolligen Foundation, Princeton, 1967.
4. Mary Lutyens, *The Years of Awakening*. (New York: Avon Books, 1975), 293-297.
5. Robert Bly, *Men and the Wild Child*.
6. Bly, *The Naive Male*.
7. Ibid.
8. "While Drinking All Night With A Friend, We Go Out In A Boat At Dawn, To See Who Can Write The Best Poem." Reprinted from *Silence in the Snowy Fields*, Wesleyan University Press, Middleton, CT.
© 1959, 1960, 1961, 1962 Robert Bly. Reprinted with the permission of Robert Bly.
9. "Laziness and Silence," Reprinted from *Silence in the Snowy Fields*, Wesleyan Uniiversity Press, Middleton, CT.
© 1959, 1960, 1961, 1962 Robert Bly. Reprinted with the permission of Robert Bly.

10. "Aban Kavost and Ivar Oakeson," from *Sleepers Joining Hands* by Robert Bly. Reprinted by the permission of Harper Collins Publishers, Inc.
11. "Snowbanks North of the House," from *The Man in the Black Coat Turns*. © 1981 by Robert Bly. Used by permission of Doubleday, a division of Bantam Doubleday Dell Publishing Group, Inc.

Conclusion

1. Robert Moore and Douglas Gilette, *The King Within*. (New York: William Morrow and Company, Inc., 1992). Limbic system diagram reprinted by permission of William Morroe & Company, Inc.

Source Data on Birth Charts

Robin Williams. Rodden Birth Certificate.

Bobby Fischer. From the book: *Profile of a Prodigy* by F. Brady.

Leo Buscaglia. Linda Clark quotes Mr. Buscaglia.

Joseph Campbell. Erin Cameron quotes his mother. (1981)

Robert Moore. From Robert Moore himself.

Jimi Hendrix. Rodden Birth Certificate

Marilyn Monroe. Rodden Birth Certificate

John F. Kennedy. From the book: *The Fitzgeralds and the Kennedys* by Doris Kearns-Goodwin (New York: Simon & Shuster, 1987)

Adolf Hitler. *The Circle Book of Charts*, revised edition (Temple, AZ: AFA, 1972). They quote "Baptismal records from Braunau" from Howe, *Astrology: A Recent History.*

Carl G. Jung. 7:32 pm given by his daughter, Grett Baumann from the book, *Carl Gustav Jung: Leben Werk Wirking* by Gerhard Wehr. This was adjusted from Berne time to 7:40 L.M.T. for accuracy.

Krishnamurti. From Le Gross, Dell Horoscope. May '63. Dated records obtained from the Theosophical Society.

Robert Bly. Rodden Birth Certificate.

About the Author

Daniel Lorey, IV is an astrologer with over 15 years of active research, counseling and lecturing to his credit. The origins of his astrological ideas trace back to the old Fagan/Allen school of thought and then venture into exciting new territory. He has taken the thoughts of such notables as Michel Gauquelin, John Addey, Robert Moore, Douglas Gillette and John Bradshaw and synthesized a unique system of astrological interpretation that transcends the traditional zodiacs.

Mr. Lorey's fresh, novel approach to astrology draws upon a rich background of experience. He is a Traditional Reiki Master as well as a Certified Iridologist and Herbalist. He is actively involved with Men's Groups and alternative healing methods. In addition, he is an accomplished musician, poet and songwriter. Mr. Lorey was born in 1958 and he makes his home on Long Island. His hobbies include collecting exotic birds, chess, Egyptology, mythology, music fitness and yoga.